What is Clinical Psychology?

What is Clinical Psychology?

FIFTH EDITION

Edited by

Susan Llewelyn
Professor of Clinical Psychology, Harris Manchester College,
University of Oxford, Oxford, UK

David Murphy
Joint Course Director—Oxford University Doctoral Clinical
Psychology Programme, Oxford Institute of Clinical
Psychology Training, Isis Education Centre, Warneford
Hospital, Oxford, UK

UNIVERSITY PRESS

OXFORD

UNIVERSITY PRESS

Great Clarendon Street, Oxford, OX2 6DP,
United Kingdom

Oxford University Press is a department of the University of Oxford.
It furthers the University's objective of excellence in research, scholarship,
and education by publishing worldwide. Oxford is a registered trade mark of
Oxford University Press in the UK and in certain other countries

© Oxford University Press 2014

The moral rights of the authors have been asserted

First Edition published in 1987
Second Edition published in 1992
Third Edition published in 1999
Fourth Edition published in 2006
Fifth Edition published in 2014

Impression: 1

Published in the United States of America by Oxford University Press
198 Madison Avenue, New York, NY 10016, United States of America

British Library Cataloguing in Publication Data
Data available

Library of Congress Control Number: 2013948982

ISBN 978-0-19-968149-5

Printed and bound by
CPI Group (UK) Ltd, Croydon, CR0 4YY

Oxford University Press makes no representation, express or implied, that the
drug dosages in this book are correct. Readers must therefore always check
the product information and clinical procedures with the most up-to-date
published product information and data sheets provided by the manufacturers
and the most recent codes of conduct and safety regulations. The authors and
the publishers do not accept responsibility or legal liability for any errors in the
text or for the misuse or misapplication of material in this work. Except where
otherwise stated, drug dosages and recommendations are for the non-pregnant
adult who is not breast-feeding

Links to third party websites are provided by Oxford in good faith and
for information only. Oxford disclaims any responsibility for the materials
contained in any third party website referenced in this work.

Preface to the fifth edition

'*What is Clinical Psychology?*' is a question that we continue to be asked by a range of people including patients who are referred to see us, undergraduates and postgraduates considering a career in this field, colleagues in other health or social care professions, and interested family or friends. The aim of this book is to provide a broad but well-informed outline of the activities that clinical psychologists perform, and also to give a 'feel' of what it is like to practice as a clinical psychologist in different fields.

Clinical psychology is one of the fastest growing health professions in the United Kingdom and in many countries elsewhere in the world. The first psychological clinic was only established a little over a hundred years ago in the USA and the profession of clinical psychology has only been formally recognized in the UK for some 60 years. Nevertheless, the size of the profession in this country has more than quadrupled since the publication of the first edition of this book in 1987. Moreover, the profession has extended into a wide range of new settings and client groups. This edition contains new chapters on working with trauma, and clinical psychology and diversity. In addition, given that the last edition was written more than 7 years ago, we took the decision to approach new authors to completely rewrite the majority of the existing chapters, while the remaining chapters have been significantly updated by the previous authors. We therefore believe that the content of this book represents a comprehensive and contemporary account of the profession today. Although many examples are drawn from UK practice, most of the approaches and theories are shared internationally, and we have been conscious throughout the book to bear international readers in mind by providing explanation of UK context where appropriate.

In the 27 years since the first edition of this book was published, there have been numerous other books published in the field of applied psychology. These books fall into two broad categories: first, those that offer a detailed account of theory and practice of a particular specialist area of practice, presenting problem or therapeutic modality, and second, those that have a broader remit and attempt to cover a field of applied psychology, such as mental health or health psychology, normally for the purpose of teaching. The specific aim of this book is somewhat different in that we aim to provide a living account of the day-to-day activities of clinical psychologists across a wide range of different areas. In doing so, we have tried to convey not just what a clinical psychologist does but importantly why they do so, by linking in the underlying psychological models and theories that are applied in their work. We also aim to look ahead to identify emerging trends and drivers of clinical psychology practice in each area of specialist practice in the years ahead. This is undoubtedly an ambitious task and could only ever realistically be achieved by calling on the collective knowledge and experience of a number of authors, each of whom is a leader in their particular field.

This book does not need to be read from beginning to end, although most readers will find it helpful to start with Chapters 1 and 2 before proceeding further, since these provide the context for contemporary clinical psychology practice and describe the essential competencies that provide the foundation for practice with the different populations and presenting problems described subsequently. At the end of each chapter there is a list of key references and suggested further reading on the material covered. These have been chosen to be accessible to non-specialist readers.

This is the fifth edition of this text, and we are indebted to the editors of previous editions, Professor John Hall and Dr John Marziller, who have handed responsibility for this next edition to us. We hope that this book will be as helpful as the previous editions have been in presenting the profession clearly and informatively to our readership. Across all five editions of this book the editors have been fortunate to be able to call upon clinical psychologists who are at the cutting edge of their specialist fields to contribute their own particular, up-to-date perspectives, which we believe is a unique strength of the book. Clinical psychology continues to be a rewarding and challenging career, which is still evolving.

There are now opportunities to work in new areas and to use innovative approaches that were not conceived of, or only aspired to, at the time of the first edition. We hope that in this book we have conveyed at least a sense of our excitement and enthusiasm for the profession as it continues to develop.

We are grateful to all of the authors in the book for their willingness to contribute and for their dedication. We would like to thank Martin Baum and Charlotte Green of Oxford University Press for their support and encouragement through the process.

Oxford	SL
July 2013	DJM

Contents

Contributors *xi*

1 Introduction: what is clinical psychology? *1*
David Murphy and Susan Llewelyn

2 Competencies and models in clinical psychology *17*
Susan Llewelyn and David Murphy

3 Working in primary health care *37*
John Cape and Yvonne Millar

4 Working with children and young people *53*
Duncan Law

5 Working with severe mental health problems *69*
John Hanna and Alison Brabban

6 Working with older people *85*
Cath Burley

7 Working with eating disorders *103*
Hannah Turner

8 Working with people with intellectual disabilities *119*
Steve Carnaby

9 Working in forensic mental health settings *137*
Jeremy Tudway and Matthew Lister

10 Working with addictions *153*
Frank Ryan

11 Working with trauma *169*
Nick Grey and Sue Clohessy

12 Working with people who have physical health problems *187*
Elenor McLaren and David Murphy

13 Working in clinical neuropsychology *205*
Katherine Carpenter and Andy Tyerman

14 Clinical psychology in teams and leadership *223*
Susan Llewelyn

15 Working with cultural diversity *237*
Kamel Chahal

16 The future of clinical psychology *253*
David Murphy and Susan Llewelyn

Appendix 1
Becoming registered as a clinical psychologist in the UK 269

Index *273*

Contributors

Alison Brabban
Clinical Lead, Early Intervention in Psychosis, Tees, Esk and Wear Valleys NHS Trust, Honorary Senior Lecturer, Durham University, St Aidans House, 2a St Aidans Walk, Bishop Auckland, County Durham DL14 6SA
abrabban@btopenworld.com

Cath Burley
The Chair—Faculty of Psychology of Older People, Division of Clinical Psychology, British Psychological Society, 48 St Andrews House, Princess Road East, Leicester LE1 7DR
cathburley@hotmail.com

John Cape
Head of Psychological Therapies, Camden and Islington NHS Foundation Trust, St Pancras Hospital, 4 St Pancras Way, London NW1 0PE
j.cape@ucl.ac.uk

Steve Carnaby
Consultant Clinical Psychologist, Autism Anglia and Affinity Trust, and Honorary Senior Lecturer, Tizard Centre, University of Kent, Unit 3 Old Pharmacy Yard, Church Street, Dereham, Norfolk NR19 1DJ
scarnaby@autism-anglia.org.uk

Katherine Carpenter
Consultant Clinical Neuropsychologist/Trust Head Psychologist, Russell Cairns Unit, Level 3 West Wing, John Radcliffe Hospital, Oxford OX3 9DU
katherine.carpenter@ouh.nhs.uk

Kamel Chahal
Chartered Clinical Psychologist, South Lambeth Recovery and Support Team, South London and Maudsley NHS Foundation Trust, 380 Streatham High Road, Streatham, Lambeth, London SW16 6HP
kamel.chahal@slam.nhs.uk
kamelchahal7@gmail.com

Sue Clohessy
Consultant Clinical Psychologist, Oxford Institute of Clinical Psychology Training and Oxford Health NHS Foundation Trust, Isis Education Centre, Warneford Hospital, Oxford OX3 7JX
susan.clohessy@hmc.ox.ac.uk

Nick Grey
Consultant Clinical Psychologist,
Centre for Anxiety Disorders
and Trauma, South London and
Maudsley NHS Foundation Trust,
99 Denmark Hill, London
SE5 8AZ
nick.1.grey@kcl.ac.uk

John Hanna
Consultant Clinical Psychologist/
Lead Psychologist for Acute
Division, Camden and Islington
NHS Foundation Trust, Acute
Inpatient Clinical Psychology
Service, Highgate Mental Health
Centre, Dartmouth Park Hill,
London N19 5NX
john.hanna@candi.nhs.uk

Duncan Law
Professional Lead for Psychological
Service (CAMHS), Hertfordshire
Partnership University NHS
Foundation Trust, Hoddesdon
Health Clinic, EN11 8BE
Clinical Lead for CYP-IAPT,
The Anna Freud Centre,
12 Maresfield Gardens, London
NW3 5SU
Duncan.law@hpft.nhs.uk

Matthew Lister
Consultant Clinical Psychologist,
Forensic CAMHS/Forensic
Adult Services, Oxford Health
Foundation NHS Trust,
Marlborough House Medium
Secure Unit, Milton Keynes
Hospital Campus, Standing Way,
Eaglestone, Milton Keynes
MK6 5NG
matthew.lister@oxfordhealth.nhs.uk

Susan Llewelyn
Professor of Clinical Psychology,
Harris Manchester College,
University of Oxford, Mansfield
Road, Oxford OX1 3TD

Oxford Health NHS Foundation
Trust, Chancellor Court, 4000
John Smith Drive, Oxford
Business Park South, Oxford
OX4 2GX
susan.llewelyn@hmc.ox.ac.uk

Elenor McLaren
Principal Clinical Psychologist,
The Pain Management Centre,
The National Hospital for
Neurology and Neurosurgery,
University College London
Hospitals NHS FT, Queen Square,
London WC1N 3BG
ellie.agar@gmail.com
elenor.mclaren@uclh.nhs.uk

Yvonne Millar
Consultant Clinical Psychologist,
Community CAMHS, Northern
Health Centre, 580 Holloway
Road, Islington, London N7 6LB
yvonne.millar1@nhs.net

David Murphy

Joint Course Director—Oxford University Doctoral Clinical Psychology Programme, Oxford Institute of Clinical Psychology Training, Isis Education Centre, Warneford Hospital, Oxford OX3 7JX
david.murphy@hmc.ox.ac.uk

Frank Ryan

Consultant Clinical Psychologist, Substance Misuse and Forensic Division, Camden and Islington NHS Foundation Trust, 108 Hampstead Road, London NW1 2LS
f.ryan@imperial.ac.uk

Jeremy Tudway

Consultant Clinical and Forensic Psychologist, Clinical Director, Phoenix Psychology Group, 73–75 Priory Road, Kenilworth CV8 1LQ
jeremy.tudway@phoenixpsychology.com

Hannah Turner

Consultant Clinical Psychologist, Specialist Eating Disorders Service, Southern Health NHS Foundation Trust, April House, 9 Bath Road, Bitterne, Southampton SO19 5ES
hannahturner0@gmail.com

Andy Tyerman

Consultant Clinical Neuropsychologist/Head of Service, Community Head Injury Service, Buckinghamshire Healthcare NHS Trust, The Camborne Centre, Jansel Square, Aylesbury HP21 7ET
andy.tyerman@buckspct.nhs.uk

Chapter 1

Introduction: what is clinical psychology?

David Murphy and Susan Llewelyn

1.1 What is clinical psychology?

Helen's day begins with a visit to a large secondary school where she is meeting teachers to discuss Jodie, a 14-year-old girl who is currently suspended from school after violently assaulting another pupil. Last week Helen met with Jodie and carried out a clinical interview and psychometric assessment, and she hopes that the formulation she has developed about Jodie's specific learning difficulties and deficits in social perception will help the school in developing an effective approach both to manage her behaviour and to improve Jodie's engagement with school work.

Chris is sitting in a consulting room in the outpatients department of a local hospital with Rajiv, a successful 34-year-old advertising executive who has obsessive compulsive disorder. Rajiv avoided touching the door handle when he entered the office but Chris is explaining a behavioural approach that will eventually require Rajiv to touch the outside of doors, including the toilet door in the hospital, and then resist the urge to wash his hands. Chris is also collecting data on the outcome of the intervention, which will be used in a current research project to investigate key components of the treatment.

Jana is sitting at Colin's bedside in a hospital spinal injuries unit; Colin was involved in a car accident 6 weeks ago which left him paralysed from the neck down. Jana has been asked to see him as the unit staff are very concerned about his mood and low motivation to participate in rehabilitation. Colin has refused to allow his fiancée to visit him as he believes he is 'no longer the man she wanted to marry' and 'doesn't want her pity'.

Alice is carrying out a training session at a nursing home to help the staff develop the skills to effectively manage challenging behaviour in people with dementia whilst continuing to maintain respect and dignity. A member of staff at the home has recently been reprimanded for shouting at an 80-year-old man who had thrown yoghurt at her during meal time. Alice is also building a database on effective systemic interventions for use when disseminating psychological skills to care staff.

Although they are working in very different environments and with quite different populations, Helen, Chris, Jana, and Alice have one thing in common, they are all clinical psychologists. Indeed, these four clinical psychologists are fairly representative of the profession in the UK. Prior to training as a clinical psychologist almost all have undertaken an undergraduate degree in psychology which confers eligibility for Graduate basis for Chartered Membership (GBC) with the British Psycholgical Society (BPS), or a joint degree with a sufficient coverage of the core areas in Psychology to be awarded GBC. However, Chris undertook a first degree in law and subsequently undertook a conversion diploma course to obtain GBC, whereas Jana completed her undergraduate psychology course in another European country before coming to the UK, where she worked first as a health care assistant on an inpatient mental health unit and later as an assistant psychologist before starting her postgraduate clinical psychology training.

At present in the UK all clinical psychology training programmes are 3-year full-time doctoral courses (D.ClinPsych). They generally consist of an average of 3 days a week of clinical training on placement and 2 days a week of formal teaching at the university (see Appendix 1 for further details of training procedures). All programmes include undertaking a piece of research which forms the basis for a dissertation and also a shorter service evaluation project. Many other countries have now established similar training curricula and courses, at either doctoral or master's level. Successful completion of the doctoral programme in the UK gives eligibility to apply to the Health and Social Care Professionals Council (HCPC) for registration as a clinical psychologist. This registration is required by law in order to practice as a clinical psychologist, and indeed 'Clinical Psychologist' is one of the seven practitioner psychologist titles that are protected by UK law, and, as such, non-registered individuals inappropriately using the titles are liable to criminal prosecution.

The primary aim of this text is to provide an insight into the nature of the profession of clinical psychology and what it is like to be a clinical psychologist. As the preceding four short descriptions illustrate, clinical psychology is an enormously diverse profession. This introductory chapter will include a general overview of how the profession of clinical psychology has developed since its beginnings in the early 20th century and the current state of the profession in the 21st century, and will then scope out how psychologists work in practice, particularly in the UK's NHS. There will also be an overview of the ethical and value base of the profession, and an examination of the possible impact on practitioners themselves. Subsequent chapters each focus on a different setting in which clinical psychologists work, which we hope will help to provide a vivid but informed picture of what this work involves.

1.2 **The emergence of psychology as a distinct discipline**

Psychology as an undergraduate subject is now among the most popular subjects studied in universities in the UK and elsewhere. There are currently approximately 70,000 full- or part-time students studying psychology at undergraduate level in UK universities. However, despite its popularity, psychology is still a relatively young subject. In textbooks it is quite rare to find references to any work before the 20th century.

The first person to refer to themselves as a 'psychologist' was the German physicist and physiologist Wilhelm Wundt who had been a student of the physicist Hermann von Helmholtz. Wundt established the world's first experimental psychology laboratory at the University of Lepzig in 1879.

In the UK, experimental psychology evolved as a distinct discipline in the very early years of the 20th century, initially at University College London (UCL) where James Sully established a psychological laboratory in 1889, about 10 years after Wundt, and then at the University of Cambridge where a psychological laboratory was established in 1912 by Charles Spearman who had trained as a physician but who then developed an interest in psychology. Spearman later served as a consultant psychologist to the British Army in France during the First World War and went on to write the first scientific paper describing the condition known as 'shell shock'.

In 1928, a separate Department of Psychology was created within London University, and Spearman was made Professor of Psychology, going on to develop the concept of general intelligence for which he is best remembered.

The first meeting of what was to become the BPS took place at UCL in 1901, and the Society was formally established in 1906. Although the Society was formed only from teachers of psychology, of the ten founder members present at the first meeting five had trained as medical practitioners. Only one was female, Sophie Bryant, the headmistress of North London Collegiate, an independent girls school.

1.3 **Psychology in practice**

Psychology was applied in practice very shortly after its establishment as a distinct academic discipline at the end of the 19th century, although psychology practice occurred only on a very small scale until the latter half of the 20th century. Whereas today the dominant areas of psychological practice are probably within adult mental health and psychological therapy, in fact the early application of psychology in practice was mainly driven by the emergence of *psychometrics* and also the *preventative principles* of the mental hygiene movement in the USA, and focused predominantly on children rather than adults.

The development of psychology practice came about as a result of the work of a number of pioneering individuals originating from a wide range of academic backgrounds, who all became influenced through various means by the emerging discipline of experimental psychology, and then developed innovative ways of applying psychological principles to people's lives.

One of the first of such individuals was Alfred Binet who graduated from Law school in France in 1878 and, after studying natural sciences at the Sorbonne, developed an interest in psychology and educated himself through reading early textbooks at the National Library in Paris.

A chance meeting on a Paris railway platform in 1891 with Dr Henri Beaunis, then Director of the Experimental Psychology Laboratory at the Sorbonne, led to Binet being appointed associate director of the Laboratory. Towards the end of the 19th century, the French Government introduced a law requiring all children from the ages of 6 to 14 to receive state education. In 1901 Binet was asked by the Department of Education to develop a standard test to identify children who would require additional educational support. Binet took on the challenge and the result was the world's first IQ test, the Binet-Simon Scale. This test was soon adapted by American psychologists Lewis Terman and Robert Yerkes who constructed measures that were administered on a very large scale to prospective recruits to the US Army, thereby firmly establishing the applied use of psychometrics.

The application of the psychometric method in the UK owes much to the work of Cyril Burt who graduated in Philosophy from Oxford in 1906. Although a formal degree course in Psychology was not established at Oxford until after the Second World War, Burt developed an interest in the newly emerging field of Psychometrics fostered by William McDougall who had been appointed as a reader in Mental Philosophy (psychology was generally regarded as a branch of philosophy at the time).

After graduation, Burt worked with McDougall on a national survey measuring mental and physical attributes of the general population (together with Charles Spearman). In the summer of 1908, Burt visited the University of Würzburg, Germany, where he first met the psychologist Oswald Külpe who had been an assistant to Wundt at Lepzig and further influenced Burt's interest in psychometrics.

In 1913, Burt took the part-time position of a school psychologist for the London County Council (LCC), with the responsibility of identifying 'feeble-minded' children, in accordance with the Mental Deficiency Act of 1913. The fact that some of his later work was discredited should not obscure the significance of his earlier contribution.

The first use of the term 'clinical psychology' is widely credited to Lightner Witmer in the USA, who founded the world's first psychological clinic in 1896 at the University of Pennsylvania. Witmer, whose first degree had been in economics followed by graduate studies in political science, had become interested in remediation of educational difficulties whilst working as a school teacher and where he had assisted a 14-year-old boy overcome specific language difficulties. He subsequently joined the experimental psychology laboratory at Pennsylvania as an assistant to James Cattell, another former student of Wilhelm Wundt, and indeed Witmer himself also spent a year as a student of Wundt in Lepzig.

Subsequently Clifford Beers founded the mental hygiene movement in America as a result of witnessing and himself experiencing maltreatment while hospitalized because of depression and paranoia. Starting in the 1920s, mental hygienists promoted a therapeutic perspective toward the everyday problems of children with the aim of prevention and early intervention. The US National Committee was also instrumental in the establishment of Child Guidance clinics.

In the UK the children's department at the Tavistock Hospital was founded in 1926 and was staffed by doctors, social workers, and also psychologists whose role was 'the carrying out of psychological tests and the ascertainment of intelligence quotients'.

Shortly afterwards the Notre Dame Centre in Glasgow opened in 1931 and was the first Child Guidance Clinic to be directed by a psychologist, Sister Marie Hilda, and is still operating today. Child guidance clinics provided services for children with a range of problems, from bed-wetting and stammering to delinquent behaviour. In addition to conducting psychometric tests, psychologists used play therapy to understand the nature of the children's difficulties.

Despite these early steps towards applying psychology in practice, the discipline of psychology in the UK remained very small until after the Second World War: the number of members of the BPS stood at only 811 in 1941.

The focus of academic psychology was understandably drawn towards military issues during this period, particularly selection and support for the forces. However, in the aftermath of the war the National Health Service (NHS) was created and this presented an opportunity for psychologists to formally establish a new profession: clinical psychology.

1.4 Clinical psychology in the National Health Service

It was only after the war that UK psychologists began working in the field of adult mental health. An informal 'Committee of Professional Psychologists (Mental Health)' formed within the BPS, and held its first meeting in 1943. The inclusion of 'mental health' created an explicit link with the establishment of the National Association for Mental Health (NAMH), assembled from a merger of the three main national voluntary mental health organizations of the time: the Central Association for Mental Welfare, the National Council for Mental Hygiene, and the Child Guidance Council (interestingly in 1972 the NAMH was renamed MIND and remains a major mental health charity today).

The BPS Committee was initially made up of a fairly small group of educational psychologists, mainly women, and was chaired by Lucy Fildes. Fildes was another pioneer in the application of psychology for children's difficulties: she had initially worked as a researcher at Cambridge under C.S. Myers and later Frederic Bartlett, and subsequently went on to become the head of psychology at the London Child Guidance Clinic. Much of the administration of the committee was undertaken by May Davidson. Davidson grew up in South Africa and studied psychology at UCL. She went on to be appointed as Educational Psychologist for the City of Oxford in 1946 and later to the Warneford Hospital where she began working with adults and then to develop pioneering clinical psychology services. She was subsequently appointed as the First Consultant Adviser on Clinical Psychology to the Department of Health and Social Security 1973–1980, for the first time explicitly marking the involvement of psychologists in national policy making.

In an article written when she was President of the BPS, Davidson eloquently captured the tension that has always existed between the scientific foundations of psychology as an academic discipline and the application of psychology in practice. *'A psychologist educated in the British academic tradition normally internalizes a demand for certainty and acquires the expectation that human behaviour will be fully explained. The student who then obtains training in applied psychology enters a state of conflict brought about by the ambiguities and uncertainties of practical work, and colleagues and clients who do not share the value system that requires scientific explanations of human behaviour'* (Davidson, 1977). This is a theme that will be returned to elsewhere in this book.

The first ever trainees in clinical psychology in the UK started at the Maudsley Hospital in 1946 and the course was formalized in 1949 into a 13-month postgraduate diploma course awarded by the University of London. From the outset the course was led by Monte Shapiro who had come to the UK after completing an undergraduate degree in South Africa. Clinical work amongst psychologists at the Maudsley Hospital was initially confined solely to psychometric testing. Indeed, the then head of the Psychology Department, Hans Eysenck, initially argued against psychologists taking on any therapeutic role, claiming that therapy was 'essentially alien' to a scientific discipline like psychology. There was certainly no pressure for psychologists to take on therapeutic roles, since psychotherapy remained the exclusive preserve of medically qualified psychiatrists who showed no indication that they wished to relinquish their monopoly.

Nevertheless, Shapiro developed a person-centred clinical approach based on a hypothesis-testing single case experimental methodology. Initially, this approach was restricted to assisting in establishing a diagnosis, but the conditioning principles identified by Pavlov and others presented an opportunity to apply the approach to intervention.

Subsequently, Eysenck also began to modify his views after visiting the University of Pennsylvania in 1949, where clinical psychology was developing a much more directly therapeutic role (perhaps unsurprisingly since it had been the base for Witmer's first clinic some 50 years previously). Indeed, in 1958 Eysenck delivered a lecture at the Royal Medico-Psychological Association (which later became the Royal College of Psychiatry) in which he described the emerging field of behaviour therapy and argued that psychiatrists should focus on disease processes, whilst psychologists should modify learned responses. Subsequently, the application of learning principles to treatment of phobias and other anxiety disorders was developed by H. Gwynne Jones and Vic Meyer, two clinical psychologists working at the Maudsley Hospital in London.

Although the Maudsley course was the first formal clinical psychology training course, other related courses developed at around the same time from very different traditions. An adult-focused training course developed from the existing child-focused course at the Tavistock Clinic, which had been founded in 1920 and was strongly influenced by the psychodynamic models developed by Sigmund Freud.

A different approach to clinical psychology was also developing contemporaneously at the Crighton Royal Hospital in Scotland where the psychologist John Raven had been invited to set up a department of psychological research in 1943. This programme was heavily influenced by humanistic psychology, an approach that rejected much of what it saw as the reductionism of experimental psychology, valuing instead intuitive forms of knowledge and the importance of personal relationships and self-understanding.

From the very beginnings of clinical psychology in the UK, and indeed in the USA, a number of approaches have therefore influenced the nature of the profession, although the behavioural and later cognitive-behavioural model emerging from the Maudsley was more dominant in the UK, whereas the psychodynamic model remained the dominant influence in the USA. This may help to explain why the cognitive approaches of Aaron Beck (an American psychiatrist) and Albert Ellis (an American psychologist) became much more quickly and readily adopted into mainstream clinical psychology training in the UK than in their homeland.

1.5 Subsequent professional developments

Based in the UK, a working group of the BPS Committee of Professional Psychologists (Mental Health) (CPP-MH) was formed in 1950 of psychologists working with adults, which then led directly to a highly significant event on 7 February 1952, when the first Whitley circular (PTA 10) was published by the Department of Health, and which officially recognized the existence of clinical psychologists within the NHS. It specified the minimum qualifications required for employment as an honours degree in Psychology, and a grading structure—entry level (£380 per year), basic grade (£520 per year), senior (£810), and top grade (£1,300).

In September 1957, the Department of Health officially approved named training courses, three of which were 'general' courses (Institute of Psychiatry, Tavistock Clinic, and the Crichton Royal) in that they provided training with children and adults, whereas four courses were in Educational Psychology and provided training with children only.

The additional 'probationer' route to enter the profession, essentially a supervised apprenticeship with no formal assessment, remained available throughout the 1970s.

Despite the emergence of clinical psychology as a distinct entity soon after the birth of the NHS in 1946, a separate Division of Clinical Psychology was not established within the BPS for another 20 years, until 1966. However, the two annual UK professional achievement awards currently presented by the BPS Division of Clinical Psychology are still named after the pioneers May Davidson and Monte Shapiro.

The clinical psychology profession continued to develop at a fairly slow but steady rate through the1970s and 1980s, although through the 1990s and the first half of the next decade there was a very substantial and sustained increase in the number of training places (see Figure 1.1), and thus the profession. Progressively all the training courses evolved into university-based master's courses, and eventually into 3-year doctorates.

Fig. 1.1 Clinical psychology training places in the UK. Data reproduced from Clinical Psychology Training Clearing House (<http://www.leeds.ac.uk/chpccp/>).

1.6 **Current context of clinical psychology practice**

Although the number of clinical psychologists working within the NHS has increased dramatically since 1998, the numbers are still relatively small in comparison to the number of people in the general population who experience psychological difficulties. For instance, based on large-scale prevalence studies, it is estimated that there are over 6,000,000 individuals currently experiencing depression or anxiety disorders in England alone. This equates to less than one practising clinical psychologist for 600 people with common mental health problems, not counting any other type of presenting problems. The *New Ways of Working in Applied Psychology* report produced jointly between the Department of Health and the BPS in 2008 highlighted the need for a mix of skills within the psychological workforce, and the need to utilize flexible approaches to service delivery (see also Lavender, 2009).

Then in 2008, the Department of Health in England launched a major programme of new investment in psychological therapies provision (Increasing Access to Psychological Services or IAPT) which consisted of an additional £900 million of funding allocated over 6 years. A key objective of the programme was to produce 6,000 additional psychological therapists including clinical psychologists and other mental health professionals, trained to deliver formal evidence-based psychological therapies. Another aim was training psychological wellbeing practitioners, via a 1-year training programme, to deliver low-intensity psychological interventions such as guided self-help and group-based psycho-educational programmes under supervision, within a 'stepped-care approach'. This stepped-care model was recommended by the National Institute for Health and Clinical Excellence (NICE) and had two essential principles:

1 The intervention provided must have the best chance of delivering positive outcomes whilst simultaneously placing the least possible burden on the patient.

2 There must be a system of scheduled review to detect and act on non-improvement to enable 'stepping up' to more intensive treatments; 'stepping down' where a less intensive treatment becomes appropriate; and 'stepping out' when an alternative treatment or no treatment become appropriate.

While the IAPT programme is limited to England, similar stepped-care programmes to expand access to evidence-based psychological therapies have been developed in other nations within the UK. In particular the NHS in Scotland has developed a very comprehensive framework across a range of client groups for matching the appropriate level of intervention to specific psychological difficulties (NHS Education for Scotland, 2011).

1.7 **Current interface between science and practice**

The scientific foundations of clinical psychology have developed very significantly since the early application of psychometrics and classical conditioning. The impressive development of the profession has resulted from a dynamic interaction between psychological research and clinical practice.

Recent examples of such innovation have included work in the field of post-traumatic stress disorder by Emily Holmes, a clinical psychologist, who has undertaken research based on cognitive neuroscience (Holmes *et al.*, 2009). She has developed a novel treatment for the prevention of post-traumatic stress symptoms, building on research that has demonstrated that the brain has selective resources with limited capacity, and that new memories consolidate in the brain over a period of about 6 hours. Holmes reasoned that it might be possible to develop a 'cognitive vaccine' which would selectively compete for resources required to generate mental images and thereby to disrupt the consolidation of flashback memories in the immediate aftermath of a traumatic event. Holmes and colleagues showed in an experiment with normal volunteers that undertaking a visual spatial task, based on the computer game Tetris, for just 30 minutes after watching a film showing traumatic events led to significantly fewer flashbacks being experienced in the following week. Thus an intervention that was developed directly from predictions from psychological theory may in the future be shown to prevent the occurrence of psychological disorders in practice, and become incorporated into clinical protocols designed to help people who have experienced traumatic events (see also Chapter 11). Similarly, other observations and insights from clinical practice may be used by clinical psychologists to modify existing theories about the causes, maintenance, and effective treatment of psychological disorders. For instance, psychologists such as David Fowler, Phillipa Garety, and Elizabeth Kuipers have conducted influential research questioning existing psychiatric diagnostic approaches to schizophrenia, instead developing therapeutic interventions for people experiencing psychosis by modification of distressing symptoms, or by helping people to change their understandings of these symptoms (see Fowler *et al.* (1995) and also Chapter 5).

1.8 **Integration within and contribution to mainstream health care**

As this brief historical outline of the profession has shown, clinical psychology is a relative newcomer to health care, creatively finding its place alongside the giants of medicine and nursing, together with many other well-established but smaller professions such as occupational therapy, speech and language therapy,and physiotherapy. Clinical psychology also claims its own unique contribution as an applied science, drawing on the science of psychology (see Chapter 2 for more discussion of this issue). In some cases, psychologists have taken on and developed tasks previously carried out by other groups (testing children or psychotherapy, for example), while in other instances they have become service innovators (for example devising many original behavioural treatments and neuropsychological assessements). In most cases clinical psychologists have worked with others in multi-disciplinary teams, and have contributed to team work by adding their essential psychological perspective to the care of patients. Although their early work was often linked with mental health difficulties, currently psychologists work in a wide range of health care settings, including paediatrics, palliative care, spinal injury, burns, and diabetes units, for example, demonstrating the growing integration of the profession with mainstream services. Broader developments in health care mean that psychological issues are nowadays given far more recognition than they were hitherto, opening numerous avenues for psychologists to make contributions to the welfare of people in distress or pain. Fifty years ago it would have been quite rare to meet a clinical psychologist anywhere at all: now psychologists play an accepted role in most modern health care services and settings.

One question that arises as a consequence of this relatively recent professional arrival is, what constitutes psychologists' special contribution, or 'unique selling point', amongst all other health care providers? The issue of professional identity is hotly debated, but most psychologists would point to their particular ability to provide detailed, theoretically derived assessments or formulations, and complex evidence-based treatments for a range of patients, together with a scientific approach to clinical problems, drawing on advanced clinical research skills. So, for instance, Helen, Chris, Jana, and Alice (introduced earlier in this chapter) all apply unique clinical formulations to their patients' difficulties and develop personalized treatment plans, but they also seek to use their skills to further develop the evidence base for use by other clinical professionals in future. Of course there are also a range of other branches of applied psychology, such as educational, organizational, and counselling, and all share many similarities: the core feature of clinical psychology, however, is its focus on working clinically within the health care context and its use of a range of therapeutic models, together with a research or evidence-based orientation to clinical problems or phenomena.

1.9 Ethics and values of the profession

The key professional values of clinical psychologists are contained in the BPS Code of Ethics and Conduct (2009), comprising the need to meet standards of respect, competence, responsibility, and integrity. This means that psychologists 'value the dignity and worth of all persons, with sensitivity to the dynamics of perceived authority or influence over clients, and with particular regard to people's rights, including those of privacy and determination' (p. 10). In practice this means taking scrupulous care to respect confidentiality and always to obtain informed consent for interventions, and to work to advance client autonomy wherever possible. Psychologists need to be mindful of boundaries which protect both them and their clients, and to be aware of the impact of their own beliefs and values on their work. They have to avoid being drawn into 'sides' and to maintain objectivity when possible. Having regular supervision is essential here, with the recognition that professional learning is a life-long requirement. Psychologists must not take on work that is outside their own sphere of competence, and should aim to work collaboratively with others, including staff, carers, and families.

1.10 The impact of becoming a clinical psychologist

Working with psychological issues can be a demanding experience, especially for trainees when they embark on the career and as they move from placement to placement, learning new skills with a range of clients in novel contexts, and managing the anxiety of seemingly repeatedly being moved back to square one for every new clinical experience, while at the same time being assessed by stringent university procedures and requirements. Trainees are expected to take on a variety of new challenges and responsibilities, including encountering human distress in a variety of forms, which means that they may have to confront issues such as mortality, abuse, or trauma, which do not normally form part of most people's daily working lives. In addition, some trainees find it hard to maintain as much contact as they might like with family or friends living elsewhere, and time is limited for socializing. Nevertheless, trainees do progressively attain many transferable skills and gain in confidence as they master the core competencies, as well as developing their own particular set of interests in specialist clinical areas. Training programmes have evolved a variety of approaches to encourage the development of personal and professional competencies, for example some courses fund confidential personal learning sessions for trainees, whilst others provide small groups run by an external facilitator, so that trainees can learn about themselves within a confidential small group setting. The good news is that, despite the heavy demands, very few trainees fail to complete their clinical training, and the vast majority, once qualified, continue to work as clinical psychologists for the rest of their working lives.

Over a career, clinical psychologists can expect to gain competence and skills in a range of ways of approaching and reducing human distress. This is a highly fulfilling career, deepening the psychologist's understanding of what it means to be human and to confront and survive distress. Experienced psychologists often report developing greater respect for individual differences and increased tolerance towards others, as well as having many valued memories of client triumphs. The demands of work are often considerable, and while financial rewards and the physical environment are not always as good as many would (understandably) prefer, nonetheless most psychologists consider their work to be a privilege, as well as being a source of constant stimulation and value.

References

British Psychological Society (2009). *Code of Ethics and Conduct*. BPS, Leicester (<http://www.bps.org.uk/sites/default/files/documents/code_of_ethics_and_conduct.pdf>).

Davidson, M. (1977). The scientific/applied debate in psychology. *Bulletin of the British Psychological Society*, **30**, 273–278.

Fowler, D., Garety, P., and Kuipers, E. (1995). *Cognitive Behaviour Therapy for Psychosis*. Wiley, Chichester.

Holmes, E.A., James, E.L., Coode-Bate, T., and Deeprose, C. (2009). Can playing the computer game 'Tetris' reduce the build-up of flashbacks for trauma? A proposal from cognitive science. *PLOS ONE*, **4**, 1–6.

Lavender, T. (2009). Reflections on the impact of new ways of working for applied psychologists. *Journal of Mental Health Training, Education and Practice*, **4**, 23–28.

NHS Education Scotland (2011). *The Psychological Therapies Matrix* (<http://www.nes.scot.nhs.uk/education-and-training/by-discipline/psychology/matrix.aspx>).

Further reading

British Psychology Society Division of Clinical Psychology (2010). *The Core Purpose and Philosophy of the Profession* (<http://www.bpsshop.org.uk/clinical-psychology-the-core-purpose-and-philosophy-of-the-profession-p1394.aspx>).

British Psychological Society History of Psychology Centre (<http://hopc.bps.org.uk/>).

Hall, J. (2007). The emergence of clinical psychology in Britain from 1943 to 1958 part I: core tasks and the professionalisation process. *History and Philosophy of Psychology*, **9** (1), 29–55.

Hall, J. (2007). The emergence of clinical psychology in Britain from 1943 to 1958 part II: practice and research traditions. *History and Philosophy of Psychology*, **9** (2), 1–33.

Improving Access to Psychological Therapies (IAPT) (<www.iapt.nhs.uk>).

Chapter 2

Competencies and models in clinical psychology

Susan Llewelyn and David Murphy

2.1 Introduction

The professional activities of most contemporary clinical psychologists are underpinned by the *reflective scientist practitioner* model, an approach that integrates evidence-based practice with awareness of the importance of context and an ethical and value base. In applying this model, psychologists generally employ an iterative cycle of psychological competencies (assessment, formulation, intervention, evaluation, communication/consultation, and, if appropriate, service development) using interventions that are all to a varying extent based on psychological theory and empirical evidence. These competencies are used in order to understand how to resolve a range of psychological difficulties, in a variety of clinical settings. Exactly how all of these competencies are employed varies according to the specific therapeutic model used, and as applicable to a specific clinical presentation. In addition, the work is always subject to the psychologist's own scrutiny and questioning about the underlying values and purpose of the work, and in whose interests the work is being carried out.

2.2 Psychologists as reflective scientist practitioners

Although most clinical psychologists aim to integrate the two aspects of the reflective scientific practitioner model, these are quite distinct perspectives and there is potentially a tension between the two. The *scientist practitioner model* was first articulated as an outcome of the Boulder Conference, held in 1949, which determined the content of clinical psychology training in the USA, and was subsequently enormously influential elsewhere. The model assumes that we will find the most helpful possible way to help a patient or family if we consistently apply and refine theories and practices about what works best, supported by evidence. In contrast, the *reflective practitioner model*, building on the work of Donald Schön (e.g. Schön, 1983), accepts that there are always a variety of ways to intervene, that no one position can ever be 'right', and that what we mean by 'what works best' depends on whose perspective is being taken. Striking a balance between these perspectives provides a fascinating dimension to clinical work, and means that, although drawing on a common evidence base, no two psychologists will practice exactly alike.

In practice, the 'scientist' aspect of the model refers not only to the psychologist's attempt to base his or her professional interventions on evidence, but also, and in fact more crucially, to his/her aim to approach each new client, patient, or family like a scientist might approach a research question. Thus a psychologist will select an intervention based on a theoretically derived hypothesis, and apply it in a particular case, which may then be accepted, changed, developed, or rejected depending on the outcome. So, for example, when asked to help a boy with nocturnal enuresis (bed wetting) a psychologist will first talk with the family and develop a hypothesis about what is causing the problem (for instance, that the boy had never learned to associate the sensation of bladder fullness with the need to wake up and urinate). At this point the psychologist might suggest a programme of therapy (for example, using a bell and pad), implement this with the boy, and assess whether or not the treatment has had any impact. If it has, this at least partially confirms the psychologist's hypothesis, and the therapy will continue until the problem is resolved. If it has not, the psychologist (using the scientific method) will seek to develop another hypothesis which may imply the need for a different type of intervention. For example, the child's level of anxiety at school or in the home might be identified as impacting indirectly on his difficulty in developing bladder control, so the next stage of intervention may focus on anxiety management.

The reflective aspect of the model is an essential part of professional practice. Psychologists need to be aware of the limits of what they are offering, and how values and beliefs shape understanding of what should be provided; hence reflection is a crucial component of their work. For example, a focus simply on the child with enuresis might deflect attention from a wider systemic problem in the family, or could obscure evidence that he is being expected to gain bladder control at an early age because of a shared cultural belief despite this being beyond his current ability. Having reflective capacity ensures that psychologists think carefully about their work to ensure that they practice in an ethically aware and culturally sensitive way, and in a way that allows for modification and development of theory and practice to fit individual circumstances. Reflection essentially means questioning, and having sensitivity about professional and clinical issues, and awareness of the values and assumptions that underpin all our actions.

Nonetheless, the profession of clinical psychology also affirms certain overarching values, based on the fundamental acknowledgement that all people have the same human worth and the right to be treated as unique individuals. Clinical psychologists therefore aim to treat all people with dignity and respect, and to work collaboratively in partnership, to reduce psychological distress, and to enhance and promote psychological wellbeing, while being sensitive to the social circumstances within which people live. Supervision is seen as a life-long process which aids thought and promotes good professional practice, and as such provides an invaluable aid to effective reflection.

As both scientist and reflective practitioners, psychologists also always attempt to link theory and practice, and to increase understanding of how best to intervene. They therefore evaluate the outcomes of interventions so that services offered to similar patients in future will improve (clinical audit), whilst knowledge about the conditions or therapy will also increase (clinical research). In addition to benefiting the individual client, these processes benefit both future clinical services and the development of psychological theory more generally.

2.3 Competencies and models within clinical psychology

During their training, clinical psychologists develop a set of core clinical competencies. The specific application of these competencies depends on the nature of the client group. For example, an assessment with a client who has sustained a mild brain injury is more likely to involve paper and pencil psychometric tests than would an assessment with a client with a severe learning disability. Furthermore, the nature of assessment undertaken also reflects the theoretical perspective adopted. For example, if a systemic perspective is taken, then the focus is likely to be on patterns of interaction between family members, whereas a cognitive-behavioural perspective will require greater focus on an individual's negative cognitions. This chapter introduces these issues and thereby forms the foundation for all the other chapters, in which applications of a range of competencies and models to specific clinical presentations are explained.

2.4 **The core competencies**

Assessment involves gaining an understanding of a person or situation, as well as of change and stability, and may involve contrasting the individual's performance or results with those of comparable others. Assessment is normally the first step in any psychologist's work, and forms the basis of what follows, although assessing the progress and outcome of any subsequent intervention is also routine. In the UK, the Health and Care Profession Council's Standards of Proficiency state that clinical psychologists should '*be able to choose and use a broad range of psychological assessment methods, appropriate to the client, environment and the type of intervention likely to be required*'. The Clinical Psychology Benchmark Statements (Quality Assurance Agency, 2004) provide a concise statement of the practice and purpose of assessment:

- ♦ the development and use of psychometric tests (including an appreciation of the importance of sound psychometric properties of test instruments, such as reliability and validity);
- ♦ the application of systematic observation and measurement of behaviour in both daily life contexts and other settings (for example, comparing interaction patterns between a child and her peers in a nursery, before and after an intervention designed to decrease expressed hostility towards other children);

- devising self-monitoring strategies for individual service-users, such as recording of daily activities or thoughts;
- the use of formal and informal interviews with clients, carers, and other professionals.

Carrying out meaningful assessments requires psychologists to develop an effective alliance with clients, families, or carers, and to understand the context of the presenting difficulty. For example, a psychologist might administer a widely used depression inventory, and a standardized cognitive battery of other tests, when trying to understand the problems of an elderly man who is becoming increasingly withdrawn and non-communicative with his family. However, when doing so, the psychologist will also seek to gain an understanding of his history, and current family and personal circumstances. Psychologists may also devise and use one-off, individualized assessment procedures. Working with a child with a specific but uncommon fear of butterflies, for example, might require the development of an individualized scale around the fear-inducing characteristics of butterflies to assess the child's progress. As another example, a psychologist aiming to reduce self-harming in a learning-disabled man might carry out an observational assessment of the sheltered accommodation in which the man is living, using a specific schedule to investigate the unique working patterns of the staff in that particular unit.

According to the model used, the psychologist will pay particular attention to the ways in which clients, carers, or families describe themselves and their difficulties, and will consider if there are any patterns to their responses. For example, if employing a cognitive model, the psychologist may seek specific examples of how a young person interprets her social experiences, and may try to uncover some of her negative assumptions about herself in relation to peers. However, a psychologist employing a psychodynamic approach would pay more attention to the client's way of seeking to relate personally to the psychologist. If applying a systemic therapy approach, a psychologist would probably assess the client together with significant family members or peers, and observe the nature of the interaction that takes place. No matter which model is used, a risk assessment will also be conducted whenever there is any suggestion that harm is a possibility, or in contexts where the client or others may be vulnerable.

Although assessment invariably takes place at the start of an intervention, it is also an on-going process occurring throughout, as the psychologist seeks to ensure that the intervention is having the desired effect. Generally an initial assessment will be conducted in a single session, although some therapeutic approaches also suggest that formal assessment should take place over several sessions so that enough information can be obtained to produce a reasonably comprehensive formulation. As new ideas or information emerge during the intervention, it is often necessary to reassess the difficulty. For example, someone who presents with depression might reveal after several sessions of therapy that they have experienced traumatic sexual abuse as a child, which will undoubtedly need further exploration, and will probably suggest changes to the intervention offered.

The assessment phase normally also involves the psychologist informing the client about the likely course and outcome of the intervention as well as gaining informed consent (or that of appropriate family members or carers).

Formulation is a specific psychological process which brings together and integrates information gained during assessment, with relevant psychological theory and data, in order to provide an individually derived working model of the causal factors leading to and maintaining the problem. This model can then be used to plan an individualized approach for intervening. As such it is the cornerstone of professional practice, and has sometimes been seen as the key distinguishing feature of clinical psychology.

Different theoretical approaches will of course focus on different possible causal and maintaining factors, and will draw upon different types of supporting evidence. But whatever the model used, formulation is central to any intervention. This ability to 'access, review, critically evaluate, analyse and synthesise data and knowledge from a psychological perspective is one that is distinct to psychologists' (Clinical Psychology Benchmark Statements (Quality Assurance Agency, 2004)). Formulation is also probably the most creative aspect of a clinical psychologist's work. It is normally carried out in collaboration with the client, and aims to make sense, for both client and psychologist, of the presenting difficulty.

Formulation is a process distinct from that of diagnosis, which is a procedure particularly associated with a medical model. However, psychologists may use diagnostic frameworks in addition to formulation, and in many ways the two processes can be seen as complementary to one another. Arriving at a diagnosis essentially involves using one of the two internationally recognized classification frameworks for mental health difficulties: the International Classification of Disease (ICD) published by the World Health Organization, or the Diagnostic and Statistical Manual (DSM) published by the American Psychiatric Association. This is done in order to locate an individual's presentation within a category or group of similar presentations. Making a diagnosis allows a clinician to draw on existing evidence about prognosis and likely effective interventions, and to facilitate communication between clinicians and with third parties, as well as to make threshold decisions about whether intervention is appropriate. Diagnosis is essentially a 'top-down' process involving matching an individual's presentation to a pre-existing category, whereas psychological formulation is a 'bottom-up' process which involves creating a unique, tailored model based on the information presented by the client. Clinical psychologists can, and do, use both approaches in their work; however, in using a diagnostic framework psychologists are required to be mindful of the limited reliability and validity of many discrete diagnostic categories within mental health, and the potential negative effects of the use of diagnostic labels in terms of stigmatizing a client and/or inappropriately locating a problem within one particular individual within a system (British Psychological Society, 2012).

When developing a formulation, attention is paid to background, *predisposing* factors which provide the setting, or sensitizing context, for the problem to develop, any *precipitating* factors which triggered the current concern, the *presenting* problem itself, and the *perpetuating* factors that maintain it. *Protective* factors will also be noted. By contrast, systemic approaches particularly focus on identifying the client's unique narrative, seeking out personal or culturally specific understandings.

Other issues frequently included in psychological formulations are accounts of how physiological, behavioural, cognitive, and affective reactions all interact in maintaining distress. Some approaches to treatment (for example, the cognitive) provide a diagrammatic representation of the problem which is shared with the client. This diagram will illustrate the links between previous experience, the formation of dysfunctional assumptions or behaviours, how they were triggered by critical incidents, how this led to distressing thoughts or imagery, and how this may then have led to the mental health problem. This is linked to behaviours (such as avoidance or checking of bodily sensations); physical reactions (such as increased arousal); cognitions (such as rumination or focusing on body changes); and affect (such as anxiety or depression). Some therapeutic approaches (for example, cognitive-analytic therapy (CAT)) involve providing a written reformulation of the client's difficulties, which is a short, sympathetically written prose account of when and why the client's problems arose, and how the client's symptoms may be a dysfunctional but understandable attempt to resolve problems that unfortunately trap the client into perpetuating the problem. Psychodynamic formulations will not normally be shared with clients, but will likewise represent the psychologist's provisional understanding of the conflicts experienced by clients, normally in terms of unresolved or unexpressed wishes or fears, with symptoms conceptualized as symbolic manifestations of conflict.

The next core competence, *intervention*, involves using a psychological model or approach to facilitate some desired change. Intervention will normally be based on the formulation (which may alter in the light of developments or new information gained during the subsequent intervention), although some approaches (for example, solution-focused therapy) do not consider formulation a prerequisite for intervention. However, for most psychologists, formulation provides an effective springboard for action. For instance, the formulation of the withdrawn elderly man already described might suggest that he has become depressed as a result of growing isolation, as well as his belief that as an older person he no longer has any value; hence a cognitive-behaviour therapy (CBT) approach to modifying his self-defeating beliefs might be implemented to help him. If a psychodynamic model was considered more appropriate, the intervention chosen might be life review, allowing the man to gain a better understanding of his relationships and values, whereas a systemic model might suggest working with those around him to develop a more supportive and stimulating environment. Alternatively, further assessment might have revealed some cognitive impairment related to an underlying dementia, in which case the intervention might alter to a discussion with him and his relatives about the likely prognosis and outcome of his condition, as well as a referral for other possible treatments or services. Any of these interventions are tests of the provisional hypotheses contained in the formulation, and are always subject to modification in the light of experience and new information.

Interventions do not just involve individual clients, but could also involve the provision of training and support for others, such as staff, relatives, and carers. An important role for a clinical psychologist is often the dissemination of psychological knowledge through teaching, supervision, and consultation. For example, a psychologist may have been asked to contribute to the therapy of an adolescent with anorexia, but after assessment and formulation, the psychologist may decide that the most appropriate form of intervention is to offer supervision to a dietician who has already made a good relationship with the client, and who is eager to implement a psychologically based treatment programme herself. Likewise, much work with children may be most effectively carried out by parents or teachers, although with help and directive guidance from the psychologist.

Duration, model, and mode of intervention vary, according to the presenting problem and the nature of the intervention provided. Many clients are seen on a one-to-one basis, whereas others, particularly children or people with learning disabilities, may be seen together with their families or carers. Interventions may be brief, although may be extended for people with psychotic symptoms, or with a range of complex problems, or for those with major social and economic difficulties. Infrequent although regular contact with those with learning disability and some types of physical disability, such as spinal cord injury, may last several years. Another crucial component of intervention is recognizing when not to intervene, or when further intervention will not be helpful. Awareness of this is an important aspect of reflective competence.

Evaluation is a central and integral part of the clinical psychologist's work, which takes place both during and after intervention. Both the effectiveness of any specific intervention and any on-going needs may be evaluated. Clinical outcomes are normally assessed by using standardized measures of symptomology, while patient experience and qualitative aspects may be assessed using satisfaction questionnaires, or by interviewing participants. Where the psychologist has administered psychometric measures or some individually derived measure prior to treatment, these will normally be repeated on termination, together with qualitative reports of improvement. In addition to evaluation of single interventions, whole treatment programmes or services may be evaluated. Comprehensive service evaluation can encompass several dimensions including a variety of therapeutic outcomes (as measured by standardized measures), as well as functions such as treatment fidelity, uptake of the programme by different social demographic groups, drop-out rates, and accessibility.

A related and also highly important activity is that of *research* into the nature of the psychological problem, or the effectiveness of interventions. Research includes investigation of psychological processes and outcomes (basic research), the development and evaluation of specific psychological interventions (primary research), and the consolidation and evaluation of primary research (secondary research). When carrying out research, clinical psychologists may also go beyond evaluation or audit of the effectiveness of specific interventions or services, to an investigation of the operation of underlying psychological issues or processes, thereby contributing to theoretical development and to new intervention models.

This aspect of psychologists' work is critical for the development of knowledge, although obtaining time and funding may be difficult, especially in publicly funded services. The establishment of clinical guidelines and evidence-based treatment manuals has been a highly significant outcome of research carried out by clinical psychologists (and also of course by others). The rapid growth of the profession, referred to in Chapter 1, may in part be due to its success in being able to demonstrate its clinical effectiveness, through well-publicized research and outcome studies. The development of qualitative approaches has further enriched the research output provided by psychologists, especially where it contributes greater understanding of service user perspectives. Nevertheless, the assumption that clinical work can ever be entirely based on evidence has also been disputed: a clear instance of the tension between the reflective and scientist-practitioner aspects of the professional role already discussed.

Communication/consultation and service delivery are areas of competence that are central to many aspects of clinical psychologists' working lives. Most straightforwardly, this involves writing reports about work done with clients, their families, and professional staff (such as general practitioners or community mental health teams). Reports may be addressed to the referring person or, in more complicated cases, to a wider set of services. For example, a mother receiving therapy for depression may in addition have a child receiving help from a family service, who may also be working with the school. The family may be in receipt of input from the probation service and have support from social services in connection with a child protection concern. The mother may also be receiving occupational therapy and physiotherapy services for mobility problems. In situations such as these the clinical psychologist is likely to be involved in on-going communication across health, social, and educational service boundaries, and any therapeutic input provided by the psychologist will comprise only a small element of the team's response to the presenting difficulties. A key skill is therefore that of being able to express psychological ideas succinctly, and the ability to formulate and present psychological reports in ways that make sense to the wider care network as well as to clients themselves.

At a more complex level, psychologists may use their communication and organizational skills to facilitate the effective delivery of some aspect of a specific health care system, for example by facilitating a staff support group or helping a service to implement a therapeutic programme for residents. It is therefore important that psychologists feel comfortable when communicating with others, both directly (face-to-face) and indirectly via all forms of electronic communication. Equally important is the ability to teach and present information to other staff, as well as to disseminate research findings through discussion or publication. Psychological interventions are clearly not the prerogative only of psychologists: many other professional groups also have competence in the delivery of psychological care. Therefore clinical psychologists need to be good team players as well as effective individual therapists, and need to be able to demonstrate sensitively their unique contribution to the delivery of care. Most clinical psychologists are involved in supervising others, especially trainee clinical psychologists, so it is vital that they have the ability to explain what needs doing and why, to a variety of audiences, and to develop the ability to nurture and facilitate the development of skills of others.

Finally, *leadership* is increasingly recognized as a core competence: the Clinical Psychology Leadership Development Framework (British Psychological Society Division of Clinical Psychology, 2010) highlights the development and application of leadership competencies at all stages of a clinical psychologist's career, beginning during post-graduate training, and becoming more central as the psychologist gains experience and competence over the years of practice. These issues are considered throughout in this text, but particularly in Chapter 14.

2.5 **Therapeutic models**

This chapter now turns to an overview of the main therapeutic models used by clinical psychologists. The application of each model is different depending on the specific context, but the essential components are outlined here, with specific instances and applications being covered in subsequent chapters. At a broad level, clinical psychologists tend to use what is described as a *biopsychosocial approach*. This means that all aspects of a person are weighed up and considered, including the influence of *biological* factors (such as any physical disease processes, legal and illegal substance use, and prescribed medication); *social* factors (such as employment status, ethnic origin, poverty, social class, and sexual preference); and the more obvious *psychological* factors. A wide range of specific models of psychological therapy exist, but, for the sake of clarity, in the rest of this chapter only the major models are outlined, which will be expanded further with clinical examples in other chapters.

Behavioural approaches

Historically the first major contribution to interventions made by clinical psychologists, and still widely in use today, is the behavioural approach. This focuses on modifying current behaviour, via the encouragement of new learning or modification of existing maladaptive patterns of behaviour. Using both operant and classical conditioning paradigms, the psychologist will attempt to understand and alter the cues that elicit either dysfunctional or adaptive behaviour. Therapeutic techniques arising from behaviour theory include functional analysis, selective reinforcement, shaping, modelling, and extinction. Examples of applications include using reward schemes to build up pro-social behaviour, the development of language in people with learning disabilities, and parent training programmes using selective reinforcement designed to improve children's conduct. Aspects of behavioural approaches are also incorporated in many other psychological interventions, as, for example, in dementia care, or as part of rehabilitation programmes for people with neurological disorders. They may also form part of wider treatment approaches such as the use of behavioural activation for people presenting with depression.

Cognitive-behaviour therapy and cognitive therapy

Developing from an awareness of the limitations of a purely behavioural approach, the most prominent therapeutic model applied by contemporary clinical psychologists across the lifespan is probably CBT, nowadays often developed to emphasize primarily the cognitive component, and known as cognitive therapy (CT). The predominance of this model is partly explained by the well-established evidence base for treatment, but also because of the ready applicability of specific cognitive models which provide a clear framework for intervention and evaluation (Roth and Fonagy, 2004). Although other professional groups also use CBT and CT, and clinical psychologists are required to have proficiency in more than one model of therapy, CBT/CT is the one model in the UK that is specified within the Standards of Proficiency for Practitioner Psychologists (Health and Care Professions Council, 2009) as essential for practice as a clinical psychologist.

The fundamental assumption of CBT and CT is that psychological distress is best understood and resolved by addressing the cognitions (thoughts, meanings, and beliefs) the person has about him/herself and his/her difficulties. An additional assumption (building on behavioural models) is that many psychological difficulties have developed via maladaptive learning, and that solutions to these may also be understood and learned. A good therapeutic relationship is seen as an important foundation for treatment, but not as being therapeutic in and of itself. Essentially, therapy involves a careful assessment and specification of how problems arose, and how faulty cognitions as well as inappropriately learned behaviours may be maintaining the problem. This is followed by joint examination of the cognitions or inappropriately learned behaviours, and the development, through homework and experimentation, of alternative, more functional ways of thinking and behaving. A collaborative stance is central, with an emphasis on problem-solving in the present, rather than aiming for either profound personality changes in the client or an understanding of the past.

How this is achieved will vary depending on the developmental stage and difficulty presented by the client. Normally therapy commences by carefully noting the history of the client's symptoms and beliefs, and assessing their current and earlier life circumstances. This leads to formulation, and re-casting symptoms in terms of the model, which is then shared with the client (known as socialization to the model). Next is a series of negotiated challenges to the client's current ways of thinking and acting, through guided discussion (often via a process known as Socratic questioning) during which clients are invited to examine the rational basis and evidence for and against their beliefs, or by behavioural experimentation, a key aspect of which is generating predictions about a specific situation and then testing this out (for example by approaching an avoided object or situation). Gradually the client is encouraged to revise any inappropriate strategies or beliefs and to develop new less restrictive understandings and behaviours. Finally, provision is also made for maintaining therapeutic gains after the end of therapy, by anticipating future challenges and planning for ways of coping with them. Hence therapists may provide a 'blueprint' of therapeutic principles for the client to use after termination, as a way of preventing relapse. For children or young people, the parents may be closely involved in the therapy; likewise interventions may be carried out in collaboration with carers or staff when working with people who are living in residential units.

CT, in particular, has developed enormously since its early application to depression in the 1970s, and there are now a range of models and therapeutic approaches proposed for most mental health difficulties, in both adults and children. More attention has recently been paid to process issues and how the therapist–client relationship may affect outcome. Different aspects of a client's experience, such as imagery, are also now being included in CT, for example when working with post-traumatic stress or eating disorders. Upsetting images, which are assumed to be stored and activated precognitively and therefore are less easily available for rational examination, are addressed and modified, in addition to observable behaviours. For further detail of these developments, see Chapters 7 and 11.

One of the undoubted strengths of the cognitive approach has been the development of specific models of particular presentations. For example, social anxiety, according to the cognitive model, results from a strong desire to fit in and to convey a particular or favourable impression of oneself to others, combined with insecurity about one's ability to do so. When faced by a social situation, the person believes that other people will notice their anxiety symptoms, such as sweating, shaking, speaking quickly, or blushing, and that they will make a fool of themselves, leading to rejection and ostracism. Self-focusing, combined with a range of behaviours adopted to cope with the situation, leads to a vicious cycle in which the anxious person feels as if they are indeed the centre of negative attention, which leads to higher levels of anxiety and increased self-consciousness. This is made worse by the person conducting personal 'post-mortems' after the event about how they behaved in recent social situations. Therapy involves shifting the attention focus from the self to the environment, and developing more realistic cognitions about self and others.

Psychodynamic therapy

Psychodynamic approaches are used by a number of clinical psychologists working with both adults and children, although only a small minority provide classical psychoanalysis (in which clients might be seen daily, or at least a few times a week, over some years). Hence clients nowadays are normally seen weekly for a much shorter duration (for instance, Brief Dynamic Interpersonal Psychotherapy is a 16-session evidenced-based therapy for depression), and are unlikely to be asked to lie on a couch, or to recount dreams. The psychodynamic model assumes the importance of unconscious material and the centrality of intrapsychic conflict, as well as the importance of interpersonal relationships and attachment patterns. Therapists aim to gain understanding of the dynamics that underpin symptoms, and to resolve them by helping the client obtain insight into the unconscious conflicts that have led to the symptoms. Understanding the therapeutic relationship itself is seen as a significant vehicle of change and as a method to work through the meaning of the client's difficulties. For example, a man presenting with repeated urges to harm himself might be encouraged to explore his feelings of self-hatred and their origins, as well as any possible angry feelings towards others, including the therapist. This is achieved via analysis of the 'transference', i.e. the client's feelings towards the therapist, and the 'counter-transference' which is vice-versa. Another example is a client who appears increasingly anxious to please her therapist and who brings in an expensive gift. The psychologist will seek to understand this as a strategy, possibly developed earlier in life as a response to the client feeling unloved, and will help the client explore the fragility of her self-esteem, with the aim of increasing her self-acceptance. In addition, psychodynamic therapists aim to understand and control their own reactions to clients, for example a wish to 'rescue' a client, which may impede therapeutic progress or obscure understanding of similar unhelpful relationship patterns occurring outside therapy. Therapists normally encourage clients to stay in touch with painful or challenging emotions, in order to try to understand their origins, and hence to more fully address and accept feelings such as loss, grief, or anger. When working with children, therapists may use objects such as dolls or sand trays, applying techniques from play or art therapy to help children to express and resolve difficult feelings.

In terms of outcome, there is less published research on the efficacy of psychodynamic therapy, although such evidence certainly exists, particularly for more recent time-limited modifications, for example, brief interpersonal dynamic psychotherapy (Roth and Fonagy, 2004). Although not necessarily accepting all aspects of the model, most clinical psychologists nowadays appreciate the importance of the client–therapist relationship, and of early attachment patterns, and how addressing difficulties within therapy, including the exploration of 'difficult' emotions within the therapeutic relationship, may significantly improve the effectiveness of a range of treatments.

Systemic and group approaches

While many psychologists work with clients on a one-to-one basis, others work with families, or with groups such as residential home staff, based on the evidence that modifying environments or systems can sometimes be much more effective in changing behaviour than individual work. Systemic approaches are based on the theoretical assumption that people are best understood in a relational context and that distress often results from dysfunctional interpersonal processes. General systems theory proposes that systems are hierarchically organized and tend towards stability; therefore changes at one level will almost inevitably lead to changes at another. This principle is used to understand and modify dysfunctional structures and communication patterns. For example, anorexic symptoms may be seen as a form of communication attempted by a young girl to pull together a fractured family, or the challenging behaviour of an elderly woman in a care home may be understood as resulting from her sense of exclusion from her previous social group following the introduction of a new, more needy resident. Addressing the family conflict or the working patterns in the care home may well have more impact than attempting to change the symptomatic 'patient'.

Most systemic therapists nowadays draw on the social constructionist approach, which contends that no one perspective can ever be 'true'; hence clients are encouraged to recognize multiple perspectives and layers of meaning, using techniques such as hypothesizing, positive psychology, and the construction of new narratives, in order to help families or individuals to shift away from underlying possibly rigid patterns of thought and behaviour. Marital or family therapy allows the distress of clients to be addressed in the context where it has arisen, and where there are likely to be a variety of ways of seeing the same issue, as, for example, in sexual problems or relationship difficulties. Recently, innovative therapeutic work has been carried out whereby some forms of family violence are addressed psychologically, in an attempt to develop alternative, less destructive ways of communicating and relating between family members.

Clinical psychologists can also make use of group approaches. Evidence suggests that group work can be just as effective as individual work, and for some difficulties may offer additional therapeutic benefits, such as the sense of not being the only one with a problem, and enhanced self-esteem gained from helping others. Some residential units provide group therapeutic treatment for personality disorder patients, where intensive groups may be run daily, during which patients are invited to explore their dysfunctional patterns of relationships in great depth. Outpatient or community-based groups have been used with a variety of people ranging from those with chronic pain, to survivors of childhood abuse, to relatives of people with brain injuries, to parents of children with learning disabilities. The underpinning theoretical base may differ, but common benefits for clients include a sense of cohesion, opportunity for interpersonal learning, and shared experiences. The group or family format essentially allows social influence processes to modify how people think or feel about themselves, as well as offering an alteration in the underlying system or context that may be promoting or maintaining individual distress.

Eclectic and integrative approaches

In practice, most clinical psychologists draw simultaneously upon a number of different approaches to inform their therapeutic work, as appropriate to the needs of their individual clients. Whilst using a broadly cognitive approach, for instance, some psychologists also make transference-based interpretations of the client's distress, or will explore an understanding of childhood dynamics while also encouraging a client to address problems directly. For example, a female survivor of childhood sexual abuse who finds trusting men difficult might be encouraged to take small steps towards developing friendships with male colleagues at work, whilst also recounting her story of trauma to her therapist. She may thereby be helped to discover both within and outside therapy that it is possible to be vulnerable and emotionally intimate with other people without being harmed. While many psychologists work eclectically without developing any particular underlying integrative model, specific approaches such as CAT formally integrate the strengths of both cognitive and psychodynamic approaches. CAT is a time-limited focused approach which aims to help people to shift existing maladaptive patterns in significant ways in a relatively short time, and to give clients tools, or ways of thinking, that minimize dysfunctional patterns of relating. Other psychologists use behavioural or cognitive techniques together with systemic ideas. For example, some innovative approaches to the treatment of psychotic symptoms are designed both to modify individual motivation or dysfunctional symptoms in a specific patient, and to influence the emotional climate in the patient's family. This has been demonstrated to significantly influence the rate of relapse.

2.6 **Conclusion**

This chapter has introduced the basic concepts and tools that inform and shape the practice of clinical psychologists today. As reflective scientist practitioners, clinical psychologists aim to extend their knowledge, and question their work, asking how they can improve it further. Clinical psychology practice is implemented via the iterative cycle of assessment, formulation, intervention, and evaluation, complemented by the process of communicating the impact of their work to others, and encouraging ways of working that enable more psychologically informed services to be provided to more clients in future. Working with individual distress, all models affirm the ethical belief that each individual has equal worth and that the task of the psychologist is to work collaboratively to reduce that distress. Although the models outlined in this chapter differ from one another in their focus on particular aspects of human functioning, they all acknowledge, to a greater or lesser extent, that people are unique, and also that they are embedded in social and interpersonal contexts which have a significant impact on individual experience. How the competencies and models are adapted to and implemented with different client groups and in different settings is the fascinating challenge of clinical psychology in practice, and is the subject of other chapters of this text.

References

British Psychological Society (2012). *The Use of Mental and Behavioural Disorder Classification Systems by Practitioner Psychologists* (<http://www.bps.org.uk/system/files/documents/diagnosis-policyguidance.pdf>).

British Psychological Society Division of Clinical Psychology (2010). *Clinical Psychology Leadership Development Framework* (<http://www.bpsshop.org.uk/clinical-psychology-leadership-development-framework-p1388.aspx>).

Health and Care Professions Council (2009). *Standards of Proficiency for Practitioner Psychologists* (<http://www.hpc-uk.org/assets/documents/10002963sop_practitioner_psychologists.pdf>).

Quality Assurance Agency (2004). *Clinical Psychology Benchmark Statements* (<http://www.qaa.ac.uk/publications/informationandguidance/documents/clinicalpsychology.pdf>).

Roth, A. and Fonagy, P. (2004). *What Works for Whom? A Critical Review of Psychotherapy Research*, 2nd edn. Guildford Press, New York.

Schön, D. (1983). *The Reflective Practitioner: How Professionals Think in Action*. Basic Books, New York.

Chapter 3

Working in primary health care

John Cape and Yvonne Millar

3.1 What is primary health care?

Within most health care systems, a distinction is commonly made between primary care, secondary care, and tertiary care services. Primary care services are those that people can access directly, without needing a referral from a professional. Family doctors or general practitioners (GPs), health visitors, and sexual health clinics are all open access primary health care services where people can make an appointment to see a professional directly. Secondary health care services such as hospital consultants and specialist mental health professionals cannot be contacted directly in many countries; patients need to be referred by a health professional, usually the GP. Tertiary services are highly specialized services such as specialist cancer centres and adolescent psychiatric inpatient units, which require a referral from a consultant or other secondary care service.

In most Western countries, primary health care normally refers to services based around the GP or family doctor and associated health professionals, who provide open access care for a very wide range of problems, and act as gatekeepers to other health services. These characteristics shape the role of clinical psychologists working in primary health care. Like GPs they have to be generalists—able to respond to a range of problems. Like GPs they have to assess and determine whether to treat the problems themselves or to refer on to other services.

Primary health care is part of a local community. The family doctor, like the vicar and publican, is a key figure in stories and TV dramas of local community life. Modern primary health care is linked with a network of local community organizations. Links with local statutory social care services are essential in order to provide coherent health and social care, for example for children in need and older people with dementia or physical disabilities. Links with key local voluntary organizations ensure that primary health care can put people in touch with local befrienders, bereavement services or other visiting and support services. Psychologists working in primary health care accordingly liaise with local community organizations. There is a significant overlap between clinical psychology in primary health care and community psychology.

3.2 **Problems presenting in primary health care**

Primary health care deals with all ages, from babies to very old people, for a huge range of health and human problems. People come asking for help for physical, psychological, and social problems and GPs, in their training, are encouraged to view all difficulties as having physical, psychological, and social dimensions. Problems range from self-limiting minor colds and minor anxieties to severe long-term life-threatening problems such as heart disease and suicidal depression. Even when people are seen in a specialist outpatient service, they will usually continue to see their GP for the same and other problems.

Multiple problems are common in primary health care. For example, a man comes for a routine GP follow-up appointment to monitor diabetes, he has longstanding marital problems of which the GP is aware, he tells the GP on this occasion that he is depressed, and also has had a chest infection for 2 weeks. What are the relationships between these different problems and what should the GP focus on in the 10-minute consultation? Pragmatically the GP has to make decisions to focus on certain problems and ignore others, on the limited information available. Knowing the patient can and will return at a future date means the GP and patient will have a further opportunity to review and focus on other problems if needed. This characteristic way of working is shared by psychologists in primary health care, having to make choices of what to focus on in the context of greater time constraints than psychologists in secondary care. But, as for the GP, it is easier for people to return and see the psychologist at a future date if needed by virtue of the psychologist being based in primary health care.

The way people present problems in primary health care often differs from secondary care. People come feeling unwell, ill, with various physical, emotional, and social concerns, rather than with a specific, focused problem. For example, a woman with a 6-month-old baby tells her GP she feels unwell, keeps getting bladder infections, has back pain, feels exhausted, her baby never seems to sleep, and that she is worried about the baby. Over a few appointments, the GP listens to her concerns, investigates her back pain, and tests her urine for bladder infections, talks to her about being depressed, and then refers her to a group for women with post-natal depression run by a psychologist. By the time of the referral she has begun to talk about herself as having post-natal depression and this is what she tells the secondary care psychologist. Michael Balint (1964) described this process many years ago as people presenting with unorganized illness, and the family doctor creating organized illness, implying there might have been alternative ways for the family doctor and patient to characterize and make sense of the patient's concerns. Primary health care thereby shapes the ways that problems are described and classified.

Most health problems are only seen in primary health care, with a minority being referred on and seen in secondary health care. Only about 10% of adults with mental health problems are ever seen in secondary care. The majority of people with mental health problems simply see their family doctor, primary care nurse, or other primary health care professional. The role of the clinical psychologist working here is to support the primary care team in delivering psychological care and treatment to this large number and range of patients.

One might expect that primary care sees just the common, less severe, less complex problems, with more complex problems being referred on to secondary care. The reality is rather different. Many individuals and families with severe and complex problems are seen only in primary care. They may perceive secondary mental health services negatively and refuse to attend or may consider them inaccessible in terms of location or the requirement to keep regular appointments. Or they may have received treatment previously in secondary mental health services that has not been successful and have been discharged. In addition, many people with less severe and less complex problems may be seen in secondary care, largely because they are articulate and request referral.

Primary care also sees a large number of people with longstanding, chronic health problems. In developed economies, an increasing proportion of health care is devoted to chronic diseases such as diabetes, arthritis, and coronary heart disease. A developing role for clinical psychologists in primary health care is in establishing and participating in programmes of care for people with all types of chronic conditions.

3.3 Organization and staffing of primary health care

In many Western countries, primary health care organization generally centres around a practice of GPs, commonly a group partnership of 2–8 GPs. Whether the practice is a single-handed GP or a group practice, however, a primary health care team supports the practice, a team that is larger or smaller depending on the size of the practice. This team will include primary care nurses, receptionists, and administrative staff. In addition, a range of other staff (e.g. physiotherapists, welfare rights workers, social workers) might occasionally come to the practice and provide services to the practice's patients.

Clinical psychologists working in primary health care vary in the extent to which they integrate with the primary health care team. Psychologists who work most of their time in a single practice will be key members of the primary health care team, whilst psychologists who visit several general practices will inevitably be more peripheral. Some clinical psychologists liaise closely with certain primary health care team members but less closely with others; for example, clinical psychologists working with young children and families in primary care will have frequent contact with health visitors, but less contact with GPs.

Clinical psychologists will not be the only specialist psychological or mental health staff working in primary health care. Depending on the country and local health system, one or more psychiatrists, mental health nurses, mental health social workers, or mental health counsellors may also be seeing patients in the practice, or providing support to the primary health care team through supervision and consultation. There may also be staff with abbreviated mental health trainings (with titles such as primary care mental health workers, psychological wellbeing practitioners or depression care specialists) providing specific treatments or interventions.

3.4 Who do clinical psychologists see in primary health care?

Emotional, psychological, and behavioural problems are the most common problems seen by psychologists. In adults these include depression, anxiety, panic, phobias, obsessive-compulsive problems, eating disorders, and difficulties in social, work, family, and intimate relationships. In very young children the most common problems seen by psychologists are sleep, feeding, and behavioural problems, while in older children anxiety and behavioural problems predominate. Clinical psychologists in primary health care see the full range of severity of mental health problems, but they generally refer people with more severe mental health problems, such as psychosis, on to secondary care mental health services.

Physical health problems such as diabetes, arthritis, and coronary heart disease are less commonly seen by clinical psychologists in British, European, and Australian primary health care, despite the important role that they could play in helping with these problems (see also Chapter 12). This is more common in the USA, where clinical psychologists also frequently provide interventions for smoking and obesity, both major public health problems for primary health care.

3.5 Assessment and triage

Assessment and triage take place where a psychologist meets a patient for the first time, finds out about their problems, and advises the patient and primary care professionals about what best to do. In the assessment the psychologist tries to build an understanding of the problems—what are the key problems, their severity, what might have caused them, what might be maintaining them—while at the same time considering options for help. If early in the assessment it becomes clear that a secondary care or educational (school-based) or voluntary sector or other service would best help the patient, then collecting further information is not needed. The time is better spent in discussing with the patient the reasons why a referral might be in their best interest, and helping them decide whether this is the option they want to take.

Triage, the process of deciding how and where, if at all, the patient would best be helped, is a key role of clinical psychologists in primary health care. Psychologists need, from their assessment, to form an opinion quickly as to whether the problems are likely to improve without intervention or whether there are treatments or other interventions that are more likely to help. They need information about the availability of treatments locally, including social community resources. One of the options that clinical psychologists will consider will be providing further advice, intervention, or treatment themselves, but this will be only one option.

In advising patients following assessment, primary care psychologists are guided by the principles of stepped care and informed choice. The stepped-care principle is that the least intensive treatment, with fewest disruptions to the person's life, should be tried first before more intensive and disruptive treatments, if it has a reasonable chance of success (Bower and Gilbody, 2005). Thus, a psychologist might suggest the patient try a self-help approach first, and CBT later if it is not successful. The principle of informed choice is that patients are given full information about different options and are helped to choose between them.

Mr Green was a 38-year-old man who had been feeling progressively more tired and had been losing enjoyment in life over a few months. Then one weekend he began to feel extremely anxious about his health, became preoccupied with thoughts that he was dying, couldn't sleep, felt he couldn't cope, and by the following week had stopped work. His GP prescribed anti-depressants and referred him to the clinical psychologist. By the time Mr Green saw the psychologist a few weeks later he was feeling less depressed and anxious and had arranged to return to work. He described a previous time when he had been depressed and off work, and was concerned about getting depressed again in the future. He also talked about concerns about being single and failed past relationships. The clinical psychologist discussed three options with him: first, a brief CBT intervention at the GP practice looking at what happened when he got depressed and anxious and how he could prevent relapses; second, a referral for group therapy where he could explore his difficulties with relationships; third, to read self-help literature for depression and anxiety and to return in future if he felt depressed and anxious again, and be seen then for treatment. He selected to do some reading himself and see how he got on, which was also the minimal needed treatment, as he was slowly improving anyway.

3.6 Education and facilitation of self-help

Educating patients about the nature of problems and guiding them in self-help is a key role of psychologists in primary health care. Although also used in secondary care as part of other treatments, in primary health care this is frequently the sole or initial intervention in a 'stepped-care' approach, with more intensive treatment offered later if does not help. Education and facilitation of self-help may involve a single meeting or a brief series of two to four meetings. Helping people to understand the problems that have given rise to concern and distress can enable them to feel less worried and anxious, and to feel they can deal with problems that previously have felt unbearable. New ways of understanding problems can also suggest alternative and more successful ways of dealing with the problems. These alternatives were not apparent until the problems were understood in a different way.

Mrs Smith made an appointment to see the psychologist at her local health centre at the suggestion of her health visitor. Her 2-year-old daughter would not settle to sleep at night. Whenever she or her partner left her daughter, the child would cry, so they would stay in her room to reassure her until she fell asleep. But then she would wake, and they would have to return. Many times they gave up and brought her to their bed where she slept undisturbed. The psychologist explained that their attempts to deal with the problem, by staying in the room when their daughter cried, meant that she never got used to being on her own or to learn that this was nothing to be frightened about since her parents would reappear in the morning. With this new understanding of the problem, Mrs Smith was able to see a different more helpful way she and her partner could respond to her daughter not settling at night—allowing the child to cry, returning periodically to reassure her they were still there, but then leaving her on her own. At a visit 4 weeks later, Mrs Smith reported that they had carried this out, had initially found it hard to leave and to listen to their daughter crying, but over a few nights she had settled, and, since then, went to sleep more quickly.

In facilitating self-help, the psychologist's goal is for patients to learn alternative strategies for managing problems and to devise plans of action themselves. The brief intervention ends when the patient has learned some alternative self-help approaches, rather than when they are 'better', although there will often be initial signs that the patient's new approaches are starting to help.

Clinical psychologists frequently make use of a range of books, leaflets, audio, and online computerized self-help materials to help people become more skilled at helping themselves. Such materials, used by patients between visits to the psychologist and after they have stopped seeing the psychologist, extend and reinforce their understanding and encourage new ways of dealing with their problems.

Education and facilitation of self-help is also well suited to delivery in groups. Examples of groups led by clinical psychologists in primary health care are anxiety management groups, and parenting skills groups for parents who are having difficulty managing a range of behavioural problems in their children. In such groups, people obtain benefit from learning from each other in addition to learning from the input of the psychologist. Groups also help people to feel less isolated and alone with their problems.

Primary care psychologists have an additional role in providing information and education about psychological issues to groups of people who might be at risk of developing psychological problems. They may give talks to ante-natal and post-natal groups about post-natal depression and how to improve parent–child bonding/attachment, or develop educational materials around suicide for young people, or work with local voluntary organizations on providing information to older people on loss and prevention of depression. Or they may advertise and run groups in community centres targeted at the general public on coping with stress or enhancing self-esteem. In these groups, the psychologist's role is to prevent psychological problems and promote psychological health, complementing their usual role with people who already have psychological problems.

3.7 **Brief psychological treatment**

Much psychological treatment carried out by clinical psychologists in primary health care is brief, being abbreviated forms of standard psychological treatments developed and delivered in secondary care (see Chapters 4 and 5 for example). A brief CBT for adults in primary care is commonly around 6–8 meetings, while in secondary care standard CBT is 16–20 meetings. In addition, while in secondary care appointments usually last 50–60 minutes and are weekly, in primary care they are more variable, from 15–60 minutes and from weekly to monthly. This is for two reasons. First, some (but as already noted, not all) problems in primary care are less severe and less complex and do not need the same length and intensity of treatment (Clark *et al.*, 1999). Second, the goals of treatment are more modest: to help people feel more optimistic about being able to deal with problems and/or to have made some progress in dealing with some problems. Once these goals have been achieved, psychologists in primary health care are happy to leave their patients to continue on their own, with an open door to return in the future if needed. In secondary care the goals are commonly more ambitious: to help people substantially overcome problems and often also to help people deal with underlying characteristic ways of thinking or relating to others in order to reduce the possibility of further problems in future. In primary health care, these more ambitious goals are not routinely attempted, on the 'stepped-care' principle that many people will make sufficient progress on their own after brief psychological treatment not to need further more intensive psychological treatment.

3.8 **Standard and intermittent treatment**

Like GPs, the work of clinical psychologists in primary health care is not all brief: a proportion also involves longer contact, some over many years, as in secondary care settings. Psychologists may see adult patients for a 16-session standard-length CBT, or for 20-sessions of short-term psychodynamic psychotherapy. Other briefer approaches may have been tried first, but when unsuccessful, the psychologist and patient then agree to try longer psychological therapy. Or it might have become apparent at assessment that a briefer treatment would not help; hence a standard (longer) length psychological therapy was agreed at the outset. The standard psychological therapies carried out in primary care are no different from those carried out in secondary care, except that it may be more convenient for the patient to attend at their local GP's surgery. It is also usually easier for the primary care psychologist to liaise with the GP about the patient's treatment, which can be necessary when the GP is also prescribing medication such as anti-depressants.

The other way that clinical psychologists see people over longer periods of time in primary care is in 'intermittent' treatment, where people see the psychologist for a period of time, then there is a gap, then they return for another meeting or series of meetings. The initiative is left for people to return when they want, which is possible since primary care is easy to access. Intermittent treatment is especially useful for people with chronic problems that can be ameliorated with psychological help and support, but which will not 'get better'. Intermittent treatment is also often the only kind of treatment possible for people who have difficulty, for various reasons, in engaging with and sticking with psychological therapy.

Mr Brown had difficulty in engaging with treatment and was seen in intermittent treatment over several years. His GP was concerned about his anger and potential for violence and referred him after he refused to see the community mental health team. He did, however, agree to see the clinical psychologist at his GP's practice. Mr Brown described frequently losing his temper and was worried that he might harm someone seriously. He had a criminal past, including violent assaults, and knew what he was capable of. He had recently become more depressed and angry following the serious illness of an aunt, who was the one person he felt had been consistently concerned about him. His father had been mostly absent and his mother abusive. He felt humiliated by a number of childhood experiences

and was very distressed talking to the psychologist about this. The psy-
chologist asked Mr Brown how it felt to talk, acknowledging that he might
find it hard to come back and talk further about how to deal with his dif-
ficulties. Mr Brown agreed it would be difficult and indeed did not return
for his next appointment. However, 3 months later he got in contact again
and a pattern developed of his attending once or twice, then stopping,
then getting back in contact again some months later. Following the death
of his aunt 4 years later, he made contact in a particularly distressed and
agitated state, thinking of killing himself and frightened of killing others,
and on this occasion attended five appointments before not coming again.
He did not make further contact with the psychologist after this, but the
GP, who continued to see him for treatment of asthma, reported that he
was more settled, had less frequent violent and suicidal thoughts, and was
living with a previous girlfriend and their son.

Clinical psychologists working in primary health care must coordi-
nate their treatment with the GPs and other members of the primary
health care team, discussing with them or keeping track through the
common electronic consultation notes of what each is doing. If there
are issues that a patient wishes to keep confidential, it is possible to do
this, but in general there is a sharing of information to provide the best
help to a patient.

3.9 **Working with others**

One major element of work in primary health care is the need to work
with other professionals. Rather than always working directly with
patients themselves, the clinical psychologist works with others, through
consultation, training, and supervision, to help them provide better care
to their patients.

The provision of consultation and advice to GPs, primary care nurses,
and other primary health care staff takes many forms. It can involve a GP
or health visitor popping in to the psychologist's room when the door is
open, having a quick chat in the reception area or over the telephone, or
a pre-arranged time to talk about a patient. The clinical psychologist, in
whatever time is available, listens, asks questions to clarify the primary

health care team member's concerns, offers suggestions about how to better understand the patient, and what they might be able to do next. To do this, the clinical psychologist needs not only to come to an understanding relatively quickly of the patient's difficulties, but also to have an understanding of the work and roles of the primary health care team member and what is, and is not, possible to do in that role. The best way for the GP or health visitor to address a patient's problems is not the same as it is for the clinical psychologist to deal with the same problems. The GP and health visitor have different roles with patients, with distinct time constraints and different skills, and the clinical psychologist needs to think of what would work best for them in the circumstances.

Dr Elliott approached the clinical psychologist about a man who was coming to see her twice a week on average with various concerns about his health, including worries about lumps, rashes, irritations, aches, and pains, which he thought might signify serious illnesses. Dr Elliott would examine and reassure him, he would go away relieved, but then return a few days later, sometimes worried about the same symptom, sometimes by a new one. The clinical psychologist suggested to the GP that she arrange a regular weekly time to see the patient, tell him he should store up his worries for recounting then, and that he should not consult her between these weekly appointments. The psychologist knew of evidence indicating that such an approach in general practice had previously helped similar patients, for whom seeking reassurance only relieves anxiety temporarily. Dr Elliott agreed this plan with the patient and tagged the patient's computer notes so that the receptionists would know not to make an appointment with the patient outside the regular weekly time. Over the course of the following 6 months, Dr Elliott was able to decrease the frequency of regular appointments from weekly, to fortnightly, to monthly and the patient reported feeling less anxious about his health.

As well as consultation and advice, clinical psychologists provide clinical supervision to primary health care staff. This may, for example, be offered to health visitors seeing mothers with post-natal depression, or to graduate primary care mental health workers providing brief self-help interventions to adults with depression.

Teaching and training of primary health care staff by clinical psychologists usually takes place in one-off workshops or training days. Training may be for GPs on using patient self-help materials in behavioural management of anxiety, for health visitors on working with mothers with post-natal depression, for district nurses on identifying and helping people who are housebound and depressed, and/or for receptionists on dealing with anxious and agitated patients. Some psychologists are also involved in formal training schemes for new GPs and family doctors.

3.10 **Developing systems of care**

Clinical psychologists in primary health care, as they become more experienced, commonly take on roles working with general practices and primary care to develop improved systems of care. This may involve working with a single general practice to improve the system of care of that particular practice, or across several general practices or with the wider community. Examples are:

- Contributing to the development of a register to monitor the practice's adult patients with severe and enduring mental illness.

- Establishing a programme across several local GP practices for the practices' primary care nurses to screen all patients with diabetes, and to provide those found to be depressed with both self-help materials and follow-up support.

- Facilitating the setting up of a local self-help group for people with agoraphobia and related problems, working with a national self-help organization.

3.11 **Audit and research**

Clinical psychologists can also contribute to the evaluation of care provided by primary health care services. Examples are auditing how many mothers with post-natal depression are receiving the agreed number of 'listening visits' from their health visitor; and checking how many parents of pre-school children attending day nurseries, who have been identified by both parents and teachers as having behavioural problems at home and school, have been offered the opportunity to talk with a psychologist about their child's behaviour problems. When an evaluation indicates that care could be improved, the psychologist will discuss this with relevant staff.

As most health problems are treated in primary care, research into how primary care can better identify and treat health problems has the potential to benefit very large numbers of people. Even when an intervention has just a small effect, or only on a small minority of people, if it is quick and cheap to provide, then it can have a large population impact. An example is research concerning the benefits of GPs asking routinely about alcohol consumption, and giving brief advice to those reporting above recommended limits.

3.12 Balancing roles—the individual patient and the population

A common dilemma for all psychologists is how much time to spend seeing patients directly and how much time to spend in other work that may indirectly help patients—liaising with other staff, developing systems, evaluation, and research. Within primary health care this dilemma is especially acute given the very large numbers of people who have psychological problems. Is the psychologist's time better spent seeing a few more patients or in possibly helping a larger number of patients through working with other primary health care professionals, or developing better systems of care? The psychologist's dilemma reflects a core dilemma of all those working in modern primary health care, which attempts to offer both personal care to individual patients, and care for a designated population of patients (the population of patients registered with the general practice and its local community). What should the balance be between responding to individual patients' health concerns and developing systems in the practice and with the local community to improve the health of the practice population and community as a whole? The challenge for clinical psychologists in primary health care, together with other primary care colleagues, is in bringing together a skilled highly personal approach to individuals' concerns and a population-based public health approach to the problems of a community.

References

Balint, M. (1964). *The Doctor, his Patient and the Illness*, 2nd edn. Pitman Medical, London.

Bower, P. and Gilbody, S. (2005). Stepped care in psychological therapies: access, effectiveness and efficiency. *British Journal of Psychiatry*, **186**, 11–17.

Clark, D.M., Salkovskis, P.M., Hackmann, A., Wells, A., Ludgate, J., and Gelder, M. (1999). Brief cognitive therapy for panic disorder: a randomized controlled trial. *Journal of Consulting and Clinical Psychology*, **67**, 583–589.

Chapter 4

Working with children and young people

Duncan Law

4.1 Introduction

There is no period in a person's life in which there is greater psychological development than during childhood. Children and young people are shaped by every interaction they have with the world and the world has with them; they are constantly changing and developing: physically, socially, and psychologically. Experiences in childhood will have a profound, and lasting, impact on their psychological health for the rest of their lives, and in turn will shape the lives of their children, and their children's children. It is during childhood that the building blocks of psychological health and resilience are laid down, and equally where the roots of psychological distress can take hold. It is for this reason that it is vital that the skills and knowledge of clinical psychology are applied, not only to offer interventions when things go wrong, but crucially also to advise and shape a child's world to give them the best chance of things going right. Due to the complex and dynamic nature of the worlds of children and young people, there are few areas in clinical psychology where the role of psychologist as applied scientist is more evident and more applicable. A clinical psychologist's training equips them with the scientific knowledge and clinical skills to draw upon a whole range of sound psychological theory and scientific evidence; to understand, and then apply solutions to complex issues of emotion and behaviour.

4.2 Wellbeing and psychological resilience

All children experience varying degrees of psychological and emotional distress during the normal turbulence of childhood and adolescence: a baby crying because it is suddenly hungry, a young child's sadness at the loss of a favourite toy, the uncertainty on the first day at a new school, pain from a scraped knee in the playground, grief from the death of a beloved pet. Although all of the above examples are likely to be psychologically distressing, the distress is a normal reaction to common childhood experiences. Indeed it is through normal stressful experiences that children learn psychological resilience—but they do not learn this on their own; how children learn to deal with distress and upset is shaped by the reactions and care they receive from their caregivers. From the first moments of life, the building blocks of a baby's psychological resilience are laid down, moulded by their attachments and by the quality of care they receive from the adults around them. For the majority of children these attachments are good enough—however, for a significant minority, particularly those who experience abuse and neglect, the relationships and the psychological environment they experience can have a significant negative impact on both their psychological development and their physical brain development (Perry, 2002).

Sadly, for the small but significant minority of children who receive poor quality care, there is a role for psychology. In exceptional circumstances the quality of care is so poor as to cause significant psychological harm to the child, to the extent that they are removed from their biological parents, as part of a safeguarding plan, and placed in foster care to prevent further harm. Here psychologists can work with social workers and foster carers to understand the reactions to care of these 'looked after children' (LAC) and to create an environment that can lead to the development of trust and the building blocks of better attachment relationships and, in turn, to better psychological health. By understanding what leads to good quality attachment relationships being formed between parent and child, and how these are shaped and maintained by good parenting, psychologists can work with parents, carers, and others to influence the environments in which children are raised in order to optimize healthy development.

Around all children are 'families' of one form or another. The shape of these families will vary considerably: from biological families of origin, through single-parent families, to families reconstituted through new partners coming together (same sex or otherwise), foster families, children's homes, adoptive families, boarding schools, and communes. Wherever on the spectrum of family life a child is raised, the family around a child will have influence on their psychological health, and it is not the shape of the family but the quality of care that matters. Around the families are other systems—school, peers, and community—which in turn will also have influence on the child. To understand children we must understand them as individuals—their way of thinking, their psychological strengths and difficulties—but we must also understand the systems in which they exist. Formulations of children's lives and the problems they might experience must take a broad systemic view—taking in family, school, and peer relationships, at the very least—to more fully understand psychological difficulties: what maintains them, and what resources and possibilities there might be in the system that could potentially change to have a positive impact on the child.

We know that the wider context, outside the immediate family, within which children and young people live, can help or harm their psychological wellbeing. Communities in which there are high rates of violence and crime, poverty, unemployment, and substance abuse tend to have a negative impact on children's mental health. More stable, integrated communities, in which the habitants experience better physical health, tend to have a positive impact on emotional wellbeing. In understanding wellbeing in children, clinical psychologists must also consider the wider community. This approach draws on the related field of community psychology (Orford, 1992) which focuses on the impact community has on individuals, including their mental health. Community psychology should be of interest to clinical psychologists as, if mental ill health is a consequence of community, then whole community interventions may prove an effective and efficient way of promoting psychological wellbeing across communities including children. There is still much work to be done to understand the complex relationships between community and children's psychological wellbeing, and perhaps because of this complexity, clinical psychologists historically have tended to focus on smaller parts of the system—families and schools—to create change and promote resilience and wellbeing. There are examples of these different *layers* of intervention in the next section.

4.3 Clinical psychology settings

Clinical psychologists working with children and young people and the psychological problems they encounter practice across a range of settings and presenting problems. These areas range from advising on common childhood problems such as toileting and feeding difficulties and temper tantrums, through to serious emotional and behavioural problems including substance misuse, in settings that include LAC teams, forensic settings, school-based behavioural support services, paediatrics, neuropsychology, research and academic institutions, as well as the more traditional Child and Adolescent Mental Health Services (CAMHS), across inpatient and outpatient settings. The majority of clinical psychologists working with children in the UK work in community-based CAMHS. These tend to be arranged into targeted (tier 2) or specialist (tier 3) services. The former tends to be commissioned to focus on mild to moderate mental health difficulties—e.g. a child who has developed a phobia around needles that prevents him keeping up to date with his vaccinations or blood tests, or an adolescent who has repeated episodes of low mood that are beginning to interfere with her academic success and social life. Targeted services are often characterized by clinicians working on their own, often in schools or GP surgeries, usually with a time- or session-limited model. Specialist CAMHS tend to be focused on working with children with moderate to severe difficulties—e.g. a young person who is depressed and self-harming, or more severe anxiety disorders—although in reality the distinction between targeted and specialist services, on grounds of severity, is often blurred.

Specialist CAMHS tend to be located in health centres or hospital settings. Within these settings psychologists normally work closely with other members of the multi-disciplinary team—for example, a psychologist might offer individual work to a teenager with an eating disorder, alongside a systemic family therapist working with the whole family, and possibly a nurse specialist who monitors weight and physical health.

Another example would be offering family interventions for a child with attention deficit hyperactivity disorder (ADHD), alongside a psychiatrist prescribing medication. Psychologists in either setting would tend to offer direct assessment and interventions with young people and their families, and supervision to other psychologists and professionals in the team, and consultation and training to other members of the team working in a variety of settings—typically teachers, social workers, GPs, and paediatricians.

Across each of these settings, a significant amount of work for a clinical psychologist comprises direct, face-to-face therapy with young people, either in individual work or in work with whole families or groups. Such interventions are often effective; however, the scope of the clinical psychologist's roles are not limited to the direct provision of therapy. There is a move towards the profession adopting a much wider focus to the application of skills and knowledge, to apply the science of clinical psychology as effectively and broadly as possible. In work with children and young people a significant amount of work is undertaken in *indirect* interventions with others who have contact with children and young people: from working with parents, foster carers, and residential staff in order to create therapeutic environments for young people, to working with whole school interventions (Stallard and Buck, 2013). On a bigger scale still, there are whole community approaches to improving psychological wellbeing—notably the El Sistema movement (Tunstall, 2012) started in Venezuela and now with projects across the globe. In Scotland the project is know as The Big Noise, and encourages whole communities to become empowered and take an active role in their lives and community. The vehicle for this change is music, giving instruments to children and encouraging them to put on concerts, pulling together the community and engendering feelings of self-efficacy and wellbeing—with results that should be of great relevance to clinical psychologists (Scottish Government Social Research, 2011). Finally, there are also national and global interventions that apply psychological theory to advise governments and international organizations on health, social, and economic policy, designed to facilitate good mental health and wellbeing in children.

4.4 **Choosing the best interventions**

Although most children and young people experience good mental health, there is a significant proportion who do not. Best estimates of mental health problems in children and young people suggest that at any one time in the UK around 10% of 5- to 16-year olds will have a mental health problem (Green *et al.*, 2005) and the prevalence of mental ill health amongst children seems to be increasing. Over the course of their life, between a quarter and half of people of all ages are likely to experience some form of mental ill health (Andrews *et al.*, 2005; McManus *et al.*, 2009), and the majority of these difficulties will begin before a person's 18th birthday (Kessler *et al.*, 2007; Kim-Cohen *et al.*, 2003).

Fundamental to the task of determining the best interventions to implement is the use of psychological theory to fully understand the problems encountered, applied within the framework of scientific evidence. Most people consider randomized control trials (RCTs) to constitute the scientific 'gold standard' of evidence, which point to the most efficacious interventions for particular problems in particular contexts (this is known as evidence-based practice). In addition, evidence gathered from everyday clinical practice through the systematic collection of clinical outcomes data provides evidence of the effectiveness of interventions applied in routine clinical practice (this is known as practice-based evidence). Practice-based evidence has shown that a wide range of psychological interventions have a positive effect on child mental health (Wolpert *et al.*, 2012) not just those interventions proven through RCTs. The best psychological practice should draw on information from both types of evidence in choosing an intervention.

In children's services this necessarily includes integrating information from all aspects of a child's world to develop a biopsychosocial formulation of the presenting problem that points to possible intervention options. Take as an example a 13-year-old girl who is experiencing distressing and worrying thoughts that she cannot explain. These thoughts started a year or so ago and have begun to impact on her socially: she has stopped seeing her friends and is generally losing interest in life. We might say she is anxious and depressed, and if we take a narrow view of the problem, best scientific evidence might suggest that CBT is the best intervention. Indeed it might be, but if we look more closely at the problem, a more detailed assessment reveals that the problem onset coincided with the girl starting secondary school. Further exploration through a cognitive assessment suggests the girl has a learning difficulty, masked by reasonable verbal abilities. We also hear that both her parents had a difficult time at school and the memories of their own experiences made them fearful of speaking to the school even when they noticed she was struggling in class. The school itself is a sizeable inner-city secondary school, understaffed, and with large class sizes. Now we understand the bigger picture we can see a range of possibilities for facilitating change. Interventions might include helping the parents deal with their own fears around liaising with school—perhaps by mediating a first meeting between parents and teachers. Alternatively, or alongside, it may be helpful to liaise with the school's learning and support team, in order to help them understand the girl's difficulties better and to explore what support they can put in place around her; or, more radically, to consider a move to a specialist learning disabilities school. Taking a systemic view we can see how any one of these interventions might change the environment around the girl and, in turn, begin to have a positive impact on her mental health. There may be a need for some direct work further down the line—but equally if the system around the girl changes sufficiently, there may not be a need for any direct individual therapy with her at all.

Robust scientific psychological knowledge is applicable to all aspects of child mental health and wellbeing. Through the scientific application of psychological understanding to the particular context of a young person, clinical psychologists can tailor interventions to fit the unique context and the needs and wishes of the child and family.

The following section focuses on the main presenting problems with which psychologists tend to work clinically with children and young people.

Problems with behaviour

All children demonstrate difficult behaviour of one form or another, but most are easily dealt with by normal good parenting. When these behaviours become extreme and persistent to the point that they begin to have a significantly detrimental effect on the young person and the people around them, more targeted interventions are required. At the less serious end are toileting problems and fussy eating, which may require intervention if they persist beyond toddlerhood—but more serious are problems of opposition and aggression. Prevalence rates of oppositional defiant disorders (ODD) and conduct disorders (CD) are quite high, estimated at between 2% and 10% of children at any one time, and there tends to be much higher presentation in boys, particularly in the younger age range. Children with severe behavioural problems account for some of the highest demands on child mental health and social care services. The routes to behaviour problems are varied and the behaviour itself is best understood as a symptom of some other underlying problem—anxiety, developmental difficulties (autistic spectrum disorder (ASD) or learning difficulties (LD)), abuse, or ADHD. The role of the clinical psychologist is to assess and understand the context in which the behaviour problem presents (to formulate), before the most appropriate intervention can be applied. For example, if a child is showing very difficult behaviour as a result of ongoing abuse, the best intervention is to implement a safeguarding strategy to stop the abuse and keep the child safe.

Where obvious underlying problems have been accounted for and the behavioural difficulties persist, there is very good evidence that the best interventions are those that work with the parents directly to improve their parenting skills and change their behaviour, particularly around positive parenting. These behavioural parent training approaches have been shown to be much more effective than working with the child directly on their own (reported in Fonagy *et al.*, in press). Without intervention, children often go on to develop other associated difficulties—such as substance misuse and involvement with the criminal justice system.

Problems with emotions

Emotional problems—anxiety, low mood, and depression, often referred to as internalizing disorders—are the most common of childhood mental health problems, with estimates that one in three children will suffer with a moderate to severe emotional problem before they reach their 18th birthday.

With anxiety there is good evidence for the benefit of psychological interventions. CBT is a clear front-runner in terms of evidence from RCTs, showing good effects across a range of different anxiety disorders: social phobia, separation anxiety, generalized anxiety, obsessive compulsive disorder (OCD), and post-traumatic stress disorder (PTSD). There is also some evidence for the usefulness of eye movement desensitization reprocessing (EMDR), family-focused interventions, and, to a lesser extent, child psychotherapy.

For depression, however, the picture for best psychological intervention is more mixed. There is good evidence that CBT can be effective in both group and individual settings not only as a treatment for depression but also as a preventative intervention to stop young people with low mood escalating into full-blown clinical depression. Interpersonal psychotherapy for adolescents (IPT-A) also shows promising effects. Family-focused therapies may be helpful in more severe depression where the young person shows suicidal intent (see Fonagy *et al.*, in press).

Self-harming behaviour is often (but not exclusively) associated with emotional problems. There are a range of interventions that show some effects but no clear treatment of choice. This is possibly due to the multiple reasons and intents behind self-harming behaviour—from suicide, to the relief of intolerable psychological distress, to self-punishment. Once again, psychologists with their particular skills in assessment and formulation have a vital role in helping young people and those around them to understand the communication behind the behaviour, and to point to appropriate interventions that best fit with the particular context for that individual.

Despite the high prevalence of emotional difficulties and the evidence of good outcomes for psychological interventions, the remarkable fact is that most young people with these difficulties do not access services for help. There is a clear need for psychologists and others to find ways of identifying young people with emotional problems, and work to help them access appropriate interventions. Even when children do access services, the interventions offered do not work to improve the wellbeing of *all* children—even the most efficacious of psychological interventions for emotional difficulties only significantly improve the lives of about half those children and young people who receive the therapy. There is clearly a great need for psychologists to continue to refine and develop interventions through research and sharing best practice.

Problems with eating

At the more serious end of eating problems are anorexia and bulimia nervosa. Both are driven by a distorted body image; the former is characterized by restricting calorie intake, often to dangerously low levels, and the latter by over-eating, often followed by purging through vomiting and/or the excessive use of laxatives (see also Chapter 7). Prevalence varies greatly across the age range and across ethnic groups and nations. These problems are most common, and growing, among white Western (Europe and the USA) teenagers, and occur predominantly (90%) in girls. In both conditions the best intervention with children is family therapy—with mixed evidence about whether this is best conducted whilst the young person is in an inpatient or a community setting. CBT and other individual-based treatments also show some effectiveness (see Fonagy *et al.*, in press).

Psychosis

Psychotic problems are extremely rare in pre-adolescents, although acute anxiety states can often be mistaken for the symptoms of psychosis, particularly in pre-teens. However, from the age of 14, pre-psychotic, or prodromal states, and first onset psychosis can begin to emerge. Until recently, medication was seen as the best intervention alongside psycho-education—but these interventions have poor effectiveness on their own. As psychological scientists work to understand psychosis better, more effective psychologically based interventions are emerging, notably adapted versions of CBT (see Chapter 5). Furthermore, as the psychological understanding of the roots of psychotic problems and the complex interplay between environmental (notably abuse and trauma) and genetic predisposition improve, the possibility of early interventions is emerging that might avert and protect young people from developing psychosis (Morrison *et al.*, 2004).

Physical and developmental problems

In addition to understanding and intervening with psychological difficulties, clinical psychologists working with children have an important role to play in the management of the physical and developmental difficulties that emerge in childhood. The two most common developmental problems that emerge in childhood are LD and ASD, affecting around 4% and 1% of school-aged children respectively (Glover *et al.*, 2011). Clinical psychologists have a vital role in identifying, assessing, and diagnosing LD and ASD. Children and young people with LD and ASD are far more vulnerable than other children to developing mental health problems in addition to their developmental difficulties. Psychologists can work to help understand the nature of developmental problems, and the complex relationship between developmental and mental health problems. In this area of work psychologists might advise and support carers and teachers to understand the nature of the child's difficulties and to shape environments to make them more adaptive for the children. Alongside this, psychologists can work with the young people themselves to help them cope better with the substantial additional challenges of childhood that developmental problems bring.

Similarly, children with physical health problems are also much less likely to have good psychological health, particularly those with long-term conditions. The application of psychological understanding, in collaboration with paediatric colleagues, can help to improve the wellbeing and mental health of children coping with long-term conditions and with the often distressing physical treatments they experience.

4.5 Access, engagement, involvement, and outcomes

It is of course clear that psychological interventions are only possible if children, young people, their families, and carers have access to services. However, we know that most children with mental health problems do not access services. The reasons for this are a complex mix of poor identification of psychological problems, poor access to settings that can provide appropriate help and that are acceptable and welcoming to young people, and the stigma of mental illness that prevents young people seeking help. Here again there is a need to apply psychological understanding to overcome these barriers. Over recent years the breaking down of taboos around child mental health problems, through its coverage in children's television programmes and discussion in schools, is slowly bringing about some change. Furthermore, models of service delivery that target limited resources in the most efficient and effective ways, such as the Choice and Partnership Approach (CAPA) (York and Kingsbury, 2013), have also been beneficial.

Once children and young people do manage to reach appropriate help, there is a need to work to engage them and their families in change. Understanding the key elements of the therapy process is vital to achieve good clinical outcomes. Intervention planning needs to take into account the wishes and goals of the family. Work with families needs to be collaborative from the start, combining the expertise of the family and the therapist in a culture of shared decision-making to develop a good task alliance, or therapy contract. Getting things right from the beginning is vital, but so too is ensuring that therapy continues in the right direction—the effective use of questionnaire-based clinical feedback tools and outcome measures has been shown to improve clinical outcomes (Bickman, 2008; Law, 2012). Services that have strong programmes of involvement and participation of young service users at all levels of the organization are also more likely to provide services that are accessible and acceptable to young people. In England, for example, the Children and Young People's Improving Access to Psychological Therapies (CYP-IAPT) project has taken each of these elements of good psychological practice in child and adolescent mental health and developed a model of practice and service delivery based on best research evidence.

4.6 Early intervention

The key message in really improving the psychological health and well-being of children is to provide the right intervention, in the right way, and at the right time, and the right time is always *as early as possible*. For many this will mean a friendly word of encouragement, a comforting arm, a little more help in the classroom, and someone to listen. If we can get these small and simple things in place that promote psychological resilience and wellbeing, there will be fewer problems over time—but where problems do develop, the need for good quality child mental health services remains vital. If left untreated, childhood problems may persist throughout a person's life—the younger someone is when the problem develops, the longer it will cause distress and limit their life chances. The need for early and effective interventions to reduce the burden of human misery over a lifespan is clearly the most compelling argument for early intervention. However, in days of economic austerity, the economic argument is just as persuasive: quite simply, a small amount of money spent early in a child's life to prevent problems or to resolve them when they occur will, over the course of that child's life, have the potential to save society millions down the line (Knapp *et al.*, 2011).

It is testament to the nature of children that interventions can have such a profound and lasting impact on their lives. The most remarkable thing about children, after all, is not their vulnerability but their capacity to change and adapt to the world around them and within them. There are lessons here for those of us who work with children, young people, and their families: to learn from the children we work with. As clinical psychologists we must continually develop our practice in the light of new research and clinical evidence about what works (and what does not work), adapt to the changing and developing world within which we operate, and, like children, learn from it, shape it, and improve it.

References

Andrews, G., Poulton, R., and Skoog, I. (2005). Lifetime risk of depression: restricted to a minority or waiting for most? *British Journal of Psychiatry*, **187**, 495–496.

Bickman, L. (2008). A measurement feedback system (MFS) is necessary to improve mental health outcomes. *Journal of the American Academy of Child and Adolescent Psychiatry*, **47** (10), 1114–1119.

Fonagy, P., Cottrell, D., Philips, J., Bevington, D., Glaser, D.E., and Allison, E. (in press). *What Works for Whom? A Critical Review of Treatments for Children and Adolescents*, 2nd edn. Guilford Press, New York.

Glover, G., Evison, F., and Emerson, E. (2011). *How Rates of Learning Disabilities and Autism in Children Vary Between Areas*. Improving Health and Lives: Learning Disabilities Observatory, Durham.

Green, H., McGinnity, A., Meltzer, H., Ford, T., and Goodman, R. (2005). *Mental Health of Children and Young People in Great Britain, 2004*. Office for National Statistics. Palgrave Macmillan, Basingstoke.

Kessler, R.C., Amminger, G.P., Aguilar-Gaxiola, S., Alonso, J., Lee, S., and Ustun, T.B. (2007). Age of onset of mental disorders: a review of recent literature. *Current Opinion in Psychiatry*, **20**, 359–364.

Kim-Cohen, J., Caspi, A., Moffitt, T.E., Harrington, H., Milne, B.J., and Poulton, R. (2003). Prior juvenile diagnoses in adults with mental disorder—developmental follow-back of a prospective longitudinal cohort. *Archives of General Psychiatry*, **60**, 709–717.

Knapp, M., McDaid, D., and Parsonage, M. (eds) (2011). *Mental Health Promotion and Mental Illness Prevention: The Economic Case*. Personal Social Services Research Unit, London School of Economics and Political Science Report. Department of Health, London.

Law, D. (ed.) (2012). *A Practical Guide to Using Service User Feedback and Outcome Tools to Inform Clinical Practice in Child and Adolescent Mental Health: Some Initial Guidance from the Children and Young People's Improving Access to Psychological Therapies Outcomes-Oriented Practice (CO-OP) Group*. Department of Health/CYP-IAPT (<http://www.iapt.nhs.uk/silo/files/a-practical-guide-to-using-service-user-feedback—outcome-tools-.pdf>).

McManus, S., Meltzer, H., Brugha, T., Bebbington, P., and Jenkins, R. (eds) (2009). *Adult Psychiatric Morbidity in England, 2007: Results of a Household Survey*. NHS Information Centre for Health and Social Care, Leeds.

Morrison, A., Renton, J.C., Dunn, H., Williams, S., and Bentall, R.P. (2004). *Cognitive Therapy for Psychosis: A Formulation-Based Approach*. Brunner-Routledge, Hove.

Orford, J. (1992). *Community Psychology: Theory and Practice*. Wiley, Chichester.

Perry, B.D. (2002). Childhood experience and the expression of genetic potential: what childhood neglect tells us about nature and nurture. *Brain and Mind*, **3**, 79–100.

Scottish Government Social Research (2011). *Evaluation of Big Noise, Sistema Scotland*. Scottish Government (<www.scotland.gov.uk/socialresearch>).

Stallard, P. and Buck, R. (2013). Preventing depression and promoting resilience: feasibility study of a school-based cognitive-behavioural intervention. *British Journal of Psychiatry*, **202** (54), s18–s23.

Tunstall, T. (2012). *Changing Lives: Gustavo Dudamel, El Sistema, and the Transformative Power of Music*. W.W. Norton, New York.

Wolpert, M., Ford, T., Law, D., *et al.* (2012). Patient reported outcomes in child and adolescent mental health services (CAMHS): use of idiographic and standardized measures. *Journal of Mental Health*, **21**, 165–173.

York, A. and Kingsbury, S. (2013). *The Choice and Partnership Approach: A Service Transformation Model*. CAPA Systems, Taastrup.

Further reading

Carr, A. (2006). *The Handbook of Child and Adolescent Clinical Psychology: A Contextual Approach*, 2nd edn. Psychology Press, Hove.

Cooper, M. (2008). *Essential Research Findings in Counselling and Psychotherapy: The Facts Are Friendly*. Sage Publications, London.

Weisz, J. and Kazdin, A. (eds) (2010). *Evidence-Based Psychotherapies for Children and Adolescents*, 2nd edn. Guilford Press, New York.

Chapter 5

Working with severe mental health problems

John Hanna and Alison Brabban

5.1 Introduction

It is now widely recognized that clinical psychologists working with people with severe mental health problems make a vital contribution to both individual recovery and community mental health services. As members of multi-disciplinary teams they undertake to work through some of the most vexing challenges to be found in the field of mental health. It is a difficult, risk-laden, but extremely rewarding area. The aim of this chapter is to clarify what clinical psychologists can offer to people with severe mental health problems, and why their practice is a vital resource to service users, carers, and multi-disciplinary colleagues.

Reflecting how both services and training have been organized over the years, this chapter will primarily focus on working-age adults, starting with early intervention with adolescents and transitioning into services for older adults, although severe difficulties can arise across the age-range. Severe mental health problems significantly interfere with social and occupational functioning, and at times can pose some risk to self and others. Psychologists have made great strides in the last quarter century in working successfully with people presenting with psychosis, mood instability, personality difficulties, and complex depression and trauma. Any of these mental health problems can become severe over time, sometimes as a result of under- or improper treatment, sometimes as a result of the absence of treatment, and often in the context of persistent social and psychological stressors.

5.2 What are severe mental health problems?

The expression 'severe mental health problems' is normally used to encompass schizophrenia, bipolar disorder, and sometimes personality disorder, and is often used synonymously with 'severe mental illness'. However, many psychologists challenge the concept of 'mental illness' as it tends to imply, to the exclusion of other possibilities, a biological predisposition, an endogenous aetiology, or a brain disease; illness also separates the 'ill from the well'. Psychologists have instead found, and continue to develop, their own language for what they are working with, as best as possible co-defined with the people involved, and most now consider psychological distress to exist along a spectrum. Disputing whether these conditions should be classed as illnesses or not is related to but also distinct from a much more controversial but widely held perspective within clinical psychology, that schizophrenia itself does not exist as a single construct. This viewpoint does not deny that there are people with a diagnosis of schizophrenia, or that many people suffer with unusual experiences such as hearing voices (classed as auditory hallucinations) or feeling paranoid. The challenge is of the diagnosis itself and whether it represents a discrete entity. We know it is possible for a number of people to have a diagnosis of schizophrenia and have no symptoms in common; for their 'illnesses' to have completely different courses; and for them to respond quite differently to treatment. In short there would be more differences than similarities within the group, making it questionable as to the usefulness of saying they are all experiencing a single condition called 'schizophrenia'. Moreover, there are so many similarities between schizophrenia and bipolar disorder (and many other psychiatric conditions) that to suggest these are discrete problems is also seen as misleading. For this reason the majority of clinical psychologists in the UK do not talk about 'schizophrenia' (whilst acknowledging that it is a recognized diagnostic label) but tend to refer to 'psychosis' as an overarching term, as this in fact tends to be the most common presenting problem.

5.3 **What is psychosis?**

Psychosis or psychotic symptoms can also be referred to as positive symptoms, not because they are good, but because they are viewed as *additional*, not general, experiences. The term psychosis tends to refer to two main symptoms or experiences, hallucinations and delusions.

A hallucination is the perception of something in the absence of a stimulus, most commonly auditory hallucinations, often experienced as hearing a voice, though hallucinations can occur in all senses: visual, tactile, gustatory, and olfactory. Delusions are the other common psychotic symptom or experience. Again, there is much debate within clinical psychology about definitions (and whether delusions are separate entities from normal beliefs), but traditionally, delusions are seen as beliefs that are held with extreme conviction despite strong contrary evidence.

5.4 **What causes these problems?**

Traditionally, severe mental health problems such as schizophrenia and bipolar disorder have been considered as purely biological in nature. Consequently, many service users have been given simplistic explanations that their problems are caused by a 'chemical imbalance in the brain'. Today, however, it is generally accepted that the causes are complex and need to be understood within a biopsychosocial model, recognizing all component parts, not just the biological. Recent research has shown that schizophrenia and bipolar disorder can, and very often do, develop following trauma, especially if that trauma is extreme or persistent over time, for example childhood abuse (sexual, physical, and emotional), neglect, bullying, or the death of a parent.

Some people find it difficult to marry evidence that early adversity is linked to psychosis with evidence that neurotransmitters also play a role, and see the two theories as mutually exclusive. This is definitely not the case: since humans are comprised of biological matter, there will evidently be a physiological correlate related to psychosis (be it electrical brain activity or high or low neurotransmitters levels), as there is for every emotional state, for example, jealousy, anger, love, and sadness. Just because correlations exist between biological states and emotions, this does not mean these states necessarily *cause* the specified emotion. If confronted by a vicious, growling dog a person is likely to feel some level of anxiety. Trying to determine whether the fear is generated by *either* the dog *or* the subsequent adrenaline rush denies the complexity of the causal interactions. With psychosis, as with all emotional states, there are undoubtedly biological correlates; however, psychosocial factors are also of crucial importance when trying to understand the origins.

To complicate the picture, we also know that some people are resilient to even persistent trauma without developing longstanding difficulties, and some develop major mental health difficulties despite no history of trauma. It is generally accepted that the causes of severe mental health problems are complex and set within a dynamic, interactive biopsychosocial field, emerging in different circumstances through any and each of the component parts, not just the biological. Richard Bentall's *Madness Explained* (2004) provides a comprehensive research-based and comparative-theoretical account of the all-too-human difficulties we regularly hear people describing in practice.

Because of the historical dominance of the biological model, it has only recently become accepted that many psychotic experiences can be understood in terms of a person's life. In the past, practitioners were advised not to talk to service users about their experiences, believing this was not only a waste of time, but could actually worsen problems. Work done by the Hearing Voices Movement (Romme and Escher, 1993) and from within clinical psychology has effectively challenged this position.

Additionally, until quite recently, a clear distinction was assumed between people who had schizophrenia or psychotic symptoms and those in the general population who were functioning well. Contemporary research has shown that this divide is far from clear. Numerous surveys have shown that up to 15% of the population will experience auditory hallucinations (voices and other noises) at some point in their lives, and yet only about a third of these will be distressed or require professional help. Interestingly, there does not seem to be any significant difference in the quality of the experience; both groups hear similar things. What is different is how the voice hearer *relates* to their voices. Those who cope well with their voices perceive themselves as stronger than their voices, are not frightened, and tend to engage with, rather than trying to escape from, them, whereas those who are distressed tend to see their voices as more powerful, are frightened of them, and perceive the experience as negative. In short, symptoms themselves do not necessarily equate to psychological difficulties; it is the way people *relate* to their hallucinatory experiences that is significant.

Delusions have also traditionally been perceived as qualitatively different experiences from 'normal' thoughts. However, recent studies comparing beliefs in the general population with delusional beliefs have failed to find a clear distinction (Peters *et al.*, 1999). It seems that 'normal' beliefs are not so distinct, but are on the same spectrum as delusions. What distinguishes one from the other is not content, but the *degree* of preoccupation, the *level* of conviction, and the *amount* of distress that the belief causes.

In summary, psychologists now believe that psychotic phenomena exist on a continuum with normal experience and are not qualitatively different. This means that psychological models that are used to make sense of emotions and behaviours in people with more common mental health issues can now also be applied and adapted to make sense of what was previously classed as 'madness'.

5.5 How do mental health services help those presenting with severe mental health problems?

Service delivery continues to evolve rapidly, but several lasting trends are worth noting.

Early intervention services

Early intervention teams were established some years ago to identify and treat emergent or first-episode psychosis, irrespective of the associated diagnosis. Most people who come into these services are hearing voices or suffering with paranoid beliefs. Early intervention teams aim to help people access appropriate help as soon as possible and to provide an intensive package of care, including psychological therapies and psychosocial interventions (focused on issues such as housing, employment, and relationships), normally over a 3-year period. These teams have been found to improve clinical outcomes (Craig *et al.*, 2004), be cost effective (McCrone *et al.*, 2010), and are valued by both service users and carers alike (Schizophrenia Commission, 2012).

Generic community mental health services

In the UK, establishment of generic community mental health teams (CMHTs) followed closure of the long-stay asylums. CMHTs work with all types of service user difficulties, although in areas of high demand they have increasingly limited their caseload to more severe presentations. CMHTs are gradually being replaced by more specialized smaller teams, such as those for people with longstanding psychosis and mood instability, or personality difficulties, or mood, anxiety, and trauma-based difficulties in the absence of psychosis. Others, traditionally termed rehabilitation services, focus on service users with cognitive or more severe functional impairment, and who need weekly or daily home help or supported living. Some teams work intensively with service users identified as particularly difficult to engage; this approach is typically called assertive outreach. While early intervention services work to reduce the numbers going on to develop persistent or recurrent problems, community services remain available to people who continue to need them.

Acute crisis

Crisis teams and inpatient mental health wards are available for those who are not coping and who are acutely distressed (or sometimes acutely distressing to others). Some service users are assessed and compulsorily detained (in the UK, under the Mental Health Act) to protect themselves or others. Increasingly, acute services are attempting to reduce the duration of both crisis episodes and hospital stays. Such attempts are intended to benefit service users (provided that appropriate aftercare is arranged) whilst also saving resources.

5.6 **Working in partnership**

Health and social care are typically linked together within a defined geographical area. In the UK, for example, the NHS works with voluntary services and social enterprises offering a range of social inclusion opportunities for service users. Many social services, such as those arranging benefit payments and housing options, are provided through local authorities. The NHS also utilizes the private sector, for example extra hospital placements or long-term residential facilities. Psychologists are never far from these interfaces, and can be central to developing partnerships and peer-support programmes with voluntary and social enterprise sectors.

5.7 How can clinical psychologists help?

Psychologists intervene to promote recovery and social inclusion for service users, alongside their families, friends, and peer groups, working with their multi-disciplinary co-workers and within their communities. Practice with service users is always intended to be consensual and collaborative as this stance provides the best outcomes. Psychologists work with people individually, couples, and families, in small groups, and within neighbourhoods and communities as part of larger scale public mental health interventions. Clinical psychologists give primacy to delivering interventions drawn from the ever-developing evidence base for psychological therapies, but also give space to support their multi-disciplinary colleagues to develop competency in psychological practice through joint working, consultation, training, and supervision.

5.8 Evidence-based approaches

Research into the nature and treatment of severe mental health problems, led principally by clinical psychologists, has provided the impetus for many major clinical innovations over the past quarter century (e.g. Fowler *et al.*, 1995; Morrison *et al.*, 2003). Indeed, advances in clinical psychology stand alongside the service user movement, with its Recovery vision, as facilitating arguably the greatest social evolutionary gains in the lives of people with these difficulties since the closure of the asylums.

Psychologists use research findings, and in the UK, particularly the evidence-based guidance issued by the National Institute for Health and Clinical Excellence (NICE), to guide them toward the delivery of the most clinically and cost-effective interventions. NICE recommends that everyone with a diagnosis of schizophrenia or bipolar disorder should be offered CBT and family interventions. Roth and Pilling (2013) have developed a competency framework, drawn from trials that have informed NICE guidance, outlining the skills required to effectively deliver CBT for psychosis and bipolar disorder; family intervention for psychosis and bipolar disorder; as well as dialectical behaviour therapy, mentalization-based therapy, cognitive-analytic therapy, and schema-based therapy for personality disorder (the latter four being promising but less-well evidenced approaches). Where there is no strong evidence base, however, or where an evidence-based approach has been unsuccessful, psychologists working as scientist practitioners can adapt their practice to the particular situation, evaluating the impact by using appropriate outcome measures. By drawing on promising emerging therapies, a carefully considered, integrated approach can be adopted. It is worth noting that approaches not recommended by NICE are not necessarily ineffective, invalid, or disproven, but there may not yet be sufficient research of the required standard to determine their efficacy.

5.9 **Assessment**

Psychologists working in this field usually use open-ended questions and a flexible approach to engagement since service users are often unsettled and anxious about meeting psychologists, and, depending on circumstances, are sometimes challenging to engage. Every effort is made to be collaborative and to enhance the therapeutic alliance during the assessment process and beyond. Keeping in mind the high rates of trauma in this field, psychologists need to go to great lengths to create a safe atmosphere and to maintain a trustworthy stance, stressing the bounds of confidentiality and emphasizing a non-judgemental position.

Although psychotic symptoms are commonly experienced by those with severe mental health difficulties, they are not always the core problem. During assessment the psychologist helps the client to generate a problem list with associated goals, which together determine the aims of therapy. These frequently reflect what we would all see as our basic human needs: wanting to live somewhere safe and secure, having a job, good friends, or a partner. The problem list ensures that therapy remains focused on working towards the client's goals, not on what the therapist or team impose or consider important. Often therapy needs to address psychotic symptoms as a means to an end, for instance a person's beliefs that they will be attacked if they go out would evidently need to be tackled if they want to develop friendships with other people. Appreciating the ultimate personal goal helps people remain motivated when the therapy becomes particularly difficult or challenging.

Psychologists also gather a personal history as a means of appreciating predisposing, precipitating, maintaining, and protective factors of the service user's distress, which in turn underpin formulations. Multiple therapeutic models and orientations (once again giving primacy to the current and emerging evidence base) are blended with lived experience.

5.10 Psychometric evaluation, self-report scales, and outcome measurement

Psychologists may also provide neuropsychological evaluation which normally takes the form of screening, while more advanced practitioners will utilize a full battery of psychometrics for service users presenting with possible cognitive deficits or challenges. Self-report tools are used to measure distress relating to symptom clusters, to help analyze personality factors, and to help guide therapy. Outcomes are often measured using clinical interviews, self-report measures, feedback from others who are involved, and objective indicators, such as rate of relapse and/or hospital admission. These measures are usually administered to gather information for formulation and throughout therapy to assess cumulative outcome.

5.11 Formulation

Following assessment, a valid formulation is developed and agreed between the psychologist and service user (sometimes together with a co-worker). This provides a hypothesis to account for what has caused and what is maintaining often complex and multiple problems. By demonstrating the interaction between a number of individual factors, formulation leads to an associated care plan, typically at both psychological and social levels. This process can be brief and intensive, for example focusing on a recent emergent crisis requiring critical resolution. In longer-term work, the formulation will be re-worked through several iterations. Crucially, it should be developed collaboratively and should be understood and agreed by the service user.

5.12 Working therapeutically with voices (hallucinations)

When applied to hallucinations, the CBT model (see Chapter 2) suggests that how people think about the experience of hearing voices, and not the experience itself, determines whether or not they are distressed. For example, if someone hears a voice that no one else does and thinks 'I'm going mad', this will create additional anxiety and distress. When working cognitively with people who hear voices, the focus is discovering how they are making sense of their voices; to explore these beliefs and to help them develop less distressing alternatives. It is also important to normalize the experience by providing information on the incidence of voice hearing within the general population and about situations commonly associated with voice hearing, such as sleep deprivation and stress. The aim of CBT is to reduce distress linked to the voices, rather than to remove them.

5.13 Working therapeutically with delusions

Psychologists view delusions as extreme beliefs stemming from attempts to make sense of events. The most common form is paranoia, when individuals believe they are being unfairly targeted or blamed. People with these beliefs tend to demonstrate a number of contributing cognitive biases. For example, they are more likely to jump to conclusions (not assessing all available evidence before making up their mind), and are less likely to consider alternative explanations for what might be happening (e.g. did my neighbour ignore me because he dislikes me or because he was preoccupied, or didn't see me?). Those who are paranoid are also more likely to blame others (rather than themselves or objects) for things going wrong. Using CBT, the therapist helps the person explore their beliefs, looking at information leading to the belief and considering alternative explanations, using Socratic questioning to help clients broaden their awareness and to modify beliefs.

Psychologists also use behavioural experiments which are developed collaboratively with clients to test out beliefs. For example, if someone believes that, should they leave home, something dreadful will happen, then the therapist must discover what 'something dreadful happening' means, exactly when this might happen, and whether any specific conditions apply— would the person need to be alone, for example? Once the therapist is aware of the 'hypothesis', then experiments can be developed to test this out.

5.14 Working within teams and systems

Increasingly, psychologists are expected not simply to provide psychological input to teams, but also to promote and lead psychological services. This means shifting the perspective of teams and services towards a more evidence-based, biopsychosocial model of care and intervention, by helping the team to develop psychological skills. Psychologists value 'giving psychology away' but also maintain that they should play a unique role in leading the provision of a psychological perspective. This normally involves supporting formulation and intervention, meeting directly with the identified service user, but sometimes, when this is not possible, working through indirect consultation within individuals or teams, or in complex case review and group supervision. Psychologists can support psychiatrists by using formulation to refine diagnoses, contrasting psychiatry's quest for an optimal superordinate category (diagnosis) with a differential diagnostic approach. This dual approach helps to capture the complexity of presenting problems whilst addressing real risks of stigma inherent in simplistic labelling. A nuanced, shared understanding between lead clinicians who share a scientific orientation provides for much better service provision. Given the predominantly biological orientation towards distress held by many multi-disciplinary teams, clinical psychologists can offer an alternative to this position by engaging in constructive debate, always held in the interests of service users.

5.15 The Recovery movement and the Recovery model

The term 'Recovery' has come to hold many meanings since entering parlance in the context of an ongoing movement led by service users for human rights. Recovery means access to a life worth living through resolution or self-management of mental health difficulties, often with support from others. Many psychologists have adopted this concept as a guiding value, believing that beyond symptom reduction, a number of factors are essential for a recovered and valued life. These include improved coping, prospects for work or work-related activity, full relationship potential, and social inclusion and citizenship.

A significant obstacle to adopting this model has been the perceived poor prognosis for people with severe mental health difficulties. Harding (1994) has reviewed a substantial number of long-term follow-up studies of those receiving a diagnosis of schizophrenia, and has suggested that belief in the poor prognosis is based not on evidence, but on clinicians' biases. Indeed, research has shown that about 45% of people who receive a diagnosis of schizophrenia recover after one or more episodes, with only about 20% showing unremitting symptoms and disability, while the remaining 35% show a mixed pattern with varying periods of remission and relapse (Barbato, 1998). Those who are most frequently seen by clinicians tend to be those with recurrent distress and/or acute crises. Perhaps understandably, clinicians who are regularly exposed to this group develop a pessimistic bias toward all who attract the diagnosis of schizophrenia. Worryingly, some continue to offer prognoses on this basis, implying that all people with psychotic symptoms will be permanently disabled. Increasingly, however, recovery is becoming a more dominant narrative within mental health services.

Wherever possible, psychologists following the Recovery model work collaboratively with service users to develop psychologically informed programmes designed to enhance recovery. Making sense of and adapting to adversity is integrated with activities promoting social inclusion, so that individuals can become valid participants in all desired aspects of societal life. Psychologists apply psychological science, innovative methodology, and creativity to develop a range of Recovery-oriented services, often alongside third-sector organizations. These include peer support groups, carer support groups, programmes supporting service users to progress on from statutory mental health services, employment training and support schemes, adult education, public health interventions (designed to reduce health inequalities, including the disproportionate impact of malnutrition and addiction), and, finally, early detection and prevention interventions within schools and communities. Psychologists need to be particularly attentive to diversity with respect to underserved and more at-risk groups, such as black and minority ethnic communities, homeless populations, and transgender people.

5.16 **Training and supervision**

Clinical psychologists currently employed in mental health services face high demands for their skills and expertise, but limits to resources typically mean that not all those who might benefit from psychological interventions are able to access them. This, and the need to develop more psychologically minded services, dictates that psychologists must use some of their time to support their colleagues to deliver psychological interventions in accordance with their own professional competencies. This means providing training and supervision to multi-disciplinary staff, as well as providing formulation-driven guidance on all aspects of practical intervention, from supporting relapse prevention to achieving solutions to unmet social needs.

Multi-disciplinary colleagues inevitably possess varying levels of core psychological skills, so it is part of the psychologist's role to ensure that service provision is optimally psychologically minded. Training in fundamental *core* skills, sometimes through formal teaching but also through joint work, normally focuses on engagement, collaboration, active listening, problem-solving, solution-focused intervention, and positive psychology. All service users deserve psychologically informed interventions and support from all staff members who are employed to serve them; clinical psychologists therefore play a vital role in ensuring that this commitment is fulfilled. Services also need to increase access to more *specialist* evidence-based psychological therapies. To achieve this, psychologists must contribute to the delivery of accredited training and supervision of other therapists. Specific skills, developed once core skills are consolidated and demonstrated, include behavioural activation, activity scheduling, emotional regulation, psycho-education, relapse prevention, and some of the basic components of family work and CBT.

5.17 Leading, managing, and developing services

Psychologists' provision of leadership through case allocation and management is a key aspect of multi-disciplinary team work. Many clinical psychologists also carry out audit and research, and will train and supervise other clinicians undertaking and often leading service improvement initiatives. Beyond this, it is also increasingly important for clinical psychologists to provide leadership to devise more clinically and cost-effective services for all those with severe mental health difficulties. There needs to be a better balance between evidence-based medical services (typically available to 100% of service users at present) and psychological interventions (available to less than 50% of service users). It is crucial that clinical psychologists make this case effectively with commissioners, directors, and senior managerial colleagues to ensure that service provision is increased. This is not only in the interests of current service users and carers, but also because funding for future services depends on it. In the UK, for instance, implementation of NICE guidance to provide psychological intervention is rapidly moving from a recommendation to a mandatory requirement.

5.18 What supports the development of services?

There are currently increasingly vocal and persistent demands for psychological services from service users, carers, and families, who report how important it has been that clinical psychologists have joined them in their recovery journey. These collaborative efforts have resulted in lives much more valued, worth living, and even cherished, whereas before they often seemed to be devalued and potentially wasted. Such testimonies have galvanized the service user movement and have led to campaigns, such as that led by Mind in the UK, 'We Need to Talk', seeking to meet the growing demand for clinical psychologists' time and input. The collective voices of service users and carers rightly lead the drive for more clinical psychology and increased access to psychological therapy services.

Psychological therapies in this area have been shown to be not only clinically helpful but also cost-effective. Evidence shows that overall expenditure on public services decreases when effective treatments are provided (Andrews *et al.*, 2012). Health economists have recorded important cost savings by way of reduction of service costs, such as days in hospital, or via indirect savings resulting from a reduction in days lost from work.

5.19 **Future directions**

Besides emphasizing the need for the delivery of evidence-based therapies, and providing a full range of clinical services, more research is needed in several areas. These include promising new types of practice such as CBT 'third wave' interventions (e.g. mindfulness-based therapy for psychosis); traditional approaches whose effectiveness in this area have not yet been fully demonstrated but which may have potential (e.g. psychodynamic therapies), and 'low intensity' interventions (those that are more easily delivered by less-intensively trained multi-disciplinary staff, such as behavioural activation and relapse prevention). Ultimately this should lead to a broader range of choice of interventions for service users.

It is anticipated that service user involvement will play an increasingly vital role in the development of effective interventions, many of which can and should be peer-led. Tapping into the expertise gained through experience, the many organizations representing service users and carers will create more reliable, cross-culturally valid, and effective service delivery models in future.

This field provides psychologists with intriguing, even fascinating insights; it offers the opportunity to supportively witness, make sense of, and often to collaboratively transform poignant moments in the lives of ordinary people with extraordinary problems. There is increasing demand for and recognition of our work in this dynamic area of clinical psychology.

References

Andrews, A., Knapp, M., McCrone, P., Parsonage, M., and Trachtenberg, M. (2012). *Effective Interventions in Schizophrenia. The Economic Case: A Report Prepared for the Schizophrenia Commission.* Rethink Mental Illness, London.

Barbato, A. (1998). *Schizophrenia and Public Health*. World Health Organization, Geneva.

Bentall, R.P. (2004). *Madness Explained: Psychosis and Human Nature*. Penguin, London.

Craig, T.K.J., Garety, P., Power, P., *et al.* (2004). The Lambeth Early Onset (LEO) team: randomised controlled trial of the effectiveness of specialised care for early psychosis. *British Medical Journal*, **329**, 1067–1069.

Fowler, D., Garety, P., and Kuipers, E. (1995). *Cognitive Behaviour Therapy for Psychosis*. Wiley, Chichester.

Harding, C. (1994). Empirical correction of seven myths about schizophrenia with implications for treatment. *Acta Psychiatrica Scandinavica*, **90**, 140–146.

McCrone, P., Park, A., and Knapp, M. (2010). *Economic Evaluation of Early Intervention Services: Phase IV Report*. Personal Social Services Research Unit (PSSRU), London School of Economics, London.

Morrison, A.P., Renton, J., Dunn, H., Williams, S., and Bentall R. (2003). *Cognitive Therapy for Psychosis: A Formulation-Based Approach*. Brunner-Routledge, Hove.

Peters, E.R., Joseph, S.A., and Garety, P.A. (1999). Measurement of delusional ideation in the normal population: introducing the PDI (Peters *et al.* Delusions Inventory). *Schizophrenia Bulletin*, **25** (3), 553–576.

Romme, M. and Escher, S. (1993). *Accepting Voices*. Mind Publications, London.

Roth, A. and Pilling, S. (2013). *Competence Framework for Psychological Interventions with People with Serious Mental Illness* (<http://www.ucl.ac.uk/clinical-psychology/core/competence_mentalillness.html>).

Schizophrenia Commission (2012). *The Abandoned Illness: A Report from the Schizophrenia Commission*. Rethink Mental Illness, London.

Chapter 6

Working with older people

Cath Burley

6.1 **Introduction**

'Ageing is not lost youth but a new stage of opportunity and strength' (Betty Friedan, 1994, p. 4.)

Working with older people is fascinating, varied, and rewarding. Clinical psychologists specializing in this field have many opportunities to listen to people's stories about themselves and their families, which could span an entire century, and which often describe impressive strengths and fortitude in facing life's challenges. Those employed in this area have the huge privilege of working closely with older people to help them overcome the range of difficult issues which have brought them into health services at this particular time in their lives.

6.2 **Population changes**

All over the world, the population is living longer. For instance, people aged over 65 currently comprise nearly one fifth of the UK population. Average life expectancy at birth has increased from around 40 years in 1900 to over 85 years today, due largely to improvements in public health and childhood immunization programmes. Women outnumber men in this age group, although the gender gap has progressively reduced as men's life expectancy has risen closer to that of women. The older adult population in the UK is predicted to continue to grow until 2060, with a higher rate of increase in the 'old-old'. Indeed by 2045, the global population of those aged over 60 is expected to exceed the number of children under the age of 15. With this awareness, many governments worldwide are now working purposefully to improve the physical and mental health care of older people.

6.3 **Context**

In the previous century, most Western societies traditionally linked 'old-age' with compulsory retirement from work at age 65. However, as standards of public health, physical health, and longevity have all improved, this nominal divide has become less useful. People describe great individual differences in their perception of their physical, social, and intellectual age. The immense social and technological changes of the last century have influenced the stories older people tell, enabled their freedoms, or in some instances may have restricted their lives. As their views and expectations of family, and of ageing, have changed, older people have become one of the most adaptable groups in society. For instance, the 'young-old' may now find themselves caring both for parents and for grandchildren, with little time in between to review their own lives and meet their own needs. They are not a homogenous group, with many differences existing both between and within cohorts.

Culturally, the experiences of older people are not always recognized and valued. The media often denigrates or ridicules the 'old', while politicians build on emotional and financial fears about the potential expense of increased longevity, including the costs of pensions, health and social care, dementia provision, and residential care. Inevitably, these stereotypes affect older people themselves and those who work with them.

Despite this, many older people are still significant figures in the world, challenging perceived stereotypes of the end of life as a time of mental frailty and physical disability. The majority of older people lead active and fulfilling lives within their families and local communities, enjoying opportunities that may have not been present in their youth. The 'normal' processes of ageing may gradually affect sensory abilities and some people may develop several chronic, potentially manageable health conditions. Only a relatively small proportion of all older people are physically frail, have dementia, or live in residential care at any point; for instance, fewer than 1 in 17 people aged over 65 have dementia, the vast majority remaining largely unimpaired.

6.4 **Psychological difficulties faced by older adults**

Historically, older people's mental health services in the UK have been provided for those aged 65 and over, according to whether they are considered to have either 'functional' or 'organic' disorders. 'Functional' disorders include anxiety conditions, depression, paraphrenia, post-traumatic stress disorder, and eating disorders. These disorders often occur in the context of adjustment to significant transitions in life, for example retirement, role and relationship changes, moving home, losses and coping with bereavement, the onset of chronic physical health conditions (e.g. diabetes, arthritis, heart disease, Parkinson's disease), and the end of life. People with one long-term condition are two to three times more likely to develop depression than the rest of the population. Depression is, however, no more common than in the adult population and responds well to therapy. Generalized anxiety disorder (GAD) is the most common anxiety disorder amongst older people, although onset typically occurs earlier in life and it tends to be of long duration, spontaneous remission being unusual. A significant minority report later onset, and have a slightly different presentation with fears about their health condition or falling.

'Organic' disorders include progressive cognitive changes on a spectrum from mild cognitive impairment to severe dementia and may include younger people with early-onset dementia.

The term 'dementia' refers to a process of progressive accelerated brain cell loss affecting multiple cognitive domains. The pattern and speed of this brain cell loss determines the type of dementia. In Alzheimer's disease the typical pattern is a gradual loss of episodic memory, and changes in mood, language, and the ability to reason. Vascular dementia has a more stepwise progression, as a series of small strokes or infarcts cause damage to different brain areas. Frontotemporal dementia initially presents with changes in personality or executive functions while memory remains relatively intact. People with Lewy body dementia may experience problems of mobility, visual hallucinations, and fluctuating attention. The assessment process can help differentiate between the dementias or other cognitive changes related to strokes, alcohol or drug abuse, endocrine disorder, or damage caused by earlier traumatic brain injury.

Although some cognitive changes may occur within the normal ageing process (for example differences in speed of processing or some aspects of executive function), having memory difficulties is not necessarily something that happens to everyone as they age. There is also a growing evidence of a link between depression and dementia. Despite recovering from depression, 90% people who show cognitive impairments before recovery continued to show deficits in delayed memory, visuospatial skills, and information processing after recovery from depression (Bhalla *et al.*, 2006). In addition, a higher level of anxiety is common in early dementia.

Caring for someone with a progressive physical or mental health condition may cause a great deal of stress for carers and family, and itself results in a raised incidence of depression. Psychologists may work with carers in their own right, either individually, in family systems, or in a group with other carers. Although services may be organized around discrete problem areas or categories, people rarely fit these exactly. People presenting with anxiety symptoms and a pattern of poor sleep may have several chronic health conditions; they may be a carer for a spouse, parent, or their grandchildren. Those who are not retired might also have a variety of work commitments.

Although the suicide rate amongst older people has fallen in recent years, this is still a risk, particularly in men. When suicide is attempted by an older person, it is more likely to be successful. Risk factors include poor physical health (especially those receiving a recent terminal diagnosis including Alzheimer's disease); inability to control pain; recent bereavement (especially for men); fear of being admitted to residential care; drug or alcohol dependency; social isolation or lack of a confidante; having made a previous suicide attempt; and being a female carer.

6.5 **Settings and tasks**

Typically, most clinical psychologists work in secondary care settings as members of specialist older people's community mental health teams, working with psychiatrists, community psychiatric nurses (CPNs), occupational therapists, physiotherapists, and support workers. Referrals to the team are normally made by general practitioners (GPs), and after a team discussion, the psychiatrist and CPN will usually make a home visit to assess the older person and their circumstances. Following further team discussions, a psychologist might then see the person regularly at home with their family members, or in a day therapy setting, inpatient ward, or outpatient clinic, to carry out an assessment or to provide therapy. Part of the psychologist's role is helping the team to think about the psychological needs of the person and their carer(s), through providing a formulation, especially where there are complex needs or challenging behaviours.

Some psychologists work exclusively in one setting whereas others move across a range of settings, offering different interventions at different levels. These might include undertaking a neuropsychological assessment in a memory clinic; contributing to formulation and care planning on a ward; helping to triage referrals at an intermediate care service; providing training and supervision to staff working with people with challenging behaviour in a residential or nursing home; or contributing to an assessment about mental capacity or deprivation of liberty on an inpatient ward. As service models have changed, psychologists' work has taken on greater breadth to include working with people with long-term physical health conditions in acute hospital wards and in hospices.

Other psychologists work more closely with primary care staff in GP practices, delivering psychological interventions in settings that older people find easier to access and may have less stigma attached to them than secondary care settings. Some old age psychologists will have a highly specialist role in tertiary services, for example as a specialist neuropsychologist or a palliative care psychologist.

A typical week will include providing clinical supervision and training to colleagues; developing audits and evaluating service inputs; contributing to service developments at local and national levels; and reflecting on the impact of the work on themselves and others. Working with older people inevitably means facing issues of mortality; providing support to bereaved families or working with a dying person may cause clinical staff to think closely about their own mortality. Some may not have had a prior personal experience of death and may find it difficult to express their concerns. Psychologists may play a helpful role in supporting such staff to address these issues effectively.

6.6 **Access**

Health care settings, including those providing psychology services, should meet the older person's needs in relation to their physical or sensory abilities, cognitive capacity, and need for safety and security. Assessment and therapy processes may need to be modified for time of day, pace, length and frequency of session, sound and light levels, and removal of distractions to meet the person's preferences and requirements.

Attempts to overcome the under-referral of older people to mental health services in the UK have led to a number of innovations, for example sessions being offered in places where older people meet regularly, including clubs, Women's Institute meetings, and adult education settings. Collaborative working with voluntary organizations, for example through co-running groups, also means that older people can be seen in less stigmatizing or threatening premises. This kind of proactive management of mental health issues and promotion of wellbeing may return some sense of control of their health and their future to the older person.

In addition, the recent drive towards increasing access to psychological therapies for a greater number of people through the provision of stepped-care models and initially lower intensity interventions has effectively employed new forms of provision, such as digital technology and telephone therapy. Evidence indicates that older people can use and do benefit from computerized treatment and remote access interventions if they are given good initial support.

6.7 **Assessment**

Any assessment carried out with an older person must be carefully planned with an awareness of the wider context, and designed with a specific purpose in mind. For example, the psychologist may wish to assess a person's suitability for psychological therapy and what changes may need to be made to maximize their ability to benefit. Although any cognitive changes seen in the 'young-old' are normally relatively small and unlikely to affect engagement in treatment, some sensory changes such as hearing loss may have a negative impact. It becomes harder to test cognitive function reliably as people age; performance may fluctuate between sessions and there is huge individual variation. Nevertheless some deterioration in executive functioning may affect the older person's ability to process content in sessions and to plan, or switch between, concepts discussed. Cognitive and sensory changes can therefore have a significant effect on motivation and engagement. Optimizing communication through the use of diaries, mobile phone texts, pictorial or written explanations, a therapy folder or book, telephone reminders and prompts, or formal memory aids could make a significant contribution to the outcome of interventions, so the potential for the use of these also needs to be assessed.

The referral information initially provided to the service may not provide the whole picture. It is often necessary to consider whether possible cognitive impairment and co- morbid physical illness might obscure or compound the relatively straightforward assessment of someone's mood. Assessing a person's psychological–mindedness and ability to engage actively in a specific model of therapy, for example, may need to be deferred while a more detailed neuropsychological assessment takes place, for instance to assess attention span and recall, or the possible onset of a dementia.

It is usually helpful to explain that assessment is an on-going process, involving observation, discussion, and standardized measures, and to take time to establish the older person's concerns. Discussion with spouse or carers may help too. Risk assessment for vulnerability may be needed, given possible poor medication management, lack of attention to personal hygiene and self-care (including diet and fluid intake), possible heart problems, sleep disorders, poor pain control, or a tendency to fall. Awareness of the person's risk of physical, financial, emotional, or sexual abuse from family or paid or unpaid carers must be shared. The use of non-prescription drugs, alcohol misuse, and the cognitive sequelae of diseases such as HIV and AIDS need consideration too.

There are a wide range of potential assessment tools, and selecting, administering, scoring, and interpreting the most suitable ones comes with training, practise, and good supervision. Neuropsychological assessments are not all necessarily well standardized, or normed for different minority groups, or for those with sensory impairments, or for the 'old-old'. Observation throughout the assessment process or in people's homes or residential settings, including wards, may help to reveal practical problems that result from an underlying neuropsychological deficit. Functional analysis and behavioural rating scales can be useful for assessing people who cannot respond verbally to rating scales or more formal assessment tools.

Selecting goals and outcomes for the intervention, and agreeing which measures would constitute a good evaluation for an achieved outcome, takes time and detailed questioning. Applying measures pre- and post-therapy and making contact subsequently to review progress can reinforce the belief that change is possible and can be maintained.

Information derived from the assessment and formulation process enables choice about which steps are taken first. Stepped-care pathways imply a sequential progression through a care pathway, with one thing being tried before another. However, as older people may be seen in a number of settings concurrently, a matched-care approach may be more helpful. For instance, this might involve planning supported bibliotherapy sessions targeted to overcome cognitive difficulties (which might impair a person's understanding of their health conditions); relaxation exercises designed to reduce anxiety or to improve sleep and pain management; individual cognitive-behaviour therapy (CBT) intended to help with depression; and activity scheduling provided in a residential setting. All of these may all be delivered by different members of a team who share a common formulation and work on shared outcomes. This combined approach may be the most effective in facilitating mood and behaviour change, especially if the carer also has input.

Initial explanations must make it clear to the person (who in some cases may be lonely and socially isolated) that both assessment and treatment sessions are set up with a clear purpose and are time-limited, so that the psychologist is not seen as a surrogate child, grandchild, or friend. Plans for relapse management and management of termination of therapy should be introduced early. Supplementary bibliotherapy and telephone or email contact, involving a family member or paid carer as co-therapist, are possible ways to support memory difficulties and to back up what has been achieved in session. Poor levels of literacy and shame about this may lead to people failing to attend or dropping out of sessions if not handled sensitively.

6.8 Psychological interventions

In this section, a number of psychological treatment approaches will be briefly outlined, all of which may be helpful with the kind of issues or conditions often presented to services by older people or by those caring for them. As a systematic evidence base has grown in this specialty, modifications to existing psychological models and therapies have been shown to enhance their effectiveness and appropriateness for older people. In addition to these modifications, lifespan perpectives need to be considered, since issues such as transition, bereavement, and loss may become pertinent (Erikson, 1990), For instance, shifts between life stages may be experienced as loss, and thus grief-focused interventions may be appropriate. The experience of recent losses may also be influenced by previous major losses not yet grieved for; hence an understanding of models of attachment is important. For example, the recent loss of an occupational role or even a pet might embody the loss of an earlier, highly significant attachment to a sibling or parent that was never truly addressed. Insecure attachments made in childhood may also affect later life security and mental health, especially at a point of transition into residential care, where people are then labelled as 'needy'. Losing the protective other or one's own caring role are also frequent themes in work with older people.

Behavioural interventions

Interventions based on classical or operant conditioning may be useful for people who are unable to respond to more verbal forms of therapy. Psychologists working in residential or ward settings can use observations to choose relevant reinforcers, and by using simple ABC (antecedent, behaviour, consequence) models can help staff to see that people are not simply 'attention seeking' or 'challenging' but may be responding to other people's communications and behaviours. This often takes the emotional 'heat' from a situation where someone is hard to manage, and can provide a way for staff to develop less troubled interactions with residents. The use of detailed functional analysis may also enable people to regain skills for a period of time if tasks are broken down into small enough component parts and backward chaining or errorless learning techniques are used.

Cognitive behaviour therapy

CBT has the strongest evidence base of all models of therapy commonly used with older people. Systematic modifications to CBT for working with older people are described by James (2010) and Laidlaw and Knight (2008). These models add to the basic CBT formulation the assessment of health status, cohort effects, intergenerational linkages, and role investment/transitions. Research has shown that better outcomes are produced by taking time to develop a strong therapeutic relationship, actively involving the person in therapy, developing achievable goals, using rewarding homework, and recording tasks.

Additional modifications for working with older people include using shorter sessions, repeating presentations of key information in more than one modality (orally, verbally, visually), creatively reinforcing understanding, and using a simpler communication style. The therapeutic process can also be consolidated by using scaffolding techniques to build up questions, eliciting pleasant events, listing pros and cons, and keeping simple diaries. As in physical health settings, clinicians may sometimes struggle with the fact that some of the client's negative automatic thoughts seem to be realistic. Asking what is helpful/unhelpful about the thought can, however, often lead to solutions for appropriate behavioural change in the present.

James (2010) has also broadened the use of the CBT model to cover people with physical health conditions and people with dementia. He reinforces the importance of assessing the person's needs carefully, since people in different cohorts will have different skills and abilities and require different adaptations to therapy. James further describes the impact that continuing cognitive changes may have on engagement in therapy, affecting interpersonal relationships, problem solving, and abstract reasoning. Therapy should therefore be modified to support the area of cognition affected. For example, knowing that someone has a reduced attention span, and cannot retain verbally presented information, should prompt the psychologist to present things visually and to offer shorter, more frequent sessions.

Mindfulness techniques (Kabat Zinn, 1990) and acceptance and commitment therapy (Hayes *et al.*, 1999) can be additional powerful techniques to use with older people, since their focus on the 'here and now' helps to avoid rumination on past failures. The techniques of working alongside someone's sadness and loss, asking them to recognize their patterns of distress, learning to observe and accept their present state, and develop the flexibility and control to work towards a preferred future, can be particularly helpful when working with someone with depression and physical health conditions, as well as with those facing end-of-life issues.

Cognitive analytic therapy

Cognitive analytic therapy (CAT) provides people with an opportunity to reflect on some of the repetitive unhelpful interpersonal patterns that can develop over a lifetime, and this can be a helpful way for an older person to see their situation in a different light (Hepple and Sutton, 2004). Reformulation letters, discussion of 'exits' (ways of developing alternative relationship patterns), and goodbye letters are particularly powerful in creating and sustaining emotional change engendered by therapy. The clear, collaborative style of CAT can be particularly empowering for the older person. Discussing behaviour in terms of reciprocal roles is often helpful in couple or family interventions, and can also be used in team settings, allowing teams to understand any unhelpful relational patterns that may be developing between the team and the older person or their carers. CAT also provides a space to listen to people's stories and to encourage more insight and self-reflection. The approach can be particularly helpful for more able clients wanting to understand more about their own distress, but who may for a variety of reasons not want to work within CBT.

Interpersonal therapy

Interpersonal therapy (IPT) is a manualized intervention with a strong psycho-educational aspect which can be helpful in the management of recurrent depression in older people. The model attributes the onset of depression to difficulties in transition (retirement, becoming a carer, change in health or marital status), bereavement, conflict with others, or to deficits/life-long difficulties in making and sustaining relationships. A formulation is developed that focuses on interpersonal conflicts, building on knowledge of the person's social networks, and usually integrating common themes of isolation and loneliness. Evidence suggests that IPT is particularly acceptable as an approach to many older people, having obvious face validity for them.

Systemic and indirect approaches

Working with older people frequently involves working with both the family and wider social systems. Systemic approaches involve working collaboratively to gather information, being curious, and using questions that are designed to help to shape the system around the older person in a way that empowers them to regain control of their own lives. Having information available from all family members about the complexity of the situation gives a broader perspective, removing the pressure of seeing the older person as the 'problem'.

Likewise, indirect approaches can be designed to influence those who themselves influence the lives of the older person (including formal organizations). The competencies of clinical leadership are highly relevant at all stages; leadership is not exclusively the focus for someone with experience and seniority. Psychologists, including assistant psychologists or graduate workers in a team, often have the greatest knowledge about psychological wellbeing and can share their skills to help psychological mindedness develop throughout a service. A core part of the psychologist's role is being available for informal case discussion, making suggestions or asking questions that might clarify a formulation, and helping to choose appropriate interventions. Working jointly with other professionals, psychologists can model sensitive questioning styles and therapeutic approaches. Highlighting both poor and good practice, and sharing it through case discussion at ward rounds and in team meetings, helps to promote psychological awareness in the team. Services can be improved by using both clinical and academic knowledge to train, supervise, and support colleagues in their work in this area. Finally, knowledge of research methods and evaluation processes also can help the service to develop and plan services systematically.

6.9 Working with people with dementia

Given demographic changes, dementia has progressively become more visible and is now somewhat less stigmatized in an ageing society. The Alzheimer's Society estimates that one million people will be living with dementia in the UK by 2020. Prevalence rates of 2–4% in the population over 65 increase to 20% over the age of 85. However, only a third of people are given a clear diagnosis, and this is traditionally done in secondary care settings by neurologists, psychiatrists, or geriatricians. More recently, memory clinics have been developed to provide a 'one stop shop' for dementia assessment, treatment, rehabilitation, and support. More comprehensive services can also provide psychosocial support across the whole care pathway, from pre-diagnostic counselling to post-diagnostic support and rehabilitation.

Changes in cognitive function can have profound effects on relationships, social functioning, independence, and feelings of self-worth. Issues that need to be recognized and discussed when planning for the future include role changes, providing support for carers, the use and efficacy of medications, the advisability of discontinuing work or driving, and the need to make arrangements about practical issues such as housing, power of attorney, and living wills. Transparency is essential when people are making choices about their futures and whilst they still have the optimum level of capacity and self-efficacy.

Psychologists can provide support for those living with dementia through all stages of the care pathway. Their breadth of skills can be applied (for example) in providing pre-diagnostic counselling, neuropsychological assessment, planned behavioural interventions to enable skill retention, cognitive therapy for any accompanying depression, systemic work to cope with role change and transition, marital or group work, and a range of interventions designed to manage challenging behaviour. Younger people with dementia may require particular support in family and work settings. For example, someone with dementia in their 30s may be cared for by teenage children who risk losing their own childhood and educational opportunities in the process, and the whole family may need additional therapeutic input and support as a consequence.

Group work approaches such as cognitive stimulation therapy (Spector *et al.*, 2011) and reminiscence (Butler, 1963) can help people to retain cognitive strengths, redevelop skills, and reduce their sense of isolation, whilst providing shared support. Oral history projects and life-story books have also helped family and formal carers to better understand the person they are caring for. Additionally, psychologists may be involved in developing more supportive communities within ward or residential environments, thereby helping staff to meet the needs of people who have severe dementia and who may otherwise find it difficult to express preferences.

Although medication, in particular anti-psychotics, has traditionally been used in hospitals and nursing homes to manage challenging behaviour in dementia, psychologists have been at the forefront of those seeking alternative psychosocial approaches. Challenging behaviour can in fact be seen as a rational response, which is highly predictable when people try to cope with situations that are incomprehensible or threatening to them. Tom Kitwood (1997) has developed dementia care mapping, a detailed observational approach nowadays often used in residential settings, which trains staff to notice and respond, not only to the positively demanding behaviours shown by some elderly residents with dementia (aggression, shouting, spitting), but also to the negative ones (withdrawal and apathy). This approach has led to significant improvements in care. James (2010) has also demonstrated better ways of managing challenging behaviours through training care staff in the systematic use of functional analysis, and has suggested that monitoring emotional responses in terms of Beck's cognitive triad (for example feeling hopeless about the self, the future, and the world) may be helpful in understanding the responses of people with severe dementia to situations perceived to be threatening or distressing.

Concern about the loss of communication abilities in people with profound dementia has also led to the development of therapies such as multi-sensory stimulation and reciprocal intensive communication techniques (Astell and Ellis, 2011). Positive responses from dementia patients are rewarding for families and staff. Validation therapy also highlights patients' emotional needs, helping staff to understand what patients might be communicating about the reality of their world, for example their own need to care for others or to retain a parental role.

As anxiety and depression are both common in dementia, and as medical treatments are not completely effective, further work needs to be done on psychosocial interventions. The early evidence shows that CBT can be an effective approach for many patients, while computerized CBT for carers can offer a helpful home-based alternative to those who are unable to leave their relatives to attend clinic-based sessions.

Working with carers is integral to working with dementia, although some services make it rather difficult for carers to be referred in their own right. One third are over 65 themselves, and three quarters of carers have a greater level of distress than age-matched controls. Lack of well-being is more closely correlated with perceived stress than number of care-giving hours per se, and has a negative impact on the carer's health and immune system (Brodaty and Donkin, 2009). However, positive aspects of caring are often also reported by carers, such as feeling useful, fulfilled, and close to the person cared for.

6.10 What does the future hold for psychological services for older people?

The evidence base for the work of clinical psychologists with older adults is becoming well established. Nevertheless many older people still receive a poor level of care, in marginalized services, from staff with limited training. Ignoring the complex needs which may be part of the ageing process, and subsuming them into 'all age' services on the mistaken assumption that this promotes age equality, is to discriminate against those who may be unable to make appropriate demands for themselves. As health and social care boundaries change to meet the social and financial pressures of caring for an ageing world, it is to be hoped that older people will in future be supported in more holistic systems. Clinical psychologists need to develop a greater knowledge of health conditions and to develop more community-focused approaches, as well as competence in arguing for improvements in provision. Technical innovations in neuro-imaging, together with more sensitive neuro-psychological assessments, will undoubtedly improve the understanding of brain functioning, but without understanding the psychological impact of ageing on the person, and how they can adapt positively to changes, this knowledge may be of limited benefit to the individual. Clinical psychologists' skills must therefore continue to develop to meet the disparate and changing needs of older people. Key areas for research will be working effectively with technical innovation and with communities, improving standards in physical health settings and in residential care, developing end-of-life care, and engaging more effectively with minority groups.

References

Astell, A.J. and Ellis, M.J. (2011). The challenges of equipping care home staff with psychosocial skills: reflections from developing training in a novel approach to communication. *PSIGE Newsletter*, **117**, 26–32. British Psychological Society, Leicester.

Bhalla, R.K., Butters, M.A., Becker, J.T., *et al.* (2006). Patterns of mild cognitive impairment after treatment of depression in the elderly. *American Journal of Geriatric Psychiatry*, **17**, 308–316.

Brodaty, H. and Donkin, M. (2009). Family caregivers of people with dementia. *Dialogues in Clinical Neuroscience*, **11** (2), 217–228.

Butler, R.N. (1963). The life review: an interpretation of reminiscence in the aged. *Psychiatry*, **26**, 65–70.

Erikson, E.H. (1990). *Identity and the Life Cycle*, 2nd edn. Norton, New York.

Friedan, B. (1994). How to live longer, better, wiser. *Parade Magazine*, 20 March, 4–6.

Hayes, S.C., Strosahl, K., and Wilson, K.E. (1999). *Acceptance and Commitment Therapy: An Experiential Approach to Behaviour Change*. Guildford Press, New York.

Hepple, J. and Sutton, L. (2004). *Cognitive Analytic Therapy and Later Life*. Brunner-Routledge, Hove.

James, I.A. (2010). *Cognitive Behaviour Therapy with Older People. Interventions for those with and without Dementia*. Jessica Kingsley, London.

Kabat Zinn, J. (1990). *Full Catastrophe Living: Using the Wisdom of your Mind to Face Stress, Pain and Illness*. Dell Publishing, New York.

Kitwood, T. (1997). *Dementia Reconsidered: The Person Comes First*. Open University Press, Buckingham.

Laidlaw, K. and Knight, B. (eds) (2008). *Handbook of Emotional Disorders in Later Life*. Oxford University Press, Oxford.

Spector, A., Gardner, C., and Orrell, M. (2011). The impact of cognitive stimulation therapy groups on people with dementia: views from participants, their carers and group facilitators. *Ageing and Mental Health*, **15**, 945–949.

Further reading

British Psychological Society (2004). *On Purchasing Clinical Psychology Services for Older People, their Families, and other Carers*. Division of Clinical Psychology, Briefing Paper No. 5. British Psychological Society, Leicester.

Bryden, C. (2005). *Dancing with Dementia: Mystery Story of Living Positively with Dementia*. Jessica Kingsley, London.

Fredman, G., Anderson, E., and Stott, J. (eds) (2010). *Being with Older People: A Systemic Approach*. Karnac Books, London.

Woods, R.T. and Clare, L. (2008). *Handbook of the Clinical Psychology of Ageing*. Wiley, Chichester.

Useful websites

<www.alzheimers.org.uk>—the UK Alzheimer's Disease Association which provides information, advice, and support to people with dementia and their carers and encourages relevant research.

<www.lifestorynetwork.org.uk>—describes training and research in the use of life-story work with a range of people.

<www.psige.org.uk>—the British Psychological Society, Faculty of the Psychology of Older People.

Chapter 7

Working with eating disorders

Hannah Turner

7.1 Introduction

Although public awareness of eating disorders has increased considerably in recent years, many myths continue to surround these often severely debilitating disorders. Commonly misconstrued as 'a diet that got out of hand', the concept of an eating disorder can leave many of those involved feeling frustrated and perplexed, as they struggle to understand what appears to be an extraordinary state of obsession with food and weight. However, beneath this there often lies a story of insecurity, anxiety, and fear. No one just wakes up one morning with an eating disorder—rather these are complex illnesses that develop over time and often as a result of multiple influences. The range of causative factors can be diverse and may include genetic and biological factors, cultural and social pressures, personality traits, and adverse life events. People with eating disorders often experience intense feelings of inferiority and worthlessness. The all-consuming nature of an eating disorder means it invariably has a profound impact on sufferers' lives, including their education, employment, and social relationships, as well as on the lives of partners, families, and friends.

Working in this field can be challenging, frustrating, and rewarding. Challenging, because a range of issues need to be untangled; frustrating, because you can't make people change; and rewarding, because when they do, you share in the development of a life less constrained by food, and enhanced by freedom and choice. Clinicians and those who have experienced an eating disorder agree that recovery is a multidimensional concept that involves a range of areas, including reduction of life-threatening consequences, cessation of weight-controlling behaviours, the development of a more positive opinion of one's appearance, and improvements in psychological, emotional, and social functioning (Emanuelli *et al.*, 2012). Working in this field is about actively engaging with people. Through developing an alliance based on openness, honesty, and trust, a clinical psychologist can offer support while the process of exploration, understanding, and recovery begins. Throughout this process, it is important to be mindful that responsibility for change remains with individuals; our role being to empower those with whom we work to take control of their lives and their recovery.

7.2 Definitions and key clinical features

The main *Diagnostic and Statistical Manual of Mental Disorders (DSM-V)* diagnoses (American Psychiatric Association, 2013) and their key characteristics are now described.

Anorexia nervosa

Behaviourally, anorexia nervosa is characterized by extreme dietary restriction, such that individuals maintain a significantly low body weight. Weight loss is commonly achieved through avoidance of 'fatty foods' and dietary intake is often limited in the range of foods eaten. A sub-group of patients will also engage in driven exercise, self-induced vomiting, and/or laxative misuse. From a cognitive perspective, patients often experience intense feelings of fatness, as well as extreme fears concerning loss of control over eating and weight gain. These patients also tend to evaluate themselves almost exclusively in terms of their weight, shape, and ability to control food.

The pathway into an eating disorder can vary. For some, natural bodily changes that accompany puberty or a negative weight/shape-related comment may lead to a conscious decision to diet. For others, an episode of physical illness with associated weight loss, such as glandular fever, may lead to more intentional dieting. Commonly occurring in the context of low self-worth, positive feedback regarding weight loss initially serves to reinforce dieting behaviour and further weight loss. Patients often report a sense of euphoria at being in control of their weight and for some it brings feelings of success and a fleeting sense of superiority at achieving something few in the general population can accomplish.

As the illness develops, so food begins to permeate all areas of life through its dominance of thoughts, feelings, and actions. Behaviours around food become increasingly rigid and deceptive, and the range of acceptable foods slowly diminishes. Cognitive rumination about weight and shape becomes all-consuming and an increasing amount of time is given to thinking about food. Over time, general functioning becomes increasingly impaired, interest in other areas of life fades, and day-to-day routine becomes characterized by social withdrawal and isolation.

It is widely recognized that individuals with anorexia nervosa tend to be perfectionists. They may also present with obsessive-compulsive personality traits, often evident in a variety of rigid, ritualistic behaviours. Difficulties identifying and managing emotions is also common and an avoidant style of coping may predominate in everyday life.

Bulimia nervosa

Bulimia nervosa is characterized by two key features; first, recurrent episodes of binge eating, during which an objectively large amount of food is consumed with associated loss of control; and second, compensatory behaviours aimed towards the avoidance of weight gain. These may include self-induced vomiting, misuse of laxatives or diuretics, excessive exercise, dietary restriction, or, in the case of those with diabetes, insulin misuse. As with anorexia nervosa, those with bulimia nervosa tend to evaluate themselves almost exclusively on the basis of weight, shape, and ability to control food.

Although most people with bulimia nervosa tend to fall within the normal weight range, the illness is characterized by an initial period of dieting. However, the extreme nature of this invariably leads to episodes of binge eating. Plagued by fears of weight gain, some begin to use compensatory behaviours, such as self-induced vomiting, in an attempt to 'undo the damage' caused by bingeing and over time a vicious cycle of dietary restriction, bingeing, and purging develops. This cycle of behaviour invariably has a detrimental impact on other areas of functioning, such as work and social relationships. People with bulimia nervosa tend to 'value' their symptoms less, compared to those with anorexia nervosa, and often binge and purge in secret. Feeling too guilty and ashamed of their condition to ask for help, many often live with their disorder for years before seeking treatment.

Evidence suggests that a proportion of people with bulimia nervosa have difficulty regulating their emotions, and for many, bingeing may serve as a form of emotional regulation. A sub-group will also present with co-morbid depression and/or borderline personality disorder, and many of these will engage in a range of self-destructive behaviours, such as cutting, overdosing, and substance misuse, the dominant behaviour changing over time.

Binge eating disorder

The key feature of binge eating disorder (BED) is regular episodes of binge eating. However, unlike those with bulimia nervosa, patients with BED do not regularly engage in compensatory behaviours. Other key characteristics include eating much more rapidly than normal, eating until feeling uncomfortably full, and feeling disgusted with oneself after over-eating.

Atypical eating disorders

Described as 'atypical' or 'eating disorder not otherwise specified' (EDNOS), this category consists of a number of sub-groups, a proportion of which comprise all but one of the key features of anorexia nervosa or bulimia nervosa. Other groups include those who chew and spit food rather than swallowing it, and those who purge after eating a small amount of food.

7.3 The issue of history and culture

Anorexia nervosa has a relatively long history, dating back to 1873, when Lasegue published his seminal paper on 'anorexic hysterique', a condition in which patients presented with amenorrhoea, weight loss, and restlessness. Although many of these symptoms are still recognized today, key features have been shown to vary with time and place. Initially viewed as a 'Western' syndrome, there is now growing evidence that anorexia nervosa can be found in diverse cultural settings, including

Asia, South America, and Africa, although the exact incidence and prevalence remains unknown. The detail of the clinical picture also remains unclear; for example, clinical accounts from non-Western countries indicating that symptoms of weight phobia and body image disturbance are absent in those presenting with sustained low body weight have led some to suggest that the 'weight phobia' commonly associated with anorexia nervosa may be culture specific.

By comparison, bulimia nervosa has much more recent roots. Although an increasing number of case reports of bulimia nervosa-type syndromes were published in the 1960s, this cluster of symptoms were initially viewed within the context of anorexia nervosa. The psychiatrist Gerald Russell is widely regarded as responsible for the identification of the modern-day syndrome. In 1979 he published a case series of 30 patients presenting with what he described as 'bulimia nervosa', the key features of which remain central to the present diagnostic criteria. It is most commonly seen in young females living in Western society. However, in the UK, Muslim Asian women have been identified as a particularly 'at risk' group. Further detail regarding the history and culture of eating disorders can be found in Fairburn and Brownell (2005).

7.4 **How common are eating disorders?**

Females are ten times more likely to be diagnosed with anorexia nervosa than males. During their lifetime, 0.9–2.2% of females and 0.2–0.3% of males will be diagnosed with anorexia nervosa. The rate at which new cases occur has not changed over the past five decades, although the incidence among adolescent girls may have increased a little. Bulimia nervosa affects 1.5–2% of females and 0.5% of males. The incidence increased rapidly in the 1980s but currently appears to be stable or has even decreased slightly since the late 1990. Onset is usually in late teenage years, later than for anorexia nervosa, which tends to occur earlier (most common age of onset is 15 years, range 9–24 years) (Birmingham and Treasure, 2010). The prevalence of EDNOS remains unclear, although reports suggest it is the most common presentation seen in clinical practice.

7.5 **Who is at risk of developing an eating disorder?**

A number of risk factors have been identified. Some are general factors, such as being female and living in Western society, whilst others are more specific, reflecting adverse early experiences such as childhood sexual abuse or parental neglect. A number of risk factors have been identified for bulimia nervosa, including early menarche and childhood obesity, whilst a number of pre-morbid traits, such as perfectionism, have been associated with the development of anorexia nervosa. A more detailed summary can be found in a review by Fairburn and Harrison (2003).

7.6 **Eating disorders across the lifespan**

Although typically associated with the young adult population, eating disorders can present in varying forms across the lifespan, from young children to older adults. Although bulimia nervosa is rare in children under 14 years of age, when it does present, the clinical picture tends to be the same as that found with later onset. In contrast, although the psychological features associated with early-onset anorexia nervosa mirror those seen in adults, children and younger adults may also present with stunted growth or delayed puberty, and it is often parents or teachers who raise initial concerns. For some, their illness may be an attempt to arrest development linked with puberty, whilst for others it may constitute a means of negotiating developmental tasks associated with adolescence, such as separating from parents and developing an increasingly independent identity.

A number of other types of childhood eating disturbance have also been described in the literature, the most common being food avoidance emotional disorder (FAED) and selective eating (Lask and Bryant-Waugh, 2013). FAED is recognized as an emotional disorder in which food avoidance constitutes the key presenting feature. Children with FAED have a history of faddy eating and food restriction but fail to meet the criteria for anorexia nervosa. In contrast, selective eating is a term applied to those who eat only a very limited range of foods. Although this group do not tend to cause concern in relation to physical health, as they get older they often experience difficulties in relation to social situations (e.g. birthday parties) where they might be faced with having to eat foods that are outside their limited range. Although a large percentage eventually grow out of selective eating, this disorder can become increasingly problematic for those in whom it persists into adulthood. More recently a new term to describe eating problems in children has been proposed. Avoidant/restrictive food intake disorder (ARFID) refers to eating or feeding disturbances that occur in the absence of weight/shape concern and lead to persistent failure to meet appropriate nutritional and/or energy needs. Such disturbances may include an apparent lack of interest in eating or food; avoidance based on the sensory characteristics of food; or concern about aversive consequences of eating, for example choking.

In relation to later stages of life, eating disorders among middle-aged and older adults are not always recognized and therefore may go untreated. For those in their 40s and 50s, life events such as divorce, grown children leaving home, and physical signs of ageing may leave some feeling that life is increasingly out of control. For them, an eating disorder may serve to engender a sense of control over life and/or represent an attempt to slow down realities of ageing. For older adults, underlying factors are also likely to relate to life circumstances. Social burden and financial strain, as well as the physical and cognitive abilities required to prepare a meal, may all contribute to decreased food intake among this group. Eating disorders for older people may also serve as a protest against living conditions (e.g. a nursing home), an attempt to get attention from family members, or reflect a lack of enthusiasm for life.

7.7 The setting for clinical work

Before describing how clinical psychologists might work within this field it is important to outline the clinical context. Until the last few decades of the twentieth century, anorexia nervosa was primarily managed by physicians, with treatment principally comprising bed rest and re-feeding on medical wards. This was followed by the development of specialist units in which supportive nursing formed the cornerstone of treatment. Predominantly led by psychiatry, treatment programmes were primarily based on behavioural principles, whereby weight gain was rewarded with activities such as home leave. Inpatient units have since moved towards a more holistic treatment ethos, with programmes aiming to address underlying psychological issues, as well as eating disorder behaviours and physical health.

The past two decades have also seen a significant increase in the number of people treated on an outpatient basis, and treatment is now commonly delivered by specialist community eating disorder services. Such services are also moving towards developing more intensive day care programmes, aimed towards those who would otherwise require inpatient admission.

7.8 **The role of the clinical psychologist**

Although eating disorders have serious medical consequences, psychological interventions remain at the core of treatment options for the majority. Clinical psychologists have a central role to play in the implementation and evaluation of evidence-based treatment. Hence clinical psychologists work in all of the settings already described. For some, the focus may be concerned with delivery and evaluation of individual psychological therapy, whilst others may be more involved in setting up day services, or providing individual and group therapies in an inpatient setting. Clinical psychologists may also provide consultation and supervision to other professionals, including nursing staff, GPs, and other mental health professionals working in the community. Senior psychologists are also likely to be involved in service planning and development, and may well fulfil the role of service and clinical lead.

7.9 **Additional knowledge and skills**

Although medical responsibility for patients remains with medical practitioners, clinical psychologists should have a basic understanding of the physical complications associated with eating disorders (Birmingham and Treasure, 2010), as well as a working knowledge of other physical health conditions that sometimes present in the context of eating disorders, such as chronic fatigue syndrome and type I diabetes mellitus.

This can be invaluable when liaising with medical colleagues, although it is important to be clear about the boundaries of expertise. Given that a shared understanding is essential if a cohesive package of care is to be delivered, it is imperative that clinical psychologists draw upon their communication skills to articulate and communicate a clear and logical psychological formulation to all involved. The complex picture often seen in clinical practice means it is not uncommon for professionals within and between teams to be divided in their clinical opinion, and such differences need to be contained and addressed if treatment is to stand a chance of success. Given that clinical psychologists working in eating disorders often form part of a multi-disciplinary team, it is also essential that time is taken to develop an understanding of how other colleagues work—this not only facilitates development of comprehensive packages of care, but also provides a multitude of opportunities for further learning.

7.10 **Clinical assessment and formulation**

People with eating difficulties often feel ashamed of their symptoms and many are ambivalent about seeking treatment. Hence establishing an effective alliance and developing a shared understanding are crucial parts of the therapeutic process. When assessing people with eating disorders it is important to cover psychological, social, and physical needs, as well as assessment of risk to self and others. From this should emerge a comprehensive personal history in which themes, patterns, and current life situations can be understood, including the development of self-identity, and the individual's personal style in areas such as coping, emotional expression, and communication. The development and course of the eating disorder should also be covered, including any history of dieting and/or eating disorders within the family. It can be additionally helpful to ask patients what functional role(s) they believe their eating disorder serves. Examples of these roles are shown in Figure 7.1.

Alongside developing a thorough formulation and identifying treatment goals, it is also important to consider medical risk, as this will further inform therapeutic options. Although the assessment of physical risk will involve liaison with medical colleagues, information relating to

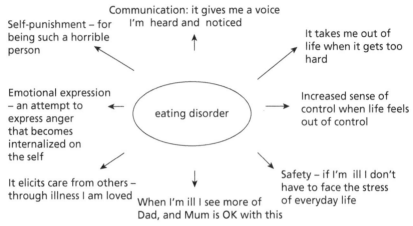

Fig. 7.1 The possible functional roles of an eating disorder.

height and weight, menstrual status, blood potassium level, and other physical diagnoses, such as diabetes, should all be obtained, usually from other members of the treating team.

7.11 **Approaches to treatment**

The last decade has seen a steady increase in the range of psychological therapies developed and applied to the treatment of eating disorders. Some of the key interventions and their application to eating disorders are outlined below.

Transdiagnostic cognitive-behaviour therapy (CBT)

Over the past 10 years CBT for eating disorders has moved away from being diagnosis specific, instead focusing more on core cognitions that are common to patients regardless of diagnosis. Such 'transdiganostic' models allow for a better understanding of how physiology (e.g. the effects of starvation), cognitions (e.g. extreme fear of uncontrolled weight gain), behaviours (e.g. dietary restriction), and emotions (e.g. anxiety) all serve to maintain the illness, as well as identifying general antecedents, such as core low self-esteem.

Emily was a 23-year-old trainee accountant who lived with her partner. At assessment she described being obsessed with food. She tried to restrict her intake to 700 calories a day through avoiding 'high' fat foods, but this led to episodes of binge eating. Driven by an intense fear of weight gain, Emily routinely made herself sick. Whilst this made her feel better in the short term, in the longer term it made her feel worse. She felt emotionally and physically drained; her mood and self-esteem were low and her behaviours were beginning to have a negative impact on her social relationships. Emily explained that recently she had also noticed herself bingeing when she was upset. Emily reported feeling fat and disgusting most days, commenting that if only she were thinner she would feel better about herself and life would be OK. Drawing upon a transdiagnostic cognitive model, it was hypothesized that Emily evaluated her self-worth almost exclusively on the basis of her weight and shape. This in turn drove strict dieting and rules around eating that reflected dysfunctional styles of reasoning as well as disturbances in information processing, such as black-and-white thinking, over-generalization, and errors of attribution (e.g. foods can only be 'good' or 'bad'; 'I must restrict my intake to 700 calories a day'; 'I mustn't eat after 6 pm'). Emily's dietary rules were unattainable and increased her vulnerability to bingeing in two ways: first, they made her feel hungry, a powerful physiological trigger; and second, the beliefs she held about food meant that even minor transgressions were viewed as catastrophic and grounds for abandoning the rule and then bingeing. Such transgressions not only promoted further concern about weight and shape, but also left Emily feeling increasingly negative about herself. It was further identified that Emily's binges sometimes served as a form of emotional release, often triggered by arguments with her partner.

During the initial stage of treatment the CBT model was explained and therapeutic goals agreed. The therapist worked collaboratively with Emily to develop the formulation. Emily was encouraged to normalize her dietary intake, reduce her eating disorder behaviours, and challenge her dysfunctional beliefs about food, eating, and weight. This involved drawing on psycho-educational material, completing food diaries, and weekly weighing, as well as using well-established CBT techniques, such as exposure and behavioural experiments. The overall aim of this was to reduce dietary restriction, normalize dietary intake (including regular *carbohydrate intake), and reduce associated anxiety. The therapist supported Emily through meeting with her weekly, and she gradually began to feel more in control of her eating, to reduce her bingeing and vomiting, and to increase the variety and quantity of foods she could eat. Emily progressively learned that these changes did not lead her to gain weight uncontrollably. Following this, treatment moved on to address prompts for residual bingeing, which were often linked to difficult emotions triggered by interpersonal difficulties. Through exploring these areas, Emily was able to begin to develop alternative coping strategies, as well as to challenge the central importance of weight and shape. In the final stage of treatment Emily was encouraged to practise the techniques learned, her concerns about ending treatment were discussed, and a relapse prevention plan was agreed.*

CBT is an active therapy and patients are encouraged to complete collaboratively agreed homework tasks between sessions. It is important that any therapy-interfering behaviours, such as not completing homework tasks or irregular attendance, are addressed, as these could have a negative impact on the effectiveness of treatment.

Cognitive analytic therapy (CAT)

Over the past 10 years CAT has become more widely used in the treatment of eating disorders, particularly anorexia nervosa. When applied in practice the initial task is to support the patient to identify their problem behaviours, which are likely to be linked to their eating disorder (e.g. dietary restriction, self-induced vomiting). The therapist then supports the patient to identify problematic patterns of relating, and the effect these patterns might have on relationships and other areas of life, which in turn may serve to maintain the eating disorder. In the early stages of therapy, the therapist takes a detailed history of early life experiences, including the development of the eating disorder, and the patient completes the Psychotherapy File, a tool that lists commonly occurring interpersonal difficulties. The patient is then invited to consider their current situation, and list patterns of thoughts, feelings, and behaviours that may be serving to keep them stuck in their illness. A reformulation letter describing key eating disorder behaviours and problematic interpersonal relationships is written to the patient. In it, clear links between past and present are made, and goals for change are suggested. Patients are subsequently encouraged to recognize when they are re-enacting past relationship patterns. It is through this process of refor-mulation and recognition that a therapeutic alliance is formed, and this forms the vehicle through which the therapist and patient work together to develop ways of revising problematic relationship patterns, which in turn allows the patient to give up their eating disorder.

Interpersonal psychotherapy (IPT)

IPT is a time-limited, goal-focused treatment that targets interpersonal problems. Within an IPT framework, it is assumed that eating disor-ders develop in a social and interpersonal context, the maintenance of the disorder and response to therapy all being influenced by interper-sonal relationships between the patient and those around them. The primary aim of therapy is to alter the problematic interpersonal pat-terns and life situations in which the eating disorder is developed and maintained. This is achieved through the resolution of problems within four possible domains: grief, interpersonal deficits, interpersonal role disputes, and role transition. An interpersonal inventory is conducted, which includes a review of the patient's past/current close relation-ships and social functioning, along with a chronological timeline of significant life events, changes in mood and self-esteem, interpersonal relationships, and eating disorder symptoms. The therapist then makes connections between life experiences and the eating disorder symp-toms, the aim being to link the eating disorder with one of the four interpersonal domains. Although patients' accounts may fit into several problem areas, one or at most two problem areas must be agreed as the focus for therapy. The therapist then draws on a range of strategies specific to that problem area. Towards the end of therapy the patient is encouraged to describe specific changes to their eating behaviours. Termination issues are addressed and a relapse prevent plan agreed. Throughout therapy the focus remains on the interpersonal context of the patient's life, rather than the eating disorder or related behaviours and cognitions.

Working with families

In the last 10–15 years the evidence base for the effectiveness of family therapy in the treatment of adolescent anorexia nervosa has steadily increased. Historically anorexia nervosa was viewed in the context of dysfunctional family interactions; however, recent writings have emphasized the importance of understanding how the family environment changes in its attempts to cope with the arrival of a chronic illness; a process that invariably culminates in the illness taking centre stage. Family therapy is therefore now less concerned with untangling causal dynamics, focusing instead on supporting families to generate solutions that will help them negotiate the transitional stages inherent in normal family life, and enabling them to play an active role in supporting recovery. There is anecdotal evidence to suggest that systemic therapy may constitute a useful intervention in the treatment of adults with eating disorders, and as such this forms an important avenue for further research.

Working in an inpatient setting

Intense interpersonal dynamics, competition between patients, and high levels of emotion can all make the inpatient setting a difficult place to be for both patients and staff. Many clinical psychologists work in inpatient settings, and key roles may include providing advice on implementing psychological interventions or behavioural programmes, and providing individual therapy for patients. The psychologist may also be involved in providing supervision and support to unit staff responsible for day-to-day care. This can take the form of group sessions, the aim being to support staff through helping them to understand team dynamics as well as their own reactions towards patients. The potential for staff splitting, for example where one staff member may be erroneously informed by a patient that another member of staff has made a particular decision, makes team time an essential part of any inpatient service.

7.12 Supervision and team-work issues

Working in eating disorders can be anxiety provoking and draining, and thus a space for regular clinical supervision is essential. Clinical psychologists are often involved in providing supervision for others and they can play a useful role in mapping team issues, which can help team members understand the potentially destructive dynamics frequently enacted in eating disorder teams, which can mirror those seen in the families of the patients treated.

7.13 **Ethical issues**

Anorexia nervosa has the highest mortality rate of any psychiatric illness and although a proportion of those avoiding therapy can be engaged through a genuine alliance, there remains a minority of patients who refuse to engage in treatment despite their physical health becoming seriously endangered. For this group, it may be necessary to consider compulsory treatment under the Mental Health Act. Whilst some authors argue that compulsory treatment forms a breach of autonomy and human rights, others remind us that for some patients this forms a necessary and essential part of recovery. For those locked deep in their illness, compulsory treatment can be viewed as an act of compassion, in which professionals realize the seriousness of the situation and are willing to enforce intensive support. In some cases compulsory treatment can be met with a sense of relief by patients and their families, who can temporarily hand over responsibility to health care professionals.

7.14 **Conclusion**

The past 20 years have seen a significant development in both the provision of specialist services for people with eating disorders and the development of psychological therapies. Consequently, the contribution of clinical psychologists continues to develop and expand. Alongside our professional colleagues we have a key role to play, not only in advancing treatment and knowledge, but also in influencing the commissioning, provision, and development of services. Although often challenging, eating disorders can be a richly rewarding and varied field within which to work.

References

American Psychiatric Association (2013). *Diagnostic and Statistical Manual of Mental Disorders (DSM-V)*, Fifth Edition. APA, Washington, DC.

Birmingham, C.L. and Treasure, J. (2010). *Medical Management of Eating Disorders*, 2nd edn. Cambridge University Press, Cambridge.

Emanuelli, F., Waller, G., Jones-Chester, M., and Ostuzzi, R. (2012). Recovery from disordered eating: sufferers' and clinicians' perspectives. *European Eating Disorders Review*, **20** (5), 363–372.

Fairburn, C.G. and Brownell, K.D. (2005). *Eating Disorders and Obesity*, 2nd edn. Guilford, New York.

Fairburn, C.G. and Harrison, P.J. (2003). Eating disorders. *The Lancet*, **361**, 407–416.

Lask, B. and Bryant-Waugh, R. (2013). *Eating Disorders in Childhood and Adolescence*, 4th edn. Routledge, London.

Further reading

Palmer, R. (2000). *Helping People with Eating Disorders: A Clinical Guide to Assessment and Treatment*. Wiley, London.

Treasure, J., Schmidt, U., and van Furth, E. (2005). *The Essential Handbook of Eating Disorders*. Wiley, London.

Chapter 8

Working with people with intellectual disabilities

Steve Carnaby

8.1 Case example: Patrick

The duty phone rang in the community team office. Patrick's keyworker was concerned, as Patrick had once again presented at the local hospital's Accident and Emergency department, insisting that a member of staff had hit him and that his family were taking his money. Patrick's safeguarding plan was put into action and the usual checks carried out to establish what had happened. As had taken place many times before, Patrick's allegations were not substantiated—the member of staff named was not on duty that day and his family were away on holiday—but the clinical psychologist arranged to meet with Patrick to see what he was really 'saying' behind the allegations. Their on-going work together had revealed a pattern of Patrick feeling unloved when his family went away without him, and unwanted when he felt that staff were giving more attention to other tenants in the housing project where he lived.

Patrick and the clinical psychologist wrote letters together, one to Patrick's family and one to the staff team, explaining how he felt and telling them how he would prefer to be more involved in what happens around him in the future. They agreed to ask everyone to meet together so that Patrick could hear what everybody thought of his letters and to draw up a plan setting out some principles aimed at helping Patrick feel he has more influence over how he is supported in future.

Patrick's story is an example of the rich and varied work carried out by psychologists working with people with intellectual disabilities. Patrick is a young man who struggles to balance the feelings he has for his family with the attachments he has formed with staff supporting him in the flat where he lives. As someone with intellectual disabilities, he has difficulties with managing his emotions and often needs others to help him make sense of the world around him. He has low self-esteem rooted in being bullied as a child, and also finds it hard to wait for the help he needs. When all of these factors come together at times of stress, Patrick turns to find help where he knows it will be guaranteed: the emergency services. In this way, Patrick 'shows' others his psychological problems and difficulties through his behaviour, since he is unable to articulate them with words.

The clinical psychologist in this example worked individually with Patrick, but also worked with those in the wider context of his life (family and support staff), always operating within local statutory safeguarding procedures and also liaising with staff from the hospital where Patrick presented. The need for clinical psychologists in the field of intellectual disabilities to adopt this multi-dimensional approach to their work is a main theme of this chapter.

8.2 Definitions and terminology

The language used to describe people with intellectual disabilities has changed many times over the years, including 'mental handicap' and 'mental retardation', the latter still being used in the USA. Historically, terms originating in the scientific community later became forms of abuse in everyday use. For example, 'cretin', 'spastic', and 'mongol' were once used as legitimate descriptors by the medical profession and regularly appeared in case notes but are now of course unacceptable and extremely pejorative.

The term 'intellectual disability' has been used in this chapter, as it is now the commonly adopted language in the international literature to describe what in the UK is known as learning disability. Using 'intellectual disability' avoids the confusion between learning *difficulties* (e.g. dyslexia or dyscalculia—where an individual has difficulties with literacy and numeracy, respectively) and learning *disabilities*, where the individual experiences significant impairments in both intellectual functioning or cognition (e.g. understanding, concentration, memory skills, and reasoning) and social functioning (i.e. coping skills and skills of everyday living). Both of these significant impairments need to have been present in childhood for a diagnosis of intellectual disability to be confirmed.

Clinical psychologists can establish whether or not an individual has intellectual disabilities by carrying out an assessment comprising three main parts:

1 *Cognitive impairment*

   In cognitive terms, the scientific community defines significant impairment as being two standard deviations from the average measure of intelligence across the population (IQ = 100), which amounts to an IQ of 70 or below. One categorization system, the International Classification of Diseases, has divided the population of people with intellectual disability into those with mild, moderate, severe, and profound disabilities. Cognitive ability is assessed using batteries of tests, usually administered by clinical psychologists trained in their use, such as the *Wechsler Adult Intelligence Scale* (4th edition).

2 *Impairment of social functioning*

   Daily life is explored using interview-style assessments, usually carried out with the individual with intellectual disabilities but also with people who know them well, often a close relative or a member of staff providing direct support on a regular basis. Clinical psychologists use their clinical interviewing skills and experience to elicit information to help complete standard assessment tools such as the *Adaptive Behaviour Assessment System* (2nd edition).

3 *Presence in childhood*

   Here the clinical psychologist is looking for evidence that the difficulties the individual is experiencing had their roots in their early years. Informants who know the individual well and can give as much detail as possible about his or her childhood are asked questions about developmental milestones (e.g. walking, talking, eating and drinking), early social interaction, and relationships. This can be a difficult part of the assessment, as it can bring up many emotion-laden memories for all concerned and can be a challenge for older parents and carers to remember details from the past.

8.3 **Causes of intellectual disabilities**

The causes of intellectual disabilities can be divided into the three main groups: pre-natal factors (occurring before birth, such as Down syndrome and other genetic syndromes); peri-natal factors (occurring during pregnancy or labour itself, such as disabilities resulting from toxoplasmosis, asphyxia, or premature birth); and post-natal factors (including environmental factors such as malnutrition or being dropped or physically abused as a baby).

8.4 **Prevalence of intellectual disabilities**

According to the British Institute of Learning Disabilities (BILD), it would be predicted that about 2.5% of the population would have intellectual disabilities. Figures show, however, that prevalence seems to be lower than this—about 1–2%, giving a total of between 602,000 and 1,204,000 people in a UK population of 60.2 million. BILD attempts to explain this difference by suggesting that not all cases of people with mild learning disabilities are identified, since a number are unknown to statutory services.

8.5 **Service settings and context**

As in many countries worldwide, UK clinical psychologists specializing in working with people with intellectual disabilities typically work in an integrated team of health and social care professionals, often referred to as a Community Learning Disability Team. Team members will usually include occupational therapists, speech and language therapists, learning disability nurses, physiotherapists, psychiatrists, and social workers. Other clinical psychologists might work in specialist hospitals or forensic services for people with intellectual disabilities. The work itself could take place in the individual's home (they might live with their family or hold a tenancy), a registered care home, an inpatient setting, or a GP practice. Clinical psychologists working in other settings (e.g. mental health settings, health psychology settings, older people's services, and physical disability settings) are also likely to come into contact with people with intellectual disabilities, particularly individuals who are more cognitively able.

Governments in many countries including the UK have set out recommendations for how people with intellectual disabilities should be supported in the community. In England, the White Papers *Valuing People* (Department of Health, 2001) and its updated version *Valuing People Now* (Department of Health, 2009) set out a clear agenda for those leading services, stating that there should be four main cornerstones for achieving quality: offering choice, empowering people who use services, aiming to increase the independence of individuals with intellectual disabilities, and ensuring that people are enabled to exercise their rights. The overarching aim is that people with intellectual disabilities live socially inclusive lives in the community. Similar guidance has been published in Wales (*Fulfilling the Promises*, Learning Disability Advisory Group, 2001), Scotland (*The Same as You*? Scottish Government, 2000), and Northern Ireland (*Equal Lives*, Department of Health, Social Services and Public Safety, 2005). The emphasis is on people with intellectual disabilities being supported to live rewarding and fulfilling lives as citizens in the community, in the same way as those without disabilities.

The British White Papers state clearly that people with intellectual disabilities should be supported in services that are led by the social care model. This means that people with intellectual disabilities are seen as primarily having needs of a social nature (e.g. housing, support with everyday living). This contrasts sharply with the historical view of medicalizing and pathologizing people with intellectual disabilities, with their care and support once being provided in large hospitals by nursing and medical staff away from mainstream community life. Current thinking is underpinned by a strong adherence to the concept of social inclusion: it is expected that people with intellectual disabilities will access health care services to meet their health needs in the same way as any other citizen, rather than having to rely on 'specialist' services.

Nevertheless, following a series of very public scandals in primary health care settings in recent years, there has been widespread acknowledgement of the importance of ensuring that health services make 'reasonable adjustments' in order to ensure that people with intellectual disabilities are able to access appropriate health care. For example, the publication in the UK of *Death by Indifference* (Mencap, 2007) and the subsequent Michael Report (2008) in particular highlighted inadequacies within health care systems and called for urgent change to avoid people with intellectual disabilities being harmed when in hospital due to inappropriate services.

8.6 Case example: Sunita

Sunita has severe intellectual disabilities and autism. This means that she finds it difficult to wait, particularly in strange or unusual surroundings, and becomes very anxious if her usual routines are interrupted. She has limited communication skills and uses a Communication Passport developed by her speech and language therapist to make her needs known to others. The staff supporting Sunita have worked with her clinical psychologist and the manager of the GP practice to make reasonable adjustments to what is provided when Sunita goes to see her GP. The GP receptionist ensures that Sunita is offered the very first double appointment; this gives her more time to communicate her needs to the GP and the waiting room will be empty. Any recommendations or treatment is added to her Health Action Plan, which provides an overview of Sunita's health and wellbeing.

On the recommendation of her clinical psychologist, Sunita makes several visits to the surgery before her first appointment to get used to the lighting, the smells, and the physical feel of the building. Her consultation with the GP is therefore more productive and helpful than it might have been otherwise.

8.7 Presenting problems and difficulties

Research suggests that people with intellectual disabilities are more likely than people *without* intellectual disabilities to have poor physical and mental health. There can be a number of reasons for this, some of which are linked to the particular cause of the intellectual disability (e.g. self-injurious behaviour in Lesch–Nyan syndrome, or overeating in Prader–Willi syndrome). Other reasons may be related to an individual's lifestyle (e.g. emotional difficulties related to relationships with support staff or other tenants with intellectual disabilities), and yet others may result from the ways in which people with intellectual disability are still perceived and stigmatized by the wider society (e.g. low mood resulting from physical and sexual abuse, low self-esteem, and bullying).

Diagnosing mental illness can be a difficult task in the field of intellectual disabilities. Psychiatrists and psychologists have become more skilled in recognizing the different ways in which mental health problems such as anxiety, depression, and psychosis can present in people with intellectual disabilities, who might not be able to use language to describe their experiences to others. There can still, however, be risks of both diagnostic overshadowing (where symptoms are explained as being 'part' of an individual's disability) or indeed undershadowing— where psychiatric disorders are diagnosed as a result of misinterpreting the ways in which the individual communicates or behaves, and attributing it to mental illness.

Clinical psychologists are often asked to provide advice and support for people with behavioural problems. Behaviour is described as 'challenging' when it threatens to exclude the individual from community life, and leads to their support becoming more restrictive. Challenging behaviour is always seen as having a communicative function, and functional analysis is commonly used to establish what the person is trying to convey through their behaviour.

Functional analysis is a method used to establish the function that a particular behaviour serves for an individual by gathering information about its nature, frequency, and duration, and about events before, during, and after the behaviour occurs. This information is then analysed within the wider context of the individual's personal history and current lifestyle. Functional analysis might reveal that internal factors such as pain, or external, environmental factors such as noise, lighting, or heat are causing the individual to present with the behaviour of concern. Equally, it could suggest that the behaviour is linked to aspects of how the person is being supported, or lifestyle events such as a bereavement or loss, or changes in structure and routine—or a combination of all of these. Understanding the function that the behaviour serves from the individual's perspective enables the clinical psychologist to work together with family and staff to design helpful interventions.

8.8 **Case example: Phil**

Staff supporting Phil are worried—he has been smearing faeces on the bathroom wall, a new behaviour, and it is jeopardizing his relationships with other tenants as well as the tenancy itself. Careful assessment from the clinical psychologist reveals a range of recent changes in Phil's life: his long-standing keyworker has just retired, one of his friends has stopped going to the employment project that he attends, and Phil's elderly mother is now only able to visit once a month instead of every week. The support team and Phil are encouraged to make a life story book together, where photos and memorabilia can be collected and assembled to help Phil make better sense of his past, present, and future. With the book used and updated regularly, Phil starts to appear calmer and less anxious; the smearing decreases and eventually stops.

8.9 **Applying psychological models when working with people with intellectual disabilities**

Clinical work in the field of intellectual disability varies according to the abilities of the individual, and can be either direct or indirect.

Direct work with individuals

The research base for direct clinical interventions with people with intellectual disabilities is still comparatively small compared with that supporting the use of direct therapeutic work with other populations. The reasons for this are likely to be manifold, but include methodological difficulties in carrying out clinical trials, the heterogeneity of the population in question, and the need to adapt clinical interventions in order to make them accessible for people with intellectual disabilities. In addition, historically there has been the phenomenon of 'therapeutic disdain' whereby assumptions have been made that people with intellectual disabilities are not able to benefit from clinical interventions—or even worse, are not deserving of the effort. Unsurprisingly, such discrimination has meant that historically the field of intellectual disability had been a relatively unpopular choice for clinical psychologists who may have been more interested in promoting quick therapeutic change.

However, this situation has changed in recent years, and enthusiasm for working with people with intellectual disabilities has grown significantly. There is now greater recognition that this area of work is exciting, challenging, enriching, and rewarding, and that it demands great commitment and creativity from clinicians. The evidence base is growing fast and there is now a significant literature supporting the use of the main psychological models with people with intellectual disabilities.

There are nonetheless some general issues to be borne in mind when working therapeutically with people with intellectual disabilities, including the following:

- *Adaptation:* people with intellectual disabilities are likely to have difficulties with memory, concentration, and attention, and often find it hard to understand abstract ideas (i.e. conversation that is not about the 'here and now'). It is unlikely therefore that a strict manualized approached to delivering therapy will be successful, or one that is simply transferred from models applicable to other populations. Thought needs to be given to the length and frequency of sessions, the location of the work, the use of language and communication, and the importance of using ideas and examples that are familiar to the individual. There also needs to be more flexibility with regard to the ways in which sessions are conducted.

- *Rapport:* therapeutic alliances are essential for all clinical interventions, but when working with people with intellectual disabilities, building and maintaining the alliance requires careful consideration. More time than is usually spent when working with other populations may be needed in order to build a relationship within which the work can be carried out.

- *Working with others:* in order for any therapeutic gains to translate into everyday life, therapists may need to involve other people in the individual's network. This might take the form of a relative or staff member attending some sessions, or holding a meeting at the beginning and end of treatment to agree with the individual and/or carers and family the support required in order to carry out homework or to practise new strategies. This needs to be handled sensitively, as people with intellectual disabilities often have low self-esteem and might find it hard to disagree with the proposal that somebody else is involved in the therapy. The approach to confidentiality and agreeing with the individual what can and cannot be shared also needs very careful attention.

- *Boundaries and attachment:* whilst the expectations around the use of the therapeutic space and function of the therapeutic relationship might be explained very clearly, individuals with intellectual disabilities may sometimes still present interpersonal boundary issues and may form inappropriate attachments to their therapists. This can of course occur with all clinical populations. However, here the context is somewhat different in that many people with intellectual disabilities have very poor or non-existent social networks, and so the sudden introduction of a regular 1:1 time where they are given undivided attention can be experienced as unusually emotional and intense. Clinical psychologists normally use their supervision to reflect on these situations, in order to devise sensitive and appropriate, boundaried interventions.

- *Thinking developmentally:* in response to the infantalization of people with intellectual disabilities that was prevalent in the institutional models of care dominating the 20th century, community-based support for adults with intellectual disabilities rightly emphasizes the importance of respect and treating individuals as adults. It is essential, however, to balance age-appropriateness with thinking about the individual developmentally, i.e. considering where their current level of skills and functioning lie on a developmental continuum, in order to make the best assessment of their behavioural and psychological difficulties, and to offer the most helpful intervention. This is particularly important when working with people with profound intellectual disabilities, who by definition are functioning at the very early stages of development and in some cases may not yet have developed communicative intent.

Some main approaches to individual therapy are now discussed in more detail.

CBT and people with intellectual disabilities

People with intellectual disabilities may struggle to identify their thoughts, feelings, and physical sensations, and so carrying out CBT can require a significant amount of psycho-educational input. People with mild intellectual disabilities are the most likely to benefit from CBT and the research literature supports this (see Willner, 2009, for an overview). The clinical psychologist may use a variety of media (e.g. photos, drawings, clips from TV soap operas) to help the individual identify emotions. These same resources can be used to agree strategies that can be practised outside of therapy sessions. Creativity will also be required when asking the individual with intellectual disabilities to keep a mood or thought diary.

A recent development in parts of the UK is to offer CBT for anxiety or depression to people with intellectual disabilities within existing IAPT (Improving Access to Psychological Therapies) services. Working inclusively and in the spirit of *Valuing People Now*, IAPT therapists may themselves be offered specialist training and support in order to help them make reasonable adjustments to their work, so that they can better meet the needs of people with intellectual disabilities, as well as of those with autistic spectrum conditions. This may also enable specialist community teams to work with individuals with more severe intellectual disabilities who might not otherwise be able to access talking therapies.

Psychodynamic approaches to working with people with intellectual disabilities

Early development and experience are undoubtedly affected by the presence of intellectual disabilities, and whilst intellectually disabled people may historically have been excluded from psychodynamic psychotherapy, there is growing evidence of the positive effects of working psychodynamically with people from this population (see report from the Royal College of Psychiatrists, 2004, for a helpful overview).

Psychodynamic work attempts to address not only common mental health problems in this group, but also specific issues relating to the disability itself. Indeed, these concerns may be the main focus of therapy—for example, perhaps exploring the ways in which the individual feels about being perceived by others as a 'disabled' person, and using the therapeutic relationship as a means for doing this. The challenge for clinical psychologists working psychodynamically is to modify the delivery of therapy in order to accommodate differences in intellectual ability. This may require alteration of both the content and the process of therapy, since psychotherapists adhering too rigidly to conventional models of psychotherapy may risk excluding clients with intellectual disabilities. It is generally recognized that post-qualification training and supervision from experienced clinicians are required in order to meet this challenge effectively.

Systemic approaches to working with people with intellectual disabilities

Individual systemic psychotherapy with people with intellectual disabilities focuses on the context of the presenting difficulties, and is concerned with the patterns and connections made between different elements of an individual's system or network, rather than with the behaviour, thoughts, or feelings of the individual. Clinical psychologists working systemically have described this approach through a number of case studies of systemic applications, often illustrating the use of narrative work, whereby individuals with intellectual disabilities are supported to explore the meaning of dominant narratives in their lives and to consider their helpfulness or unhelpfulness. This can then encourage a 'thickening' of positive, constructive narratives that provide a way forward, and a 're-scripting' of the person's view of themselves, their network, and the world in general. Family therapy can also be offered to people with intellectual disabilities and their families, for example to address differences of opinion within a family about whether the individual with disabilities is able to live alone or have a partner. Research and professional debate in this area continues to explore innovative ways of ensuring that the disabled individual is meaningfully involved. For an overview of systemic approaches to working with people with intellectual disabilities, see Baum and Lynggaard (2006).

Indirect work

This refers to work carried out *about* the individual that does not involve them directly, usually because the individual does not have the cognitive ability or capacity to engage in direct therapeutic work themselves. The clinical psychologist may meet with key members of the individual's network (e.g. support staff, family, and other involved clinicians or practitioners) and provide advice or guidance around a presenting problem or difficulty. Clinical psychologists new to the field of intellectual disability can find this aspect of the work ethically challenging, as the individual with disabilities is often unaware that this work is taking place. This is almost always because the individual concerned lacks the capacity to consent to intervention or lacks insight into their difficulties, so that the indirect work is therefore carried out in their Best Interests (in the UK this is described fully in the Mental Capacity Act 2005; see also Chapter 9 of this text). In order to be deemed to have capacity to consent to treatment, an individual normally needs to demonstrate the ability to:

- understand and retain information about the treatment;
- weigh up the pros and cons of having that treatment; and
- communicate their decision about whether or not to have the treatment to others.

Indirect work often requires careful initial discussion with those most concerned about the presenting problem, in order to establish the nature of the concern and the meaning currently given to what is happening by those closest to the individual with intellectual disabilities. This discussion might then reveal a need to gather more information about what is happening and the context around it—a functional analysis of challenging behaviours is typically carried out in this situation. Once the information has been gathered and analysed, the network can then reconvene and discuss the findings, and the psychologist can encourage consensus about the nature of the intervention required.

Specific systemic techniques can be employed as part of a consultation model, whereby the clinical psychologist takes a 'curious', non-expert stance which encourages the behaviours of concern, or problems, to be seen as symptomatic of difficulties within the system or network, rather being seen as intrinsic to the individual per se. This approach can be immensely empowering for all concerned, avoids a blaming attitude towards the individual with intellectual disabilities, and promotes a collaborative approach to agreeing solutions and strategies for moving forward.

Indirect work can also take the form of training and teaching others, and clinical psychologists in the field of intellectual disabilities often develop special interests in key areas such as autism, parenting, offending behaviour, or dementia.

8.10 Overview of the work of clinical psychologists with people with intellectual disabilities

People with intellectual disabilities form a highly heterogeneous population and, as a result, clinical psychologists are required to work flexibly across a range of different modes of service delivery. The main features of the role are now described.

Assessment

Assessment is an important aspect of clinical psychologists' work across all populations, but in the field of intellectual disability psychologists may also be specifically required to carry out psychometric assessments to establish whether or not an individual has an intellectual disability and meets criteria for specialist services. These assessments can be done with any adult where there is speculation about the individual's cognitive abilities. There are also a number of specific programmes aimed at school leavers who have been identified as having difficulties with learning, and who might meet criteria for adult intellectual disability services.

Another key area for clinical psychologists is dementia. People with Down syndrome are at a higher risk than others of developing Alzheimer's disease, and routinized screening has become common practice. Assessments establish a level of baseline functioning and regular follow-ups can then track the course of any deterioration observed, so that interventions and support can be recommended.

Range of direct and indirect therapeutic work

It is important to note the wide range of issues and concerns that must be addressed in all types of therapeutic work, that require the psychologist to 'join' an individual and their network in their understanding and interpretation of a given problem, in order to offer effective support. Within the course of one day, a clinical psychologist might be working with issues as diverse as faecal smearing, relationship problems, self-injurious behaviour, suicidal ideation, and inappropriate sexualized behaviour. Conversations need to be adapted to their audience and this requires great skill in order for content to be relevant and meaningful to all.

Training and teaching

Training and teaching can be a significant component of the role, and clinical psychologists might be asked to train support staff, family carers, other professionals, and their peers—sometimes with all of these groups together as part of a network. Increasingly, most modern health care settings now demand that generic services become more skilled in supporting people with intellectual disabilities, and so clinical psychologists specializing in intellectual disability are often requested to offer training, support, and consultation to other sectors such as mental health services, adult education, GPs, and primary care, homelessness services, and drug and alcohol services. Involvement in teaching and training is an important part of continuing professional development and ensures that clinical psychologists themselves keep up to date with the recent developments and current research findings.

Service development

As in many parts of the world, the field of intellectual disabilities in Britain has been transformed in recent years, as the advent of personalization (a directive from the government that offers individuals more control over their support via personal budgets and direct payments) and the transfer from registered care accommodation to supported living models have radically shaped the ways in which people with intellectual disabilities are perceived and supported. These major changes have required health and social care services to significantly adapt their ways of working, and clinical psychologists are often key players in this process. This aspect of the work might involve attending committees and steering groups, proposing new designs for service models, evaluating existing services in order to make recommendations for improvement, or creating new services in response to the publication of legislation, professional guidelines, or government policy.

A core aim in the profession of clinical psychology is the process of sharing psychological knowledge with others. This can be done through formal and informal supervision, teaching, professional meetings, mentoring, and leadership. As the landscape of the health and statutory services continues to evolve, services and support for people with intellectual disabilities will need to respond accordingly; it is likely therefore that this aspect of the work of psychologists will become increasingly important in the years to come.

References

Baum, S. and Lynggaard, H. (2006). *Intellectual Disabilities: A Systemic Approach.* Karnac Books, London.

Department of Health (2001). *Valuing People: A New Strategy for Learning Disability for the 21st Century—A White Paper.* Department of Health, London.

Department of Health (2009). *Valuing People Now: A New Three-Year Strategy for People with Learning Disabilities.* Department of Health, London.

Department of Health, Social Services and Public Safety (2005). *Equal Lives: Review of Policy and Services for People with a Learning Disability in Northern Ireland* (Chair: Professor David Bamford). Department of Health, Social Services and Public Safety, Belfast.

Learning Disability Advisory Group (2001). *Report to the National Assembly for Wales 'Fulfilling the Promises': Proposals for a Framework for Services for People with Learning Disabilities* (<www.assemblywales.org>).

Mencap (2007). *Death by Indifference.* Mencap, London.

Michael, J. (2008). *Healthcare for All: Report of the Independent Inquiry into Access to Healthcare for People with Learning Disabilities.* Department of Health, London.

Royal College of Psychiatrists (2004). *Psychotherapy and Learning Disability. Council Report CR116.* Royal College of Psychiatrists, London.

Scottish Government (2000). *The Same as You? A Review of Services for People with Learning Disabilities* (<www.scotland.gov.uk>).

Willner, P. (2009). Psychotherapeutic interventions in learning disability: focus on cognitive behavioural therapy and mental health. *Psychiatry*, **8** (10), 416–419.

Further reading

British Institute of Learning Disabilities (<http://www.bild.org.uk/docs/05faqs/factsheet%20learning%20disabilities.pdf>).

Carnaby, S. (ed.) (2011). *Learning Disability Today*, 3rd edn. Pavilion Publishing, Brighton.

Carr, A., O'Reilly, G., Noonan Walsh, P., and McEvoy, J. (eds) (2007). *The Handbook of Intellectual Disability and Clinical Psychology Practice*. Routledge, London.

Emerson, E., Dickson, K., Gone, R., Hatton, C., Bromley, J., and Caine, A. (2012). *Psychology and People with Intellectual Disabilities*, 2nd edn. Wiley-Blackwell, Chichester.

Harrison, P.L. and Oakland, T. (2003). *Adaptive Behavior Assessment—Second Edition. Manual (ABAS-II)*. Pearson, San Antonio.

Chapter 9

Working in forensic mental health settings

Jeremy Tudway and Matthew Lister

9.1 Introduction

This chapter introduces the role of clinical psychologists in forensic settings, and outlines the range of unique challenges and diverse set of forensic environments in which the profession can be practiced. Forensic clinical psychology can be defined as the intersection between clinical psychology and the justice system. Although its most obvious application involves working directly with offenders to address offending behaviour or its consequences, work is also carried out with victims and other significant people from within the systems in which offenders function.

The chapter begins by considering the range of clients seen, and issues typically addressed, by clinical psychologists working in forensic settings. Offending and anti-social behaviours occur across the age, cultural, ability, and social spectrum, and consequently all the core skills of clinical psychologists can be applied, together with additional expertise and forensic knowledge which have been developed within the sub-specialism. The most notable aspect of forensic work is probably its complexity, its duration, and the requirement to liaise closely with a range of different agencies, including the police, social services, Courts, and prisons. This requires additional knowledge of the legal and Court system, and familiarity with legal concepts or processes such as capacity to consent, caution, fitness to plead, and best interests, as well as the specific constraints of communicating with legal representatives. Hence some of these concepts will be explained later in the chapter.

The drive towards evidence-based practice has been particularly prominent among those working in forensic services since their expertise is open to intense scrutiny at tribunals and Court hearings. In addition, those who have a focus on offending behaviours are inevitably involved in addressing public safety through the routine application of risk assessment. The need to balance the traditional psychologist's role of advocate-therapist for the client, with a wider responsibility for managing risk of harm, presents a challenge to clinical psychologists in forensic settings since they routinely have to confront the manner in which risk potentially contradicts the more traditional role of the advocate-therapist.

In order to illustrate the type of clients seen, two examples are provided, one of victim-focused work and one of therapeutic work with an offender.

Ms L was a 24-year-old woman of South East Asian origin who spoke limited English and who was referred for an assessment following a request from her parents for a termination of pregnancy. Medical and nursing staff were concerned that Ms L had an obvious learning disability and was unable to provide informed consent to such a procedure which may have reflected her parents' choice, not her own. The police and Social Services were informed and it was quickly established that Ms L, who also had a sister with learning disability, had become pregnant by her brother-in-law. Suspicions were raised that Ms L was not only unable to consent to such a significant medical procedure, but also unlikely to have been able to consent to sexual intercourse, and consequently her brother-in-law was arrested on suspicion of rape. Subsequently Ms L's pregnancy miscarried, but the police wished to pursue a prosecution and the psychologist was invited to assess Ms L's intellectual ability, her understanding of sexual behaviour, decision-making, and capacity to agree to sex.

The assessment involved a widely accepted culture-free assessment of general intelligence, a test of receptive verbal functioning, and an informant-rated inventory of social and adaptive functioning. Together these confirmed that she met the criteria for a disability of intellectual functioning. Next a protocol was used to assess her experience of and capacity to make everyday choices and decision making, and again these were found to be very limited. Finally, her sexual knowledge and beliefs were assessed, and results indicated that she had only a rudimentary understanding of sexual behaviour. Taken together, the psychologist concluded that Ms L had insufficient understanding of the nature and consequences of sexual intercourse with her brother-in-law and was vulnerable to pressure to engage in sexual acts with him. This was then communicated to the police, to assist them in making decisions on the appropriate next steps.

The second example demonstrates psychological work with an offender.

Mr M, a man in his early 30s, was arrested after having assaulted a number of strangers with a machete, and having doused himself in petrol in an attempt to set himself on fire. These actions had resulted in serious injury to three police officers and the deployment of an armed response unit. At the time of his arrest Mr M was clearly extremely distressed, believing that he was being pursued by demons, and experiencing derogatory and frightening auditory hallucinations. After admission to a secure psychiatric hospital Mr M began to respond to medication and became more open to meeting a psychologist to discuss these events. Gradually a positive therapeutic relationship developed and a different explanatory framework for his beliefs emerged.

In ongoing therapy Mr M described a traumatic childhood during which he was sexually abused by a family friend, after which he had voluntarily requested being taken into care. Following school (where he was bullied) he joined the armed forces, where he excelled and was promoted to the rank of sergeant; however, he still experienced distressing flash-backs relating to his abuse. Around then he began experimenting with recreational illicit drugs, and was involved in a road traffic accident whilst under the influence of drugs, in which the driver of the other car was killed. After a dishonorable discharge, he experienced a complete psychotic breakdown in which he re-experienced the accident and developed a delusional belief that he was evil and would be pursued by the mutilated victim of the road traffic accident.

As therapy progressed, the experience of auditory hallucinations decreased, so that he was discharged as an outpatient to his own accommodation. There he settled but continued to experience distressing nightmares. The psychologist arranged for Mr M to be interviewed by the police in connection with his childhood abuse experiences, and, following this, the police opened an investigation into the allegations, also interviewing the alleged perpetrator under formal caution. Although the police explained to Mr M that a prosecution was unlikely, he reported that being taken seriously by the police, and the interview of his alleged abuser, was a tremendous relief for him. Subsequently his nightmares reduced significantly, and he successfully completed an art course and began to display his pictures in a local gallery.

9.2 **Forensic services**

Forensic services are provided in a variety of settings by a number of agencies, with different remits for public protection, offender management, and health and social services. Specialist clinical psychology forensic services can be located within a range of these settings, including prisons, community projects, secure hospitals, and secure units. Some forensic services are run in partnership with different agencies such as mental health and probation or Social Services, so service provision can vary according to local areas and need, and could be publically or privately provided. This can include youth Court diversion services, adolescent abuser projects, specialist personality disorder services, and, in some areas, specialist teams set up for Family Court work. Within most forensic settings, clinical psychologists work in multi-disciplinary teams, consisting of forensic psychiatrists, specialist social workers, psychiatric nurses, and occupational therapists.

The most common form of forensic service is the system of secure units, these being hospital units operating outside the prison system. These units aim to address the mental health needs of an individual whilst also considering the psychological difficulties that contribute to offending. The term 'secure' normally relates to the physical, relational, and procedural measures put in place to ensure that there is a safe and secure environment in which to deliver treatment. Secure services for adult mentally disordered offenders in the UK range from High Secure hospitals for those considered to represent a grave and immediate danger to the public, to Medium and Low Secure services for offenders presenting a lower risk and who require significant treatment. For adolescents, secure services include Young Offender Institutions (YOIs), secure training centres, and secure children's homes. These services differ in their remit and vary according to the needs of their clients.

Community forensic services are usually linked to secure units and provide a service to those who have usually, although not exclusively, spent time already detained within a secure setting such as a secure hospital but who no longer represent a significant risk of harm to others. These services may also offer consultation and assessment to other community services.

The inpatient forensic population differs from both the general and the prison population in several ways:

- most people in inpatient forensic services are adult males
- women typically comprise one in eight of those seen in inpatient forensic services (double the proportion of women offenders within the prison population)
- the average stay in inpatient forensic services is 5 years or less, but more than a quarter are detained for over 10 years
- most detained patients have committed violent or sexual offences
- recidivism rates are significantly lower than those associated with prison

Despite the fact that the general prison population is predominantly male, a higher proportion of female prisoners present with mental health issues and receive treatment after incarceration.

Finally, it is important to note here the consistent finding that people with mental health problems or learning disabilities in contact with criminal justice systems are much more likely to be victims of crime than to be perpetrators (Bradley, 2009).

9.3 Mentally disordered offenders and the legal context

In British law, mentally disordered offenders are broadly defined as: (1) those individuals meeting diagnostic criteria for a mental disorder who are either involved in or 'diverted' from the criminal justice system owing to the link between their mental health problems and the offences committed; or (2) those whose behaviour is very challenging and can-not be managed in other services or settings. Thus mentally disordered offenders may present with a range of offences, disabilities, and disor-ders. The intention is to ensure that everyone, including those whose behaviour is difficult to understand, control, or manage, receives treat-ment and/or justice in a fair, appropriate, and effective manner. The con-cept of someone having limited responsibility for criminal acts is based on a long history of compassion; Maeder (1985) records that, according to Ancient Hebrew laws, 'idiots, lunatics, and children' did not possess the ability to differentiate between good and evil and therefore could not be held responsible for their actions. In medieval Europe, juries are recorded as referring the accused for a King's pardon in consideration of their mental health, despite being found guilty of a crime.

In the UK, the 'insanity' defence for significant crimes is nowadays referred to as the 'McNaughten rule', derived from the case of Daniel M'Naghten. In 1843, M'Naghten attempted to kill Sir Robert Peel, the then British Prime Minister; however, in error he actually killed Edward Drummond, Peel's Secretary. M'Naghten was suffering from psychotic delusions and was acquitted of the crime of murder on the grounds that he was considered insane at the time of the offence. The House of Lords then formulated the M'Naghten (more latterly McNaughten) rules that determine whether a person should escape criminal liability on the grounds of insanity. The defence must prove that the defendant is suffer-ing from a mental disorder *at the time of the committing of the act* **and** *was under a defect of reason, from disease of the mind, as not to know the nature and quality of the act he was doing; or, if he did know it, that he did not know he was doing what was wrong.*

Subsequently most societies with well-resourced mental health care systems have been able to respond to unusual or deviant behaviour, even if criminal, by recourse to hospital or care admission; however, in the absence of adequate systems, individuals showing such behaviours may instead enter criminal justice systems. Penrose (1939) proposed that the manner in which society deals with individuals whose behaviour challenges norms is dependent upon the prevailing social and political climate, normative behaviour at the time, and the resources available.

It is notable that a reduction in psychiatric beds has been matched in recent years by a steady increase in the numbers of prisoners presenting with frank mental health problems, both in the UK and USA (Cummins, 2012). Figures show that since 2000, UK admissions of mentally disordered offenders to hospital have increased by 35% (Ministry of Justice, 2010) including admission to 'high-secure' hospitals, despite the gradual reduction in the capacity of these institutions since the late 1990s.

9.4 **Mental health legislation**

All forensic work takes place within legislative frameworks, so clinical psychologists must be familiar with legal constraints that apply where they are working. This includes understanding both long-established legal practice and all subsequent modifications. In the UK, for example, recent mental health legislation has included establishing the roles of Clinical Supervisor and Approved Clinician, both key figures within forensic settings. In many inpatient services, these roles are taken by Consultant Forensic Psychiatrists. However, legislation now means that non-medical practitioners can be appointed to these roles, offering opportunities for clinical psychologists and other mental health professionals to have much more influence over the care and treatment of offenders than previously. Intervention planning and management is central to complex forensic cases, and decisions about interventions are often appropriately informed by psychological decision-making. Nevertheless, despite such legislative changes, few clinical psychologists have as yet been appointed as Clinical Supervisors, so the impact this will have on the future development of the profession is unclear.

Additional legislative changes that currently frame practice in UK forensic settings include laws concerning deprivation of liberty and the rights of victims, as laid down in the Mental Health Act (1983). This Act concerns the circumstances under which detention and treatment without consent can take place, establishes the necessary processes that provide safeguards for individuals detained in hospitals to ensure this is legitimate, and checks that any treatment received is effective, coherent, appropriate, and humane.

The UK Mental Capacity Act (2005) is also highly relevant and introduces a statutory framework to empower and protect vulnerable people who are unable to make their own decisions, by specifying who else can take decisions, in which situations, and how they should go about this. Key principles governing implementation of this legislation are that:

+ there is a presumption of capacity
+ every adult has the right to make his or her own decisions and must be assumed to have capacity to do so unless proved otherwise
+ people have the right to be supported to make their own decisions
+ people must be given all appropriate help before authorities can conclude that they cannot do so
+ people must retain the right to make what might be seen as eccentric or unwise decisions

These aspects of legislation mean that a component of the work of some clinical psychologists in community settings is now the assessment of capacity relating to a range of aspects of interpersonal functioning, from financial decision-making to capacity to instruct a legal representative.

9.5 Examples of clinical psychologists' work in forensic practice

This chapter now provides further examples of the types of work typically carried out by clinical psychologists working in forensic settings, applying the core competencies of assessment, formulation, intervention, and communication as described in Chapter 2, albeit modified to fit the specific requirements of the forensic setting.

Risk assessment

First, offender-based work most crucially involves the identification and classification of particular risks associated with specific behaviours (such as sexual offending, fire-setting, aggression, and violence). This is often carried out with an individual prior to case review, appearance at a tribunal, or in Court, but will continue in more depth and be reviewed if the individual is taken on for treatment by a service. Research has consistently demonstrated that clinical opinion is not the most reliable mechanism for assessing risks posed by clients (Grove and Meehl, 1996). Consequently a number of risk assessment tools (e.g. HCR20, SAVRY) have been developed, although individual formulation is still needed. Clinical psychology has a lead role in the systematic analysis of offences in order to better understand the dynamics of offending and to improve risk assessment (West and Greenall, 2011).

Family Court work

A second set of tasks includes involvement within public and Family Courts, often focusing on the assessment of potential risks to children posed by adults deemed to be potentially harmful to them. For example, a family in which either one or both parents have personal histories of offences towards children (e.g. sexual or physical assault and neglect), or of behaviours associated with harm to children (domestic violence, illicit substance use), might be referred for a psychological assessment to address such key issues. This would typically involve a series of specific observations, presentation of a psychological evaluation of likely risks, and provision of a hypothetical formulation of the underlying processes. This information is then communicated via a legal report. The requirements of legal reports differ significantly from those needed in most other situations, primarily because the commissioners and consumers of the report are neither health professionals nor the clients who are the subject of the reports. Instead, these reports address specific questions pertinent to Court proceedings, and are intended to enable the Court to arrive at a conclusion, rather than being concerned with a reduction of distress to the individuals themselves. A further, and potentially more significant, issue is that the report is not confidential to the individual or their medical representative. This poses a number of ethical and practical questions, namely what are the likely implications for the person who is the subject of the report? Is it ethical to fail to report, or more likely *to* report, something likely to be contrary to the expressed wishes of the subject of the report? For example, a client in family proceedings may wish to divulge that a partner is aggressive, but simultaneously not want to do so for fear of losing custody of their children.

Working therapeutically with offenders

The third common area of work is the provision of therapy. Many psychological ideas and models found in other fields are also used across forensic settings, including the notion of 'recovery' which has become increasingly important in offender treatment and rehabilitation (Simpson and Penney, 2011). There is also growing emphasis on wellbeing in forensic settings, supported by the tradition of service-user involvement. It is worth noting that in some settings, systemic work is sometimes carried out with the families of offenders.

Within hospital settings, interventions relating to aggressive or offending behaviours frequently focus on attitudes or anger, often following extensive assessment of these issues together with consideration of the impact of a range of other interpersonal/emotional problems. There are many psychometric scales available that measure aspects of anger, attitudes, and an individual's presentation and can contribute to the clinical formulation. Aggression and violence are seen by most psychologists as learned behaviours, while patterns of aggression and offending behaviours are viewed as embedded in habitual beliefs and thinking styles. Many psychologists also work with people with severe and enduring mental health problems such as psychosis, carry out long-term work on personality difficulties, and address offence-related matters (e.g. inappropriate sexual thoughts).

In community settings, referrals may be received from other services seeking an opinion or a risk assessment, whilst others may request ongoing therapy to support recovery. In some parts of the UK specialist personality disorder services have been established which work closely with probation services. Recently, the Bradley Report (2009) argued that forensic services for Courts should be more coherently organized, resulting in an increase in provision of services such as Court Liaison and Diversion.

In prisons some psychologists provide in-reach mental health services, for instance by offering treatment for people with complex personality, mental health, and offending presentations. Others work in prison settings delivering a number of assessments and treatment programmes, many of which are manualized, reflecting an attempt to standardize evidence-based approaches to common problems (for example, Thinking and Cognitive Skills programmes; Sex Offender treatment programmes).

In the UK, a pilot Dangerous and Severe Personality Disorder (DSPD) programme was established in 2001 as an attempt to deal with individuals whose serious offending was seen to be linked to severe personality disorder. DSPD services were provided in some prisons and some hospitals, which applied a number of distinct strategies to the treatment and care for this complex and challenging group. The aims were to address the offenders' poor and unstable representation of self and others, poor self-regulation and emotional management, and interpersonal deficits, as well as addressing violence and risk. Evaluation studies suggested there were significant reductions in risk measures indicative of reduced violent recidivism; however, there was insufficient evidence to suggest this was solely the result of the DSPD treatment programme. One clear emerging finding was that DSPD units enabled the men to live well together, without resorting to institutional hierarchies, and irrespective of offending histories. This has resulted in more positive approaches to management. The longer-term effectiveness of the programmes along with the robustness of the concept are yet to be established, but alternative treatment pathways for these types of offenders are being pursued (Freestone *et al.*, 2012).

Sex offenders

Another specific area of intervention is with sex offenders, this ironically being an area that often draws defensiveness, negative attention, and criticism from the public, policy makers, fellow professionals, and clients themselves. Nevertheless this remains a very significant area for clinical psychologists to make a contribution. Empirical evidence continues to indicate that sexual offenders are at an increased risk of future offending and that this is linked with an individual's negative self-image. Jeglic and colleagues (2012) found significant levels of psychological distress, depression, and hopelessness amongst individuals with sexual offending histories, especially those living in the community and who are subject to strict legal restrictions on their movements or associations.

A recently influential theory used in therapeutic work with adult and adolescent sex offenders is the 'Good Lives Model' (GLM). This is a framework of offender rehabilitation and recovery which, given its holistic nature, addresses the limitations of the traditional risk management approach. In this model, individuals are understood to offend as a means to achieve a valued life outcome; however, due to interpersonal and environmental deficits and weaknesses, harmful behaviour occurs (for example, sexual offending). As such, sexual offending is conceptualized as a 'by-product' of a motive to address inherently human and normal desires that manifests itself in damaging and anti-social behaviours (Ward and Stewart, 2003). The GLM is based on the central notion that there is a need to develop the capabilities and strengths possessed by individuals in order to reduce their risk of reoffending. As a consequence, interventions should add to pre-existing personal functioning as opposed to either just removing or managing offending behaviour as a 'problem'. For example, it is possible to see that a man who presents a sexual risk has a desire and motivation to enjoy intimate relationships. In order to achieve this he must develop a coherent insight into how other people experience him and how his distorted beliefs, inferences, and behaviour may have undermined his motivations. Teaching him to identify how these distortions undermine his goal attainment and that he can achieve greater satisfaction through an alternative route offers a more positive opportunity to reduce specific dynamic risk factors associated with offending, and thereby to enable the individual to reduce risk, whilst also achieving a more fulfilling life, *and* protecting the public.

Consultancy, Court work, and training

Finally, as in other fields of practice, psychologists also provide consultancy and leadership. In secure settings this may involve providing input into strategic decision-making, such as the risk assessment protocols adopted by a particular unit, or the development and oversight of psychological practice, or organizing treatment programmes and the clinical supervision of both psychology and non-psychology colleagues. Within community services, however, consultancy will often be provided to other teams regarding risk issues and/or complex case formulation. An element of 'case management' may also occur in order to ensure the correct services are accessed for the client in question.

Presenting evidence to any Court (including tribunals) is a specific challenge; it is necessary to be aware of the role of the Court, and that clinical psychologists are considered expert witnesses, who are consequently required to provide expert opinions. A delicate balance must be struck between presenting various options and making a theoretically coherent and defensible statement of probability given the historic evidence, presentation, and psychometric test data.

Involvement in the training of non-psychologists and participation in various management tasks represents a final and extremely varied area of clinical leadership. It can represent something of a challenge to communicate complex psychological concepts to those who do not have a background in the subject. For example, psychologists have provided input to the training and supervision of the police in hostage negotiation and firearms situations in the UK, USA, and Canada. In addition, although controversial, psychologists have been consulted with regard to the provision of a psychological 'profile' of factors that may influence the development of 'politically extreme' views of individuals who then take part in acts of terrorism.

9.6 **The demands of working as a forensic clinical psychologist**

There are particular demands placed on the practice of clinical psychologists in forensic settings. Within a forensic population, engaging clients in assessment and therapeutic work is difficult, although it is a critical component of effective practice (Jones, 2007). Liaison with other professionals becomes vital to support engagement, but also to manage risk. However, on occasions, a clinical psychologist's view may differ from that of other professionals, and the communication of complex formulation and risk information can thus be difficult. At times it can be difficult to ensure that psychological principles are 'kept in mind', particularly when interacting with professionals who do not have training in psychology.

In some settings, such as Mental Health Tribunals (MHTs) and Parole Board Hearings, psychologists may be required to provide evidence to support decision-making related to their client's progress. At times, this places the clinical psychologist in the unusual ethical position of constructing an argument that might contradict the wishes of their client or may be at odds with the views of their colleagues. An example might be a psychologist becoming involved in a decision-making process to move a high-risk individual from conditions of greater security back into the community. This might present a potential ethical dilemma since it may be necessary to divulge sensitive information disclosed in therapy to professionals outside the service. As with any therapeutic or clinical encounter, it is essential that clear contracts are made early in therapy with clients, making it clear that there is a statutory duty to disclose any information relating to public or child protection.

Work in forensic settings requires a good understanding of the complexities of ethical codes of practice and the use of relational ethical approaches to clinical practice. It is important to argue for the introduction of dignity and human rights in the models of ethical practice, and to improve the process of ethical decision-making in all parts of the forensic system and when working with colleagues from all disciplines.

Clinical work with forensic clients provides practitioners with many challenges, particularly concerning the understanding of criminal and anti-social behaviour. Given that clinical psychology is by its very nature concerned with assisting people in distress, it can be challenging to work with clients whose behaviours are themselves likely to have caused very significant suffering to others. An important first consideration for those working with this client group relates to their capacity to reflect on their own experience of victimization, attitudes towards perpetrators, and values associated with punishment and retribution. Similarly, working with forensic populations may involve high-profile cases or acts so shocking that practitioners risk become vicariously traumatized.

Nevertheless, many clinical psychologists find working with forensic populations challenging and stimulating, and ultimately a very rewarding area of clinical psychology in which to specialize.

References

Bradley, K. (2009). *The Bradley Report: Lord Bradley's Review of People with Mental Health Problems or Learning Disabilities in the Criminal Justice System*. Department of Health, London.

Cummins, I. (2012). Policing and mental illness in England and Wales post Bradley. *Policing,* **6** (4), 365–376.

Freestone, M., Taylor, C., Milsom, S., *et al.* (2012). Assessments and admissions during the first 6 years of a UK medium secure DSPD service. *Criminal Behaviour and Mental Health*, **22** (91), 107.

Grove, W.M. and Meehl, P.E. (1996). Comparative efficiency of informal (subjective, impressionistic) and formal (mechanical, algorithmic) prediction procedures: the clinical–statistical controversy. *Psychology, Public Policy, and Law*, **2**, 293–323.

Jeglic, E., Mercado, C.C., and Levenson, J.S. (2012). The prevalence and correlates of depression and hopelessness among sex offenders subject to community notification and residence restriction legislation. *American Journal of Criminal Justice*, **37** (1), 46–59.

Jones, L. (2007). Using case formulation for assessing and intervening with engagement difficulties. *Issues in Forensic Practice*, **7**, 42–48. DFP: British Psychological Society.

Maeder, T. (1985). *Crime and Madness: The Origins and Evolution of the Insanity Defense*. Harper and Row, New York.

Ministry of Justice (2010). *Statistics of Mentally Disordered Offenders 2008 England and Wales*. Statistics available from bulletin <http://www.justice.gov.uk/downloads/statistics/mojstats/mentally-disordered-offenders-2008.pdf>, accessed December 2012.

Penrose, L.S. (1939). Mental disease and crime: outline of a comparative study of European statistics. *British Journal of Medical Psychology,* **18**, 1–15.

Simpson A.I.F and Penney S.R. (2011). The recovery paradigm in forensic mental health services. *Criminal Behaviour and Mental Health*, **21**, 299–306.

Ward, T. and Stewart, C.A. (2003). The relationship between human needs and criminogenic needs. *Psychology, Crime, and Law*, **9**, 219–224.

West, A.G. and Greenall, P.V. (2011). Incorporating index offence analysis into forensic clinical assessment. *Legal and Criminological Psychology*, **16**, 144–159.

Chapter 10

Working with addictions

Frank Ryan

10.1 **What is addiction?**

Addictive behaviours are those behaviours that persist in the face of efforts to desist, often in the context of causing harm and distress to the addicted individual, their loved ones, and others known to them. Addiction persists because core cognitive and motivational processes are subverted: the transient experience of intoxication or euphoria seems to override strongly held values and fervent beliefs. The *Diagnostic and Statistical Manual of Mental Disorders* (*DSM-5*) (American Psychiatric Association, 2013) categorizes addictive behaviours as impulse control disorders. This places addiction firmly in the clinical psychologist's domain regardless of the substance involved. Therefore, whether dependence (i.e. tolerance, withdrawal distress, and craving) is adduced, or impulsive episodic use (e.g. using cocaine at weekends) is the issue, or indeed in the absence of any substance (as with problem gambling), the clinical psychologist works with the client to enhance self-control. In many cases, for example with alcohol misuse, abstinence is not necessarily the chosen therapeutic goal, regardless of the potential benefits. Instead, *harm reduction is* a more pragmatic and flexible framework for working with people with substance misuse problems. In the same way as a clinical psychologist can intervene with clients to help them manage negative emotions, without expecting a complete remission of distress, the practitioner addressing addiction can aim for goals other than complete abstinence. These interventions can be health-promoting or indeed life-saving, as for example in those that promote safer injecting or safer sexual practices which can forestall the transmission of infectious diseases (such as human immunodeficiency virus (HIV) and hepatitis C).

Substance misuse and addiction comes at a huge human and fiscal cost. Cigarette smoking, for example, is estimated to lead to five million deaths worldwide annually (Thorne *et al.*, 2008). In the UK in 2009, 8,664 deaths were attributed to alcohol use disorders and over a million visits to hospital were deemed alcohol-related (Office for National Statistics, 2011). Addiction also incurs massive health care costs. The health care costs of addictive disorders across 30 European countries have been estimated at a total of €65.7 billion. This was significantly more than mood disorders (unipolar and bipolar depression), estimated to have cost €43.3 billion, and approaching the €74.4 billion attributed to anxiety disorders (Gustavsson *et al.*, 2011). It is estimated in the World Drug Report (United Nations Office on Drugs and Crime, 2009) that between 11 and 21 million people in 148 countries worldwide inject drugs, of whom as many as 6.6 million may be infected with HIV.

10.2 Clinical psychology and addictions

In the UK and beyond, clinical and research psychologists have provided leadership for the development and delivery of psychosocial approaches to tackling addiction. These approaches are largely derived from cognitive, social learning, and motivational theories, but are nowadays increasingly also influenced by cognitive neuroscience findings. This chapter outlines the nature of addictions and describes the role of the clinical psychologist in the substance misuse and addictive behaviours field, with particular emphasis on the application of psychological theory and research. The role of the clinical psychologist in this setting is varied but not fundamentally different in terms of core competencies from many of the other areas of practice described elsewhere in this volume. For example, the ability to form a robust therapeutic alliance and to conduct a functional analysis of behaviour are two clinical psychology core competencies that are immensely helpful with addictive disorders. The main focus in this chapter is on front-line or direct client roles, in keeping with an emphasis on clinical psychologists as reflective scientific practitioners (although there is no intention here to detract from the invaluable contribution clinical psychologists can also make through leadership, training, supervision, research, and innovation). Clinical psychologists, in whatever role, are crucial to the delivery, development, and evaluation of evidence-based treatments for substance misuse and associated psychological disorders.

10.3 Substance misuse and associated disorders

Substance misuse generally presents alongside other common mental health problems. Typically, the clinical psychologist will be one of the main treatment providers for this client group, although psychologists working in other areas (e.g. Improving Access to Psychological Therapies, IAPT) are also likely to encounter substance misuse as a collateral problem, albeit of less intensity than perhaps seen in specialist clinics. The reader need look no further than the list of chapters in this text to appreciate that substance misuse might be a factor across a diverse range of presenting problems spanning the developmental spectrum. Thus, for example, Weaver and colleagues (2003) found that 44% of attendees at a London Community Mental Health facility reported problematic drug and alcohol use within the previous year. Conversely, surveys of those in treatment for alcohol dependence and related alcohol problems show that 86% also met the criteria for one or more mental health problems:

- 19% psychotic disorder
- 32% severe anxiety
- 34% severe depression
- 40% minor depression
- 53% personality disorder

Whether assessing an adult with a mood disorder, a parent struggling to care for their child, or an older adult feeling bereft and lonely, substance misuse needs to be regarded as a possibility. This leads to the most important point in the present chapter: individuals presenting with *any* problem where affect, behaviour, cognition, or interpersonal relationships (including parental competency or capacity) is a cause for concern should routinely be asked about their use of drugs or alcohol. This always needs to be accomplished in an empathic and non-judgemental manner.

Moreover, high levels of co-morbidity require sound conceptualization and robust formulation skills on the part of the clinical psychologist.

In planning treatment it is therefore crucial to disentangle the relationship between problematic substance use and related behavioural, emotional, and interpersonal difficulties. Regardless of whether, for instance, depression clearly preceded the onset of alcohol misuse or drug addiction, or the reverse, the substance use disorder always needs to be addressed in the first instance. Embarking on psychological intervention in the context of unregulated substance use is likely to fail, or at least fail to deliver any enduring therapeutic gain.

10.4 Treatment systems in the UK

In the UK, formal treatment systems were primarily developed in the National Health Service (NHS), typically as a division of a larger mental health provider organization, delivered by a multi-disciplinary team. In recent years, independent, charitable, and social enterprise organizations have become more prominent in providing structured treatment and rehabilitation services, although historically there is a long tradition of non-statutory agencies providing mainly residential 'rehab'. Over time, a dichotomy has developed between services for those with alcohol as the primary drug of abuse as opposed to those who develop problems with illicit drugs such as the opiates (e.g. heroin) and cocaine. In many NHS and allied services, clinical psychologists work across this boundary, contributing to the work of more than one team. The work is also influenced by broader trends in patterns of drug use. The increasing use of 'club' drugs such as gamma hydroxybutyrate (GBH), its derivative gamma-butyrolactone (GBL), and of course stimulants such as cocaine and amphetamines are also reflected in the addiction clinic. It must be noted that clinical psychologists' roles are inevitably more varied than the primarily therapeutic role, because service users present with a wide range of problems. Looking at the author's own diary from last week's clinics, for example, there were clients with post-traumatic stress disorder (PTSD), depression, anger, and anxiety disorders, and suspected cognitive impairment in the context of drug and alcohol misuse. In addition to direct clinical work, clinical psychologists typically undertake a more generic case management role which involves liaison with other agencies such as housing, benefits, probation, and social services.

10.5 **The role of clinical psychologists in working with addictions**

In non-substance misuse treatment settings, for example primary-care community mental health centres, screening for substance misuse disorders can be achieved by using standard tools such as the Alcohol Use Disorders Identification Test (AUDIT) or the Drug Use Disorders Identification Test (DUDIT) (both are widely available online). Whenever the criteria for substance misuse are met, a comprehensive assessment is essential; a pragmatic quantitative approach is best practice. Typically, assessment will entail a functional analysis of the *antecedents* (social, environmental, emotional, or cognitive contexts, and triggers/cues); the *target behaviour* (the quantity and frequency of substance misuse or gambling); and the *consequences* or outcomes that ensue. Ideally the assessment is based on prospective self-monitoring, but extrapolations can also help, e.g. enquiring about a *typical* week's cocaine use, or about a time when alcohol last caused problems. The psychologist may ask the client to describe situations where substance use led to negative or harmful consequences and perhaps to contrast this with episodes of less harmful or risky substance use.

Addiction usually evolves into a stimulus-driven behaviour, and raising the client's awareness of cues is crucial in planning treatment based on coping skills in risky situations. Encouraging the client to keep a record of substance use between sessions can reveal hitherto unrecognized cues, complement self-reports, and improve self-regulation skills. Throughout, the clinician needs to be aware that, sometimes despite the client's best efforts, self-reports can be less reliable. This could be due to the disruptive effect of alcohol and other drugs on memory, the habitual and autonomous nature of addiction, or indeed a tendency for some individuals to minimize the problem. Collateral reports from partners or affiliates are useful in this regard, as are toxicology results.

With regard to emotional factors, it is important that the clinical psychologist can differentiate between the various emotional facets arising in the context of addiction. For example, addressing enduring depression linked to childhood trauma calls for a different treatment approach compared with that suited to resolving transient negativity, linked to

Table 10.1 A brief inventory of empirically supported psychological interventions for addictive behaviours

Level of intensity	Focus
Low	Giving accurate information about addiction, detoxification, and relapse to service user and family
	Brief motivational interventions
	Contingency management
	Identifying triggers and cues
	Coping skills for impulse control
	Facilitating engagement in structured self-help groups (e.g. Alcoholics Anonymous/Narcotics Anonymous)
	Cognitive Bias Modification
High	Programmed cognitive behaviour therapy sessions such as Relapse Prevention Skills Training
	Mindfulness-based cognitive therapy
	Behavioural Couples Therapy
	Social Behaviour Network Therapy

recent drug or alcohol excess. Other sources of negative emotions in the addiction treatment context include those related to the after-effects of drug intoxication and negative emotions arising from setbacks or lapses when self-control fails, sometimes labelled goal or abstinence violation effects. The clinician needs to ask about all of these issues, and thereby to develop an individual case formulation to guide intervention. Data gleaned from the functional analysis can provide the basis for generating hypotheses to inform case formulation. Table 10.1 lists some common interventions according to intensity. Typically, the clinical psychologist will be called on to deliver 'high-intensity' interventions in specialist substance misuse treatment settings. Less intense interventions can, however, prove invaluable in other settings when delivered in advance of treatment aimed at alleviating chronic depression or anxiety.

10.6 **Building motivation and maintaining engagement**

Overcoming habits (especially compulsive ones) uniquely challenges the motivation and resolve of both treatment seeker and treatment provider. This is arguably the key distinguishing feature of working with addictive disorders compared to those defined by negative affect and avoidance such as depression and anxiety. In the latter, clients have a clear motive to recover, although they might have to exert effort and to experience heightened distress in the short term. Addictions are characterized by ambivalence: the person knows they need to change but struggles to translate this into action. Historically, the ambivalence of the help-seeker was often viewed by treatment providers as a sign of limited motivation, often with negative implications for the therapeutic alliance. The current motivational enhancement approach, enacted mainly through 'motivational interviewing', is a fusion of strategies and techniques derived from counselling (especially Carl Roger's triad of empathy, sincerity, and congruence), motivational psychology, and social psychology (particularly with reference to concepts such as cognitive dissonance). Motivational enhancement approaches have been widely endorsed and feature in many guidelines for assessing and treating alcohol- and drug-related dependence and problematic use, including those produced by the National Institute of Health and Clinical Excellence (NICE). The aim is to explore ambivalence about change and elicit undertakings to enact change. In the course of a motivationally orientated encounter, the interviewer might say, 'You have some concerns about your drinking but you don't feel able to make a decision to quit today' or, in a similar vein, 'On a scale of 0–10, how ready are you to quit [drug of choice or compulsive behaviour, e.g. gambling]?' If a client gives a low rating (high ratings of course indicate that the intervention can usually proceed) the therapist can ask either 'Why not lower?', eliciting a motive or concern such as weight gain linked to alcohol excess,or follow up with 'Why not higher?,' which might reveal impediments to change such as beliefs that alcohol is an effective means of coping with stress that will be sorely missed.

10.7 **Brief interventions**

Brief motivational interventions can be structured and delivered across one or more appointments in a range of settings. The acronym *FRAMES*

(Rollnick and Miller, 1995) captures the key ingredients of Motivational Interviewing for building motivation and commitment:

F represents individualized *feedback*, focusing on risk, and in particular with regard to motivation itself.

R represents the emphasis on the client taking *responsibility* for their decision to commit to change.

A stands for the provision of clear *advice*.

M signifies a *menu* of change options. For instance, the client could be asked about the intensity, timing, and setting of any potential intervention.

E represents *empathy* and should be warm, person-centred, and accurate.

S stands for s*elf-efficacy*. It is important to bolster the client's belief that they can attain their treatment objectives, for instance by reflecting back resilience in other areas of the client's narrative.

This approach is suited to working in generic settings such as general hospitals, psychological therapies services, and primary care. Motivational interventions have also been applied across a range of presenting problems where ambivalence, compliance, or relapse is an issue, e.g. dieting, or the promotion and maintenance of behaviour associated with maintaining health and wellbeing.

10.8 Maintaining change

The following clinical example illustrates how a motivational ethos can be combined with a more behavioural approach as part of a treatment programme. The context should be self-explanatory.

Therapist: '*Thanks for coming in for your session. It's good to see you. I know from your phone message that you've had a setback.*'

Client: '*It just doesn't feel like I'm making any real progress! I seem to have no willpower when it matters most.*'

Therapist: '*It sounds like you feel you've let yourself down. I agree that in some situations you seem to reach a point of no return with the cocaine; this often happens when we come across a trigger like you did last week: it can be difficult to apply the brakes! But let's not get into the "blame game" and instead see if you can learn anything from the lapse with alcohol and cocaine. I think it would be useful to go over what led up to you using again last Saturday. This could help you to anticipate and be more prepared to cope if you find yourself in a similar situation. With hindsight, is there anything you could have done differently to maintain your goal of not using cocaine?'*

Client: *'Well, to be honest, I knew there was a chance of getting cocaine if I went to that bar, but I hadn't seen my friends there for a few weeks and I felt lonely.'*

Therapist: *'It sounds like you miss your old friends, but as it happens they are all regular cocaine users.'*

Client: *'That's the problem, although it was usually at the weekend when the real partying went on.'*

Therapist: *'I wonder if you could plan ahead so that you keep in touch with the two or three you are closest to, but meet them during the week? It would involve you being prepared to refuse cocaine, if available, and minimize your alcohol intake, since this seems to affect your ability to say "no" to cocaine. That's something we can work on in today's session.'*

The above scenario is not of course risk-free and in some cases it might be advisable for the client to avoid any situation in which the powerful incentives associated with drugs like cocaine are available. This is where a psychological perspective and sound clinical judgement are crucial. The risks for the client of engaging in further drug use need to be calibrated against their need for social interaction and affiliation. This decision needs to be taken in the context of vulnerability factors such as poor cognitive control or emotional regulation strategies. In substance misuse treatment settings, clinical psychologists are generally the most practised and knowledgeable exponents of motivational enhancement and engagement strategies. They are thus commonly required to provide teaching training and supervision of this type of work for their professional colleagues.

10.9 **Managing urges and craving**

Substance misuse and addictive disorders reflect a failure in cognitive control or willpower. Teaching the treatment-seeker strategies to manage impulses is arguably the most important contribution clinical psychologists can make to promoting good outcomes and long-term recovery. In the experience of many psychologists, it is never too early in the therapeutic journey to begin this process. Commonly a lapse into substance misuse could signal disengagement from therapy. In effect, the urgency that defines substance misuse needs to be embraced in the therapeutic encounter.

10.10 **Case example**

Gary (aged 32) started drinking alcohol when he was 13. He also used cannabis, ecstasy, amphetamines, and cocaine in social 'clubbing' contexts. He said that drugs 'never really suited him' and he became anxious and avoidant, particularly after using cannabis and stimulant drugs. Following one episode of ecstasy use, he felt unable to go outdoors, feeling self-conscious, anxious, and depressed. He also described experiencing intrusive thoughts or confusion about his sexual orientation and said that he found these thoughts repugnant and remarkably anxiety provoking. He had previously developed an obsessive-compulsive disorder when aged 18. He then stopped using cannabis and stimulant drugs but continued drinking heavily at weekends, and occasionally had periods of 5–6 days of intensive drinking, from early morning to apparent unconsciousness. When he was 28 he met Deborah, who became pregnant early on in what appears to have been intended as a casual relationship. Gary at first played an active parental role, but following a period of excessive drinking, a violent argument occurred between the couple, with subsequent involvement of police and social services. Gary agreed to quit drinking and attend the specialist unit, where the psychologist saw him.

Assessment

Detailed assessment revealed that Gary's father had also had significant alcohol problems, as had other family members, and that Gary had witnessed his father being violent in the home. His father had then died aged 41 from drowning, as a result of either suicide or an accident. Gary said that he had recently managed to remain abstinent from alcohol for 5 weeks, but knew that he needed to learn how to prevent further recurrence of his drinking.

In the first session, in advance of a complete assessment and detailed formulation, Gary was asked to describe the lead-up and context to his recent 'binges'. Some of the factors were:

- *Striving for relentless or perfectionistic standards at work and as a parent. This led to a feeling of exhaustion and stress.*

- *Tension in his relationship with Deborah because he thought that she was not contributing her fair share in terms of parenting and housework.*

- *Lack of opportunities for recreation and relaxation. For instance, Gary was a talented amateur footballer, but had drifted away from his local club and let his gym membership lapse.*

- *Feeling awkward or embarrassed when refusing alcohol in social situations.*

- *Feeling overwhelmed by craving.*

A functional analysis was then developed which guided the treatment and intervention plan. Cognitive restructuring or behavioural experiments were used to encourage Gary to reappraise the utility of his perfectionistic beliefs; then activity scheduling and problem-solving strategies were used to achieve a more balanced lifestyle; and Deborah was invited to a joint session to focus on communication and other aspects of the relationship, and as a participant in Behavioural Couples Therapy. Other potentially relevant interventions would have included social skills coaching in order to facilitate drink-refusal, or modifying expectancies, or mindfulness training applied to manage craving and impulsivity. The issue of managing craving usually needs to be addressed as a priority: for example, in the week before the next appointment it was inevitable that Gary would be challenged by an impulse, urge, or the experience of craving.

Accordingly, the psychologist asked Gary to describe his last episode of problem drinking. He said he had been abstinent for 3 weeks and that the impulse came 'out of the blue' when he was walking down the street in his

Table 10.2 Positive and negative expectancies associated with alcohol consumption

Gary's expectancies	Immediate consequences: 'Now'	Long-term consequences: 'Later'
Positive expectancies	Feeling part of the crowd; relaxation; less boredom	None!
Negative expectancies	I will feel I've let myself down; I might become argumentative.	I will probably carry on drinking. It will put my role as parent and life-partner at risk.

local neighbourhood. This is quite commonly reported and can be difficult to address psychologically. Typically, self-monitoring would be used to enable the client to recognize, anticipate, and cope with these triggers. As this was the initial session, detailed self-monitoring data were not available, and given the risk of further alcohol excess, Gary was asked to imagine himself in a similar situation in the coming week and to identify the short- and long-term consequences of the decision to drink or to abstain. Table 10.2 summarizes his responses. It was agreed that if (or more likely when) Gary experienced impulsivity, he would practise the 'Now, Later' coping strategy (see Kober et al., 2010). Cultivating mindfulness in the face of craving and impulsivity is another possible approach, outlined towards the end of this chapter.

Gary was advised that even if, or indeed especially if, he had a setback and began drinking alcohol again, he should prioritize attending the next appointment. People with addiction problems blame themselves excessively and can often feel intensely guilty when they lapse. This can lead to disengagement and resumption of addictive behaviour, and needs to be anticipated and managed.

10.11 **Psychological vulnerability factors**

As noted, many clients who present with addictive disorders also report other complex psychological difficulties. In fact, it is often these problems that trigger the treatment-seeking, e.g. anxiety and insomnia, which are linked to alcohol excess, or apparently unmanageable debt due to gambling or drug excess. Disentangling the relationship between vulnerability factors and addiction liability is a key task for the psychologist. Research can be helpful in this regard. For example, Sinha (2009) concluded that frequent exposure to adverse life experiences, linked to individual genetic susceptibility, can alter neurotransmission in stress-related pathways such as corticotrophin-releasing factor (CRF), and serotonergic and dopaminergic systems. This can sensitize the individual to subsequent exposure to potentially stressful events, and thus make 'self-medication', using alcohol or other drugs, more likely, not least because they alter neurotransmission in the same pathways. Alcohol, for instance, binds to the gamma-aminobutyric acid (GABA) system in a manner similar to that of the benzodiazepines (a class of tranquillizer medication), resulting in lowered arousal often experienced as hedonic or anxiolytic. This coheres with cognitive social learning accounts of emotional vulnerability, but also highlights the direct relationship between subjective distress and the rapid and powerful reinforcement delivered by self-administration of psychoactive substances.

10.12 Translating new findings into practice

Over the past three decades or so, psychological theory, research, and practice have transformed the field of substance misuse and addictive behaviours. As with all good innovations, enhancing motivation (as in Motivational Interviewing) and forestalling relapse (as in Relapse Prevention) now seem rather obvious, but they were not obvious at the time of their development. Clinical psychologists have been instrumental in the introduction and stewardship of these approaches. Psychological research now continues to generate new findings with direct clinical applications. Two such recent developments will now be described.

Mindfulness-based relapse prevention

Paying attention in a detached mindful manner is increasingly recognized as a means of managing the relentless urges and cravings associated with addiction. Bowen and colleagues (2010) have integrated the practice of mindfulness into extant cognitive behavioural approaches to develop relapse prevention skills training. For instance, clients are taught to distance themselves from addictive urges by adopting practices such as the 'SOBER breathing space':

Stop (or slow down).

Observe what is happening right now.

Breath focus—centering your attention on the breath.

Expanding awareness to include a sense of your body as a whole.

Responding with full awareness, asking yourself what is needed (Bowen *et al.*, 2010, p. 123).

This more acceptant stance can defuse the conditioned cue reactivity associated with high-risk situations encountered by the client. It is also less taxing than more elaborate strategies (e.g. evaluating the 'pros and cons' of resuming substance use, drinking, or gambling), thus preserving scarce coping assets for subsequent challenges.

Boosting willpower

When the Oscar Wilde character famously stated 'I can resist everything but temptation', he was presumably alluding to a lack of willpower. Viewed as cognitive control, researchers have now begun to explore ways in which willpower could be augmented. Muraven (2010), for example, evaluated the possibility that self-control training would contribute to success in quitting smoking. For 2 weeks prior to 'quit-day', he encouraged smokers who were aiming to quit to practise small acts of self-control designed to 'train' willpower, such as squeezing a bar to the point of discomfort. Other examples could include maintaining good posture when sitting at one's desk or watching television, or brushing teeth using the non-dominant hand. One month later the enhanced self-control group had indeed fared better than controls: 27% of the active 'self-control' group were verifiably abstinent from smoking compared with just 12% of the controls, who had been assigned tasks requiring some effort but not particularly entailing self-control.

Conversely, willpower can become depleted. This is particularly likely when faced with the apparently relentless urges and craving associated with addiction. Educating the client about willpower can aid recovery;

for example, explaining that it is quite common for a client to succumb to a relapse at the end of a day, after successfully resisting urges earlier in the day. It is also helpful for clients to develop realistic expectations about the extent of their willpower, and to be vigilant when it becomes depleted through tiredness, hunger, or 'overuse'. The relevant psychological processes here are working-memory capacity, goal maintenance, and selective attention (see Ryan, 2013). Although these ideas have only recently been utilized professionally in the addictions field, they can relatively easily be related to the advice that has been given to people striving for abstinence over many years by organizations such as Alcoholics Anonymous, and are represented by the acronym HALT: [never be] 'Hungry, Angry, Lonely, or Tired'. This illustrates that, in addition to teaching the client specific strategies for managing impulsivity through augmenting self-control, a broader emphasis on developing a balanced lifestyle and promoting psychological wellbeing is vital for recovery in the longer term.

10.13 **Conclusion**

From assessment to discharge and follow-up, psychological theory, research, and practice skills are crucial for engaging with the core motivational, cognitive, and behavioural mechanisms of addiction. This endeavour calls on the full range of clinical psychology core competencies and indeed has created a context within which these competencies have evolved further in the quest to deliver better, enduring outcomes. In practice, clinical psychologists will often be asked to work with service users with complex needs, spanning the spectrum of substance misuse and mental health problems. A case formulation approach is invaluable in any setting, as different strategies are needed to address the ambivalence and urgency that define addiction, alongside the broader issues of compromised emotional control also observed in other disorders. Regardless of the context they are working in, all clinical psychologists should *always* screen for or investigate the possibility of substance misuse. By applying both tried and tested as well as more innovative approaches, clinical psychologists can continue to make a valuable and distinct contribution to helping people manage and eventually overcome addictions, leading to major gains in health and wellbeing for individuals and society as a whole.

References

American Psychiatric Association (2013). *Diagnostic and Statistical Manual of Mental Disorders, Fifth Edition, DSM-5*. APA, Arlington.

Bowen, S., Chawla, N., and Marlatt, G.A. (2010). *Mindfulness-Based Relapse Prevention for Addictive Behaviors: A Clinician's Guide*. Guilford Press, New York.

Gustavsson, A. Svensson, M., Jacobi, F., *et al.* (2011). Cost of disorders of the brain in Europe 2010. *European Neuropsychopharmacology*, **21**, 718–779.

Kober, H., Ethan, F., Kross, E.F., *et al.* (2010). Regulation of craving by cognitive strategies in cigarette smokers. *Drug and Alcohol Dependence*, **106**, 52–55.

Muraven, M. (2010). Practicing self-control lowers the risk of smoking lapse. *Psychology of Addictive Behaviors*, **24** (3), 446–452.

Office for National Statistics (2011). *Alcohol-Related Deaths in the United Kingdom, 2000–2009*. The Stationery Office, London.

Rollnick, S. and Miller, W.R. (1995). What is motivational interviewing? *Behavioural and Cognitive Psychotherapy*, **23**, 325–334.

Ryan, F. (2013). *Cognitive Therapy for Addiction*. Wiley-Blackwell, Chichester.

Sinha, R. (2009). Stress and addiction: a dynamic interplay of genes, environment, and drug intake. *Biological Psychiatry*, **66**, 100–101.

Thorne, S.L., Malarcher, A., Maurice, E., and Caraballo, R. (2008). Cigarette smoking among adults in the United States. *Oncology Times*, **30** (24), 26.

United Nations Office on Drugs and Crime (2009). *World Drug Report 2009*. UNODC, New York.

Weaver, T., Madden,P., Charles, V., *et al.* (2003). Co-morbidity of substance misuse and mental illness in community mental health and substance misuse services. *British Journal of Psychiatry*, **183**, 304–313.

Chapter 11

Working with trauma

Nick Grey and Sue Clohessy

11.1 Introduction

All clinical psychologists need to be aware of the possible impact of traumatic events on individual clients, families, and communities. This chapter describes the nature of trauma and how clinical psychologists use psychological theories to formulate and intervene in a variety of circumstances. As reflective practitioners, the impact of such work upon oneself and one's practice is important to consider. The chapter also introduces some of the controversies present in this field including definitions of traumatic events, the false memory debate, and the role of debriefing treatments. A central theme is that effective clinical psychologists must be both trauma-aware and trauma-informed, and recognize the scientific and personal challenges inherent in this work.

11.2 What is trauma?

Trauma is a common term used to describe a multitude of experiences, defined by the Oxford English Dictionary as 'an emotional shock following a stressful event' and 'a deeply distressing or disturbing experience'. The terms 'trauma' and 'traumatic' seem to be used with increasing frequency in the media and casual conversation. However, such colloquial use may hide the more precise clinical term. A traumatic event in clinical terms can be associated with various mental health problems, the most common diagnosis being post-traumatic stress disorder (PTSD). The *Diagnostic and Statistical Manual of Mental Disorders (DSM-V)* (American Psychiatric Association, 2013) defines a traumatic stressor as an event in which the person has experienced, witnessed, or been confronted by actual or threatened death, serious injury, or sexual violation. Such traumatic events include physical or sexual assaults, car accidents, natural disasters, and combat experiences. However, it would not include other stressful events such as divorce or bereavement.

Reactions to traumatic events have been well documented since the 19th century, with the phenomenon of shell shock apparent in soldiers following exposure to combat experiences in World War I (for a summary of the historical context of trauma and PTSD, see Brewin, 2003). However, defining trauma and PTSD has proved controversial. Initial definitions of trauma focused on the event as being outside the range of normal human experience, and significantly distressing for almost anyone—a normal response to an abnormal event. However, this definition has evolved in light of evidence that exposure to such experiences is actually relatively common (an estimated 80% of people in a sample in the USA have experienced a trauma), but only a minority develop persistent problems with PTSD (less than 10% from the same US study). Further revisions of the definition of a traumatic event are likely.

There has also been considerable controversy in defining responses to traumatic events, with many arguing that PTSD has a political dimension. This perception is particularly based on the fact that the establishment of PTSD as a discrete category within DSM in 1980 came about after considerable lobbying by groups representing veterans of the Vietnam War for formal recognition of the psychological difficulties many returning veterans had experienced. Some have suggested that the diagnosis was included to allow access to services for veterans, whereas others have argued that it pathologized the individual, rather than acknowledging the broader political consequences of involvement in the conflict.

The scientific trauma literature differentiates between two types of traumatic experience. Type-I is a one-off traumatic event, such as a road traffic accident or assault. Type-II refers to prolonged, repeated traumatic events, such as repeated abuse or torture. Such events commonly occur in childhood, such as childhood physical and sexual abuse, but can also occur in adulthood, including the events experienced by refugees or those seeking asylum, and people experiencing domestic violence.

For some groups, such as the armed forces and emergency services, traumatic experiences are an occupational hazard. The effects of trauma can have wide impacts. Traumatized people are embedded within multiple systems, including family and friends, work, and the wider community and societal structures. Communities and societies have been through, and continue to experience the effects of, traumatic events such as natural disasters (the 2004 tsunami in Indonesia and elsewhere), civil conflict and war (Northern Ireland and the Balkan countries), state-sanctioned oppression (apartheid in South Africa), and other events such as mass shootings (Norway and the USA). The effects may include major damage to basic infrastructure, and sometimes problems meeting the needs of the general population for food, shelter, and power. Addressing mental health needs includes dealing with the impact of bereavement, low mood, intrusive images, nightmares, and widespread, often justified, problems in trusting people.

11.3 **PTSD and other effects of traumatic experiences**

A cornerstone of the work for clinical psychologists is the individualized formulation, discussed in Chapter 2. Formulation includes assessment of how people's beliefs and rules for living have been shaped by past events, including traumatic events. For example, when traumatic events occur, people may experience 'shattered assumptions' (Janoff-Bulman, 1992). Many of us hold assumptions that the world is *benevolent* (basically a good place and both people and events are generally good) and *meaningful* (there's a reason things happen as they do), and that the self is *worthy*. It may not be possible to assimilate traumatic events within these beliefs and hence beliefs must change to accommodate the trauma, e.g. the world is a dangerous place and I am weak. This process of assimilation and accommodation is natural, but difficulties may emerge if overassimilation (changing the event to fit one's beliefs, e.g. 'it wasn't really rape') or overaccommodation (completely changing one's beliefs to make sense of an extreme event) occur. Shattered assumptions will only occur in those originally holding benign beliefs, and such people are likely to have had few prior traumatic events. Many people seeking psychological help hold less benign assumptions about themselves and the world (e.g. 'people aren't to be trusted', 'I'm a bad person'), that may have developed from traumatic childhood experiences, and in such instances a further trauma in adulthood will confirm such beliefs.

11.4 **Features of PTSD**

PTSD is the most common and best-studied response to trauma requiring psychological help. The key symptom is 're-experiencing' of the trauma. Parts of the memory of the trauma are easily triggered and the trauma can feel as though it is happening again. Re-experiencing can take a variety of forms: images in any sensory modality (e.g. from a road traffic accident—hearing brakes squeal and screams, smelling fuel); nightmares that may be replays of what happened, or thematically linked (being in other accidents, or being chased); or experiencing similar feelings, physically and emotionally, as at the time of the traumatic event. For example, a man who was physically assaulted feared he was going to die, and when hearing news reports about other people being attacked, or when seeing someone wearing similar coloured clothing to his assailant, he had vivid images of the knife, his heart started racing, and he felt sweaty and threatened, just as if it was happening again.

People with PTSD also experience other symptoms, such as avoidance and numbing: trying not to think about what happened, or suppressing feelings related to the event, avoiding triggers such as people or places. Symptoms of hyperarousal are common, such as feeling on edge, being especially alert even if there is no clear need, being jumpy, and poor sleep and concentration. Recent changes in diagnostic criteria also include negative mood and cognitions. Most people with PTSD will have additional difficulties, especially substance misuse and panic attacks.

11.5 **Vulnerability to trauma and PTSD**

Epidemiological studies have shown that men are more likely to be exposed to a traumatic event, but women are more likely to develop PTSD. It is not clear why women are more vulnerable to developing PTSD; this is not explained simply by a greater incidence of sexual violence in women, pre-existing depression/anxiety, or women being more likely to disclose PTSD than men. Three risk factors, in both men and women, have been consistently identified across studies—prior personal psychiatric history, psychiatric problems in the family, and early adversity. How people respond during the trauma has also been identified as a risk factor—with higher rates of PTSD in those reporting dissociation during the trauma. Other research has identified negative appraisals during or after the trauma as significant (such as 'these memories mean I am going mad').

11.6 **Psychological theories of PTSD**

Brewin and Holmes (2003) provide a valuable summary of psychological models of PTSD. In the UK the most influential model is that of Ehlers and Clark (2000) which has led to an extensively tested cognitive-behavioural treatment (CBT). They suggest that PTSD becomes persistent when traumatic information is processed in a way that leads to a sense of serious current threat. This can be a physical and/or a psychological threat to one's view of oneself (e.g. 'I'm weak'). Due to high levels of arousal at the time of the trauma, the trauma memory is poorly elaborated and poorly integrated with other autobiographical memories, and can be unintentionally triggered by a wide range of low-level cues. In particular, there is no 'time-code' on the memory telling the individual that the event occurred in the past. Thus, when the memory intrudes, it feels as if the event is reoccurring. The persistence of the sense of current threat, and hence PTSD, arises from not only the nature of the trauma memory, but also the negative interpretations of symptoms experienced (e.g. 'I'm going mad'), the event itself (e.g. 'It's my fault'), and sequelae (e.g. 'I should have got over it by now'). Change in these appraisals and the nature of the trauma memory is prevented by a variety of cognitive and behavioural strategies, such as avoiding thoughts and feelings, places, or other reminders of the event, suppression of intrusive memories, rumination about certain aspects of the event or sequelae, and other avoidant/numbing strategies such as alcohol/drug use. In addition, PTSD is associated with various cognitive biases including selective attention to external threat, explicit memory bias for trauma-related words, over-general memory, threatening interpretive biases, and elevated expectancies for negative events.

11.7 Biological aspects of trauma

There are clear biological and neurophysiological effects of traumatic events, including a different pattern of hypothalamic–pituitary–adrenal axis response, and differential activation of the hippocampus, amygdala, and prefrontal cortex. Several neurotransmitter systems are dysregulated in PTSD. Sub-groups of PTSD patients exhibit sensitization of noradrenergic and serotonergic systems, respectively. In addition, MRI studies have detected smaller hippocampal volumes in people with PTSD. It has been shown that smaller hippocampal volume is a risk factor for PTSD, rather than PTSD 'shrinking' the hippocampus as had been previously suggested. People with PTSD often find such information both 'normalizing' and non-blaming; the implication being that their brain reacted the way it was designed, but with unfortunate side-effects which need to be addressed.

11.8 Effects of culture

Some have argued that PTSD is a Western phenomenon, having little relevance to other cultures. An individual's spiritual, social, and moral context mediates expression of psychological distress; hence responses to trauma are not uniform across cultures. However, the symptom structure of PTSD is relatively stable across cultures, and although there may be some variation in the symptom profile (e.g. increased somatization), it remains a useful concept for understanding reactions to trauma across cultures. The specific ways in which different communities and cultures react to traumatic experiences influence how people make sense of their own individual traumatic experiences, and how they can best be supported in their recovery.

11.9 Other outcomes after trauma

PTSD can only be formally diagnosed 1 month after the traumatic event. Within the first month, individuals may meet diagnostic criteria for acute stress disorder (ASD). The symptoms are similar to those in PTSD, but the presence of dissociation is specifically required. Although the diagnosis of ASD was introduced to help identify people prone to go on to develop PTSD, the utility of the diagnosis ASD has been questioned.

Type-II repeated and prolonged trauma may lead to more complex traumatic stress presentations. The events are typically the result of human mistreatment rather than accidents or acts of nature. Herman (1992) was among the first to refer to such presentations as 'complex trauma'. This is extremely likely to be formalized as a new diagnosis by the World Health Organization (WHO) in its next diagnostic manual (ICD-11). This diagnosis will require the presence of the core symptoms of PTSD, and also on-going and long-lasting impairments in affective, self, and relational functioning. This includes problems regulating emotions, having beliefs about oneself as diminished, defeated, or worthless, and having difficulties in sustaining relationships (WHO, 2013).

The problems in affect regulation specifically include dissociation. Dissociation is a normal process that ranges from daydreaming and being on 'automatic pilot' to observing yourself doing things as if from outside (an 'out-of-body' experience). Dissociation often happens when people have a high level of stress. During a traumatic event people may dissociate: the event is experienced as unreal or dreamlike, and things seem to go in slow motion. DSM-5 introduces a dissociative sub-type of PTSD, which will apply to many of the more complicated presentations following type-II trauma.

The Ehlers and Clark (2000) model, like other PTSD models, predominantly focuses on type-I trauma and does not fully account for other traumatic presentations. Type-II trauma affects attachment relationships, which is important since trauma from attachment figures is particularly likely to give rise to difficulties such as fear in close relationships that often have long-lasting impact.

Traumatic experiences are also implicated in the onset and maintenance of psychotic symptoms such as hearing voices and paranoid delusions, and help to provide psychological explanations of controversial diagnoses such as Dissociative Identity Disorder (previously known as

Multiple Personality Disorder) and Borderline Personality Disorder (BPD). Furthermore, careful assessment may indicate circumstances when problems, such as substance misuse or compulsive rituals, may in fact be responses to traumatic stress symptoms, and be coping strategies to reduce the frequency and intensity of re-experiencing symptoms.

11.10 How clinical psychologists can help with trauma

Therapeutic work for PTSD is the most common contribution made by psychologists working in this area. The UK NICE guidelines recommend trauma-focused cognitive-behavioural treatment (TF-CBT) and eye movement desensitization and reprocessing (EMDR) as first-line treatments for people with PTSD. Other forms of intervention include work with families and preventive work.

TF-CBT

TF-CBT is a psychological therapy focusing on accessing and processing traumatic memories, and changing unhelpful appraisals/beliefs associated with the trauma, and problematic behaviours (such as avoidance or rumination). The aim of treatment derived from the Ehlers and Clark (2000) model is threefold: (1) to reduce re-experiencing by elaboration of the trauma memory and discrimination of triggers, and integration of the memory within existing autobiographical memory; (2) to address negative appraisals of the event and its sequelae; and (3) to change avoidant/numbing strategies that prevent processing of the memory and reassessment of appraisals. A wide range of both general and PTSD-specific cognitive-behavioural interventions can be used to achieve such changes.

The most common procedure in TF-CBT involves the person with PTSD talking about the memory in great detail, without avoiding any emotional aspects of it, and identifying and updating the beliefs associated with the trauma (e.g. 'I'm going to die' to 'I survive/I'm going to be ok'). Alongside this, the person is encouraged to address unhelpful coping strategies such as avoidance by deliberating exposing him- or herself to situations and emotions that were previously avoided.

EMDR

EMDR also aims to access and process traumatic memories. Clients are asked to hold a traumatic memory in mind, along with associated emotions and thoughts, whilst simultaneously focusing on an external stimulus, usually the therapist's hand moving from side to side in front of the client's face. Other external stimuli, such as hand tapping, can be used. Once clients are less distressed by the memory, they are encouraged to hold the memory in mind with a more positive thought, and again focus on an external stimulus. While this is an evidence-based therapy, there is still on-going controversy about how to account for its effects at a theoretical level, and whether its effects extend beyond the role of exposure to the memory.

Working with families

Trauma can have a significant impact on families, who may not know how best to support their relative. Some may think that not talking about the event is the best approach, or respond in ways that may exacerbate the problem for the trauma survivor (reinforcing beliefs such as 'I'm to blame'). Living with someone with PTSD can be worrying and stressful, for example they may be irritable, jumpy, have recurrent nightmares or flashbacks, or avoid associated people or places. They may seem a different person, be affected by chronic physical health problems/disabilities resulting from the trauma, or be affected by other mental health problems such as depression or substance abuse. Psycho-education about PTSD and providing information and support can play an important therapeutic role.

Preventative work

Formal mental health treatment (e.g. psychotherapy) constitutes a small proportion of the efforts of society in general to improve the wellbeing of traumatized individuals and populations. Psychologists can also be involved in preventative work, ensuring that the vulnerable are protected from trauma whenever possible. Assessing for risk of trauma is an important aspect of this. Involvement in child protection aims to ensure that children are protected from traumatic events such as physical or sexual abuse. This may involve carefully assessing risk to children and young people in relevant services, or consciousness-raising and increasing public awareness about issues such as domestic violence, or ensuring those at risk are signposted to appropriate services which will ensure their safety. Psychologists can also advise professional groups who are at particular risk of exposure to trauma and developing PTSD, such as the military and emergency service personnel. Providing education about normal responses to trauma, and helpful (e.g. accessing social support) and unhelpful (e.g. excessive use of alcohol) ways of coping is another useful role.

Psychologists can additionally be involved in disaster planning: preparing how communities will cope in the aftermath of major events; what services will be required; educating relevant agencies about the impact of trauma; how to screen for PTSD; the importance of 'watchful waiting' within the first month post-trauma; and the provision of appropriate follow-up, so that those in need of trauma-focused interventions can access them in a timely way.

11.11 Providing reports to the Court

The nature of trauma work may involve legal proceedings, for example, claims for compensation. Clinical psychologists may be asked to provide expert witness reports for the Court on the consequences of a traumatic event on an individual, and the implications for their future. They may also become involved in preparing reports to the Court on behalf of asylum seekers who are applying for asylum status, providing information on their reported experiences of trauma in their country of origin, the subsequent impact on their mental health, and the potential impact of returning to their home country. There is a distinction between an expert witness report, in which the psychologist has a duty to the Court to report independently the assessment of someone with whom they have no prior relationship, and treatment reports, which are the description of assessment and treatment of clients or families with whom the psychologist has an on-going, or past, clinical relationship. An understanding of the role of memory processes and other psychological theories is necessary in order to explain possible discrepancies in verbal reports, or the previous withholding by survivors of information (for example, due to shame).

11.12 Research on trauma

There has been significant involvement of psychologists in research concerning trauma, including developing clinical theories and the treatments that follow, early intervention, and prevention strategies. Some of the key clinical psychologists who have undertaken research in these areas in the UK are Chris Brewin, David Clark, Tim Dalgleish, and Anke Ehlers. Ehlers and Clark developed the cognitive model of PTSD already noted, and the influential treatment that follows from it, while Brewin and Dalgleish, both in collaboration and individually, have been instrumental in understanding the role of memory processes following trauma, and also how these link to intrusive imagery and thoughts more generally. A final example is the experimental psychology investigation conducted by Emily Holmes and colleagues of possible risk factors for the development of intrusive memories. In non-clinical samples, increased intrusions after viewing a distressing film are associated with performing a verbal distraction task, compared with a visuo-spatial task such as playing Tetris (see also Chapter 1). Holmes' work shows that engaging the visuo-spatial scratchpad of working memory in this key early 'memory consolidation window' inhibits the later development of intrusions after viewing unpleasant events (Holmes *et al.*, 2009). This research has led to on-going investigations of the role of playing Tetris in Accident and Emergency units immediately following a trauma, as a 'cognitive vaccine' against the development of later intrusions. There is still much to learn about responses to traumatic events, and why some people are more vulnerable to developing PTSD than others, as well as investigating whether there are ways that PTSD can be averted in the aftermath of trauma.

11.13 Personal impact of this work

As reflective practitioners, psychologists will be aware of the effects of their work on themselves personally, including emotional, cognitive, and behavioural reactions (such as feeling distressed or angry with the client) during clinical treatment sessions and in other work settings. The impact of working in a helping profession can lead to 'compassion fatigue' or 'burnout', whereby empathy or caring feelings for clients diminish. Also there is the possibility of 'vicarious traumatization', having intrusive thoughts and images of the stories heard from clients. This is most likely when the client's traumatic experiences share similarity in practice or meaning with the psychologist's personal life, e.g. hearing stories about abuse of a child of a similar age to the psychologist's own child. While strong feelings engendered by work are normal, psychologists need to be aware if these negatively impact on their work (e.g. not wanting to hear details from clients) or affect life more broadly (e.g. taking extra precautions oneself). This can be addressed with regular formal supervision, informal support from immediate colleagues, and following general guidelines about self-care. Luckily secondary traumatization is not common, and is usually short lived. Less discussed is the possibility of secondary traumatic growth—the degree to which clinical psychologists can learn and develop from working with people who are overcoming the effects of traumatic experiences. Working with people who have experienced traumatic events reveals the strengths of humanity, such as kindness and courage, and also resilience in the face of adversity.

11.14 Special issues

In complex and newly articulated areas of work, competing views and controversies often exist about how best to understand the issues and what approaches are most helpful to those needing help. This is certainly true in the field of trauma.

Debriefing

There has been extensive debate about what types of intervention should be offered to people in the immediate aftermath of traumatic events. For many years it was assumed that asking people to recount in emotional detail the events that they had recently experienced (debriefing) would be helpful. Although people offered debriefing are often grateful, reviews show that individual emotional debriefing, at best, is of no benefit and, at worst, can actually impede normal recovery. A number of studies show that those who received debriefing are more likely to have post-traumatic stress symptoms many months later than those who do not. Current guidance is to offer 'psychological first aid' in the immediate aftermath of trauma, including information about possible traumatic stress symptoms and advice about maintaining routine, valued activities, and looking after oneself (e.g. eating regularly and not drinking to excess). Along with such 'first aid' there should be careful monitoring (also called 'watchful waiting'), and if traumatic stress symptoms do not quickly reduce after a few weeks, then offering prompt TF-CBT.

Power therapies

There have been many claims for 'miraculous' cures for PTSD, suggesting that in a few sessions people can be relieved of their symptoms. Collectively referred to as 'power therapies', the implication is that these are more powerful than existing treatments. Examples include thought field therapy (TFT) which involves bringing anxiety-provoking images to mind while tapping particular meridian points with fingertips, and traumatic incident reduction (TIR) where people imagine the traumatic event without verbal description, and then describe it verbally afterwards. There is no substantial evidence that these 'power therapies' are as effective, let alone more effective, than existing treatments. The mechanism of action is either unclear or seemingly related to the exposure or imagery component of the treatments, similar to that of TF-CBT and EMDR. The world of trauma treatments will doubtless attract further similar claims of powerful new treatments in the future. Extraordinary claims need extraordinary evidence.

False memory and recovered memory

The 1980s and early 1990s saw many reports of recovered memories of horrific childhood sexual abuse (often including satanic rituals) disclosed during psychotherapy. Proponents of recovered memories suggested that these memories had been repressed for many years, without the victim's conscious knowledge, until recovery during psychotherapy, using techniques such as hypnosis. Remembering earlier abuse was seen as an important therapeutic step. A powerful backlash against this view followed, particularly from families of victims, many of whom were accused of being abusers. A number of organizations were founded, including the False Memory Syndrome Foundation in the USA and the British False Memory Society (BFMS) in the UK, suggesting that these memories were not recovered but were false—induced in vulnerable patients by therapists. Many of those who recovered memories of earlier abuse had no recollection of these experiences before entering therapy, and had actually consulted their therapist for other mental health problems, such as depression, rather than PTSD. Proponents of recovered memories suggested that this backlash was a reaction to disclosures, an attempt to silence them, and a further abuse of power. Research to date suggests that although recovered memories are possible, they are very rare. Most people who were abused as children remember all or part of their experiences, although they may not choose to disclose this. Research suggests that it is also possible to create a 'false' or pseudo memory; see the British Psychological Society report (1995) for a review of this area. Clinical psychologists should be wary of sources that claim recovered memories are common, that memories of early trauma should be 'sought out' in therapy, and of suggesting to patients that such approaches should be adopted in their therapy. This debate highlights the often controversial nature of trauma treatments.

11.15 Case example of TF-CBT

Abbie was a 27-year-old receptionist, referred after she developed PTSD following physical violence and emotional abuse in a 7-year relationship with her ex-boyfriend Dan. This relationship had ended, but Abbie experienced frequent intrusions (including flashbacks) to two to three incidents in which she had believed she would die. When experiencing these memories, she 'relived' the same emotions, the meanings of which were 'I'm going to die'; 'I'm worthless/useless'. She believed these flashbacks and nightmares proved that she would never be free of Dan. She tried to avoid thinking about her experiences, but ruminated about what he had said to her—that she was useless/no good and so on.

Following assessment and formulation, Abbie was provided with information about common reactions to trauma, PTSD, and trauma memories, in order to help her understand her symptoms ('this is my mind's way of trying to make sense of what happened to me, not a sign that I'll never be free of Dan'). Abbie and her psychologist discussed her goals, and how she wanted to move on with her life (contacting friends again, renewing her gym membership, etc.). The initial focus of therapy was to help her to progress with these as quickly as possible. The collaboratively developed formulation then led to discussions about how avoiding going out, and ruminating on what Dan had said, kept Abbie stuck in the past. The psychologist then used cognitive therapy to change appraisals, e.g. 'I do have worth'; 'I don't need to listen to him'. In a few sessions Abbie was able to describe past events with less distress. Further work in sessions focused on dealing with memory triggers. Finally they developed a treatment summary (therapy 'blueprint'), listing key learning points from therapy and ways to managing future setbacks. Overall, Abbie had 13 sessions of TF-CBT, and by treatment termination, no longer met PTSD criteria, had returned to work, and was seeing her friends regularly.

11.16 Case example of work with on-going trauma in families

Clare, a woman aged 19 with very low mood, was referred to a clinical psychology trainee. At assessment, Clare disclosed that her father had repeatedly sexually abused her when she was aged between 8 and 11, although she had not disclosed this to anyone before. She also described witnessing her father physically assaulting her mother on many occasions. She continued to live at home with both parents and her younger siblings. She was planning to leave home and was concerned that her father would abuse her sister, whom she had tried to protect. She wanted the trainee's advice about what to do next.

The trainee was aware of many current risk issues in this situation. Clare was still living with the abuser, and there were other children at home. The mother was also at risk of assault. The trainee clarified to Clare that she would have to discuss this with others, beyond her supervisor, and that confidentiality could not be maintained, in line with limits explained at the start of the assessment. In addition, Clare was very low in mood, disclosing suicidal thoughts and previous self-harming behaviours.

Following discussion in supervision, the trainee contacted the local social services about this family (following established child protection procedures) who then gave Clare's mother information about refuges and local community support groups. The father left home and, although his arrest was attempted by the police, he disappeared. The trainee continued to work with Clare, helping with her low mood and feelings of guilt over having not acted sooner. Social services also provided support for the family as a whole.

11.17 **Conclusion**

Both these case histories demonstrate the role of clinical psychologists in thinking about and intervening with the sequelae of trauma. While Abbie's therapy shows the importance of formulation, the centrality of establishing a positive therapeutic relationship, and the usefulness of applying an evidence-based model, working with Clare illustrates the range of different agencies that may be involved in helping both adults and children following traumatic experiences. Both cases illustrate that psychologists need to know how to help people disclose sensitive information, to understand the correct boundaries concerning confidentiality, and to be aware of when to appropriately use supervision with more experienced practitioners, in order to aid this process and to gain personal support when working with potentially distressing material.

References

American Psychiatric Association (2013). *Diagnostic and Statistical Manual of Mental Disorders,* Fifth Edition. APA, Arlington.

Brewin, C.R. (2003). *PTSD: Malady or Myth?* Yale University Press, London.

Brewin, C.R. and Holmes, E.A. (2003). Psychological theories of posttraumatic stress disorder. *Clinical Psychology Review*, **23**, 339–376.

British Psychological Society (1995). *Recovered Memories: Report of the BPS Working Party.* BPS, Leicester.

Ehlers, A. and Clark, D.M. (2000). A cognitive model of post-traumatic stress disorder. *Behaviour Research and Therapy*, **38**, 319–345.

Herman, J.L. (1992). *Trauma and Recovery: From Domestic Abuse to Political Terror.* Pandora, London.

Holmes, E.A., James, E.L., Coode-Bate, T., and Deeprose, C. (2009). Can playing the computer game 'Tetris' reduce the build-up of flashbacks for trauma? A proposal from cognitive science. *PLOS ONE*, **4**, 1–6.

Janoff-Bulman, R. (1992). *Shattered Assumptions: A New Psychology of Trauma*. The Free Press, New York.

World Health Organization (2013). *International Classification of Diseases 11th Revision* (<www.who.int/classifications/icd/revision/en/>).

Further reading

Allen, J.G. (2001). *Traumatic Relationships and Serious Mental Disorders*. Wiley, Chichester.

Courtois, C.A. and Ford, J.D. (2009). *Treating Complex Traumatic Stress Disorders: An Evidence-Based Guide*. Guilford Press, New York.

International Society for Traumatic Stress Studies (<www.istss.org>): the largest professional organization focused on traumatic stress. The website, based in the USA, provides useful information for the public and professionals.

National Center for PTSD (<www.ncptsd.org>): this is a programme of the US Department of Veteran Affairs, which maintains the free-access Published International Literature on Traumatic Stress (PILOTS) database. This is the best place to start looking for trauma references.

National Institute of Health and Clinical Excellence (< www.nice.org.uk>): the NICE guidelines for PTSD provide a summary of PTSD assessment and treatment, and guide service provision within the UK NHS.

UK Psychological Trauma Society (<www.ukpts.co.uk>): includes listings of specialist UK trauma services.

Chapter 12

Working with people who have physical health problems

Elenor McLaren and David Murphy

12.1 **Introduction**

While the majority of clinical psychologists work with people who have mental health problems, a small but rapidly growing number work with people whose primary difficulties are related to physical health and/or disability. This work generally takes place in acute (medical) hospitals or primary care settings, in particular with people with chronic conditions such as diabetes, heart disease, or chronic pain. Here psychologists are integral members of multi-disciplinary teams, alongside other health professionals such as physicians, specialist nurses, and allied health professionals including physiotherapists, occupational therapists, and dieticians.

This area of clinical psychology has grown significantly in recent years, in part related to the changing nature of health care. As a result of medical advances and improvements in standards of living, the focus of physical health care in economically developed countries shifted dramatically during the 20th century from infectious diseases to chronic conditions. In the first half of the 20th century infectious diseases were the single most common cause of mortality, accounting for one in four deaths in the UK in 1900, whereas coronary heart disease accounted for less than one in 100. By the start of the 21st century, however, infectious diseases accounted for less than 1% of deaths in the UK, whereas cancer and circulatory diseases now account for two-thirds.

Whilst chronic conditions are treatable, they often result in residual difficulties which require adaptation and long-term management, for which psychological factors such as mood and coping strategies are important. Furthermore, the occurrence of conditions such as circulatory disease and diabetes is strongly influenced by behavioural factors (e.g. smoking, diet, and exercise), whilst effective management is dependent on adherence to medication and lifestyle changes; and here clinical psychologists can make a significant contribution by facilitating behaviour change.

The roles of clinical psychologists in this field, known as 'clinical health psychology', vary in relation to the health problems encountered, clinical activities undertaken, settings, and intervention levels (e.g. individual, group, service, or organization).

The nature of clinical health psychology has been shaped by a number of distinct influences over recent years. In the 1960s, at the same time as behaviour therapy principles were beginning to be implemented in mental health, an American psychologist, Fordyce, started to apply these principles in physical health. He developed a programme for chronic pain management based on operant conditioning principles, particularly modifying social reinforcement of 'pain behaviour'.

Through the 1970s and 1980s, psychologists' work was also informed by developments in psychophysiology, and techniques such as biofeedback became widely used in the management of physical conditions such as headache, temporomandibular joint disorder, and essential hypertension. However, some of the initial optimism faded when studies showed that, in many cases, non-specific factors rather than physiological changes mediated the treatment effects. Techniques such as biofeedback are employed much less commonly today but can be effective in specific circumstances.

A parallel strand of influence originated in the field of health psychology, which emerged as an autonomous domain in the USA in the late 1970s (although it was not formally recognized as such in the UK until 1997). Health psychologists tend to have a greater role in health promotion/illness prevention in an educational, organizational, or research capacity, and, through their research into factors that affect health, have developed theories about concepts such as stress, coping, adjustment, resilience, locus of control, self-efficacy, and quality of life, as well as theories about how people make decisions about their health. These models have led to clinical interventions and include stress-vulnerability models, health-belief models, theories of planned behaviour, and illness representations.

In recent years therapeutic developments in clinical psychology, most notably cognitive-behavioural therapy (CBT), have informed interventions for a range of health problems (e.g. White, 2001) as have mindfulness-based interventions (e.g. Kabat-Zinn, 1990). Meanwhile, acceptance and commitment therapy (ACT) (Hayes *et al.*, 1999) has become increasingly influential, while in the systemic field, solution-focused (SF) approaches (de Shazer, 1994) have also evolved for people with physical health problems (e.g. Bray, 2009).

12.2 Shifting themes

Over the past 20 years, three shifting themes have shaped clinical health psychologists' work. First is a move from instructing people (e.g. bio-feedback, guided imagery) towards developing a partnership between individuals and their medical team, including improving communication and choice, and facilitating greater self-directed care, including the development of the concept of 'expert' patients, and involving patients in decision making. This is echoed by greater emphasis on equality in therapeutic relationships, from professional expert and passive patient, to therapist and patient becoming 'collaborative empiricists'.

A second theme is greater integration of the biopsychosocial model into medical practice. This has influenced the types of questions referrers ask, from 'is the problem physical or psychological?' or 'we cannot find a physical explanation so we are referring to Psychology' to 'how can we improve this person's quality of life and engagement in significant activities?' There is also greater recognition of the psychological impact of physical illness and of the difficulty in focusing narrowly on symptom reduction or control.

The third theme concerns changing settings. There continues to be important work in both acute (e.g. outpatient clinics or hospital wards) and residential rehabilitation settings; however, the management of long-term conditions is increasingly provided in community settings with accompanying psychological care. In recognition of the need for greater, faster, and reduced cost access to intervention, there is also a move for psychological care to be provided by other professionals such as nurses or wellbeing practitioners, with psychologists providing training and supervision.

The rest of the chapter will explore a range of typical issues that clinical health psychologists address, detail some of the key therapeutic approaches that inform work in the field including how models require adjustment, and illustrate these with examples. The chapter then considers broader issues of working in teams and concludes with a consideration of future directions in the field. While this chapter is focused on clinical applications, it is also important to acknowledge the essential role of research in developing innovations and improving the effectiveness of treatments.

12.3 Key clinical issues

Clinical psychologists may focus on a range of different clinical issues, as discussed below.

Distress that interferes with quality of life

It is well documented that psychological distress following physical illness, injury, or disability can have a significant impact on the health outcomes of affected individuals. Distress can vary in severity, from normal 'adjustment' reactions to major depressive and anxiety disorders which can interfere with recovery, rehabilitation, functioning, and quality of life.

Inappropriate use of medical treatment including poor adherence

Excessive health anxiety may result in people inappropriately attending their primary care physician and/or Emergency departments to seek reassurance about symptoms. Not only can this result in unnecessary demand being placed on medical services, but also it can actually increase health anxiety over time. Psychological approaches to health anxiety have been demonstrated to be effective in reducing both anxiety and excessive consultation, even among people with established chronic health problems (Tyrer *et al.*, 2011).

Underengagement in health services is also important, such as dropping out of treatment, not attending appointments, not taking medication as prescribed, and self-discharge. There are several potential influencing factors: the unpleasantness/intrusiveness of treatment, beliefs about illnesses, the quality of relationships with medical teams, the clarity of information provided, and a person's ability to understand and act on information. For example, some people with diabetes fear hypoglycaemic attacks (which can be unpleasant) and avoid them by keeping their blood sugar level too high. Unfortunately this can lead to complications (e.g. blindness). An individual with a cardiac condition may hold a belief that physical exertion will lead to another heart attack, which may lead to inactivity and increase their risk factors (e.g. through reduced fitness or weight gain).

These examples highlight the importance of integration of psychological and physical care at the outset to optimize how people manage their physical conditions.

Preparedness and suitability for medical procedures

Medical procedures can be uncomfortable, aversive, and frightening. Psychologists can be asked to help prepare people for a treatment or manage the after-effects of procedures. Examples include using graded exposure to help people with needle phobia have injections, or preparing an individual for an MRI scan (which can be noisy and claustrophobic). Psychologists might see patients before and after an amputation or skin grafts for burns, or be asked to help individuals cope with nausea associated with chemotherapy.

Psychologists also have a role in assessing suitability for surgery, which may include examining how realistic individuals' expectations are and whether they have considered how they might proceed should the intervention be deemed inappropriate or is unsuccessful. Examples include cosmetic surgery (where body dysmorphic disorder needs to be excluded), gastric bypass surgery, or implanting of a spinal cord stimulator for chronic pain (where a determination as to whether the person has the required skills to self-manage after surgery is important). Psychologists can also be involved in genetic counselling and helping people navigate fertility decisions.

Physical presentations of psychological problems and physical conditions that respond to psychological interventions

Psychological distress is frequently accompanied by physical symptoms. Tiredness and concentration and memory problems can be signs of depression. Chest pain can be a symptom of panic attacks, tension head-aches of chronic anxiety. Many physical conditions including asthma, eczema, migraines, psoriasis, and irritable bowel syndrome can be wors-ened directly by psychological distress. There are some chronic condi-tions such as chronic fatigue syndrome which are not well understood medically but which respond to psychological interventions.

Psychological presentations of physical problems

Conversely, it is important for psychologists to be aware of possible psychological presentations of diseases that might require physical treatment. Dementias can present with depression symptoms, while hyperthyroidism can cause symptoms of anxiety or psychosis.

12.4 **Assessment**

Assessments in clinical health psychology overlap significantly with those in other adult psychology settings, and use a biopsychosocial framework to assess the parameters of presenting difficulties, their impact on life physically, psychologically, occupationally, and socially, prior history of both physical and mental health, as well as family his-tory, current relationships, and activities. At times, given the complex-ity of some physical problems, skill is required in guiding the process toward aspects relevant to distress. It is also essential to draw out areas of resilience. Assessment of risk is important because people often have easy access to lethal means of self-harm (e.g. painkillers, insulin).

Engagement is essential: people frequently (and understandably) question the relevance of the referral: 'do you think it's all in my head?' Absolute validation of the physical and real nature of the problem is cru-cial, as is the assurance that the psychologist has no reason to question this. Instead it must be clarified that entirely normal reactions can interfere with living effectively with health problems; hence psychological intervention can often be of help.

A common question from trainees considering working in physical health is 'how much medical knowledge does a psychologist need to have of specific conditions?' It is certainly not necessary to be an expert: in fact that can be unhelpful since patients normally have already had numerous encounters with medical experts and know a great deal about how the condition affects them. However, it is important that psychologists know enough to understand what patients experience in terms of daily demands, potential complications, and embarrassing or disabling aspects. A collaboration is formed by the psychologist bringing knowledge about psychological aspects of managing illnesses, whilst recognizing that the patient is an expert in the ways in which the illness impacts upon them.

Assessment may involve observations, diary keeping, reviewing medical records, consultation with other health professionals and families/significant others, as well as information gained from measures such as psychometric assessments. Questionnaires measuring depression and anxiety designed for adult mental health settings may be used; however, there are versions developed for physical health that account for the possibility that some symptoms of depression or anxiety (e.g. fatigue) may be attributable to the physical illness. Some measures are disease-specific (e.g. for cardiac anxiety), some examine particular processes (e.g. acceptance) and others examine quality of life more broadly.

12.5 **Therapeutic models**

There are a number of evidence-based therapeutic models informing interventions in this field.

Cognitive-behaviour therapy (CBT)

CBT has been applied to anxiety and depression in the context of physical health problems and also to adjustment and adherence issues. CBT can reduce distress in a broad range of health problems but is less compelling for changing relevant health behaviours or functional outcomes (Sage *et al.*, 2008).

Although the classic Beck model can be used, there are some special considerations. First, timing: distress is a normal response to receiving a serious diagnosis and immediate intervention is inappropriate. However, CBT may be appropriate when distress is prolonged and/or related to distorted thinking.

Second, the physical aspects of a person's presentation will likely affect other areas, for example, physical factors might limit activity (e.g. shortness of breath) or access to social/vocational pursuits (e.g. wheelchair accessibility). Physical issues may also affect the amount of pleasure derived (e.g. diabetes management requires reduced spontaneity) or make it difficult to fully attend to tasks (e.g. sitting with back pain). Physical aspects can convey expectations about the future (e.g. finding a breast lump) or prompt associations from the past (e.g. chest pain may trigger memories of a heart attack).

Third, it is important to avoid making incorrect assumptions about what causes distress. It is natural (but unhelpful) to assume one understands what someone is distressed about in the face of very negative/traumatic circumstances. Moorey (1996) used the example of impending death to illustrate the importance of eliciting personal meanings, arguing that death has specific meanings for different people. For example, one person might fear pain/suffering, another helplessness; a single man may fear dying alone, and a young mother may fear for her children's wellbeing.

The final issue is the nature of cognitive work; Moorey emphasized that therapy is not about 'positive thinking' or pretending things are better than they are, but rather about shifting from unhelpful to helpful responses. A 'positive thinking' approach does nothing to help people deal with intense emotional experiences or prepare them for a setback (Sage *et al.*, 2008). In classical CBT, 'dysfunctional' cognitions can often be examined in terms of their match with reality and behavioural experiments designed to test out theories. In physical health, negative cognitions are sometimes realistic, not irrational, so a pragmatic approach needs to be adopted which involves examining the cognition's helpfulness and impact on behaviour, and developing ways of accepting them (as thoughts) rather than 'challenging' them.

Coping effectiveness training (CET)

CET is a related approach based on Lazarus and Folkman's (1984) model of stress and coping, which has been applied particularly in physical disability contexts (Kennedy *et al.*, 2003). Patients learn skills in appraising stressful situations and accurately identifying changeable aspects (for which they learn problem-focused strategies, e.g. problem solving) and unchangeable aspects (for which they learn emotional-focused strategies, e.g. seeking social support). Individuals' coping styles may involve both problem- and emotion-focused coping, so it is important to promote strategies that are approach- rather than avoidance-orientated. Treatment involves training a meta-skill in discriminating between these in stressful situations and developing flexible coping repertoires.

Mindfulness approaches

Mindfulness derives from Buddhist teaching and promotes a non-striving, non-judgemental observing and accepting of experiences as they are, rather than as we wish them to be, facilitated by committed practice in 'being' rather than 'doing'. Most mindfulness approaches for physical health problems draw upon the 8-week Mindfulness-Based Stress Reduction group programme developed by Kabat-Zinn (1990), which was designed for people with chronic conditions involving fatigue, pain, and stress, and where medical treatments have not been entirely successful. People learn mindfulness practices, stretch, and yoga which are designed to enhance awareness in everyday life, and through practice, to begin recognizing their patterns of reactivity: that is, the thoughts, feelings, or urges that increase their distress.

Acceptance and commitment therapy (ACT)

ACT has been applied within a range of physical health problems particularly chronic pain (McCracken, 2011) and the main goal is to promote 'psychological flexibility' (Hayes *et al.*, 2006). In a chronic pain context, this translates to enabling individuals to respond to pain and associated thoughts, feelings, and urges in a flexible manner and to increase engagement in valued goals in the presence of these experiences, as an alternative to struggling ineffectively to reduce or control them. To develop psychological flexibility, there are six interrelated processes:

First, four mindfulness and acceptance processes including:

Willingness: openness to or acceptance of experiences that individuals normally attempt to avoid, escape, or control;

Cognitive defusion: capacity to see thoughts, images, memories, or predictions as mental phenomena rather than taking them literally;

Present moment awareness: ability to bring awareness into the present moment rather than being caught up in past regrets or future worries;

Self as observer: ability to notice stories about the self (e.g. 'I'm a person who always pushes through') that constrain or guide behaviour in directions not in line with personally held values. For example, if you had a goal of gardening daily and, in your experience, a 'little and often' approach enabled you to do this more consistently than an 'always pushing through' strategy, the capacity to notice the 'I must push through' story would enable you a space to choose whether to follow that strategy or to consider alternatives.

And second, two engagement and integration processes, including:

Values: developing clarity about what provides a personally chosen sense of meaning and vitality in life, which then becomes the focus of behavioural efforts (e.g. being a loving parent);

Committed action: taking continued steps toward chosen valued directions in the face of obstacles.

Solution-focused therapy (SFT)

SFT was developed by de Shazer and colleagues in the late 1970s and has been applied in orthopaedic rehabilitation, cancer services, palliative care, and services for those with renal failure. The approach is brief and defined by a focus on constructing solutions rather than investigating problems or developing formulations. The main therapeutic task is helping clients to envisage a 'preferred future' by defining how they would like things to be different, identifying any times when things currently are closer to this future, and examining what is distinct on these occasions. The focus is relentlessly on the client's strengths, resources, or expertise ('how do you cope at all?' 'how have you got through hard times before?').

12.6 **Examples of clinical health psychologists' work**

The next section gives three examples of how a clinical psychologist might intervene with different types of clinical presentation.

Broadening strategies

Neil, a 49-year-old head teacher, sustained a spinal cord injury playing rugby which paralysed him from the neck down. Neil had been in the high dependency unit of a hospital for weeks when the psychologist saw him, and was awaiting transfer to a specialist unit. He was referred for distress and difficulty managing long periods of slow progress.

Assessment revealed that Neil had always been an excellent problem-solver at work and home, being the person who tended to sort everything out. He typically responded to any emotional problems by undertaking practical jobs such as mending objects in his shed. His distress in hospi-tal stemmed from the limits of his ability to problem-solve, despite his desperate attempts to do so, and then becoming frustrated and anxious. This was interfering with sleep and his ability to focus on his physical rehabilitation.

The psychologist gently explored with Neil the frustrations and limi-tations of the problem-solving strategy that had previously worked so well but that was unhelpful in this exceptional situation. His reactions of anger and despair were normalized as understandable. A formulation and treatment plan informed by CET was developed collaboratively, and focused on the capacities he could develop to manage the situation more effectively. Treatment included developing emotion-focused strategies including delegation (giving key jobs to his wife) and harnessing social support from friends and colleagues, clarifying immediate goals (e.g. in rehabilitation), plus adapting other past strategies to cope emotionally (e.g. imagining mending intensive care machines). He also developed activities that were personally meaningful within his physical limitations (e.g. reading to his children).

After three sessions, Neil's mood had improved and he was focusing on rehabilitation tasks. He had effectively delegated other tasks and slept better.

Working with health anxiety

John, a 58-year-old postman, had a heart attack 2 years previously and subsequently attended a cardiac rehabilitation programme, following which he had been medically investigated and was encouraged to return to work. However, fearing that the exertion required would provoke another heart attack, he stayed off work. He often checked his pulse, asked others whether he looked pale, sought second opinions, and researched symptoms on the internet. He generally avoided exercise, and during a recent shopping trip had felt breathless and tight-chested, which further strengthened his belief that exertion might cause another heart attack. When he did go out, he took nitroglycerin spray, often using it against medical advice.

A formulation was developed with John to illustrate some of the factors that, despite having the purpose of reducing his anxiety, might inadvertently be maintaining and heightening it. For example, checking, reassurance seeking, and hypervigilance all maintained attention on difficulties, as well as his belief that not doing these things might cause feared outcomes. These processes in fact maintained anxiety (see Figure 12.1).

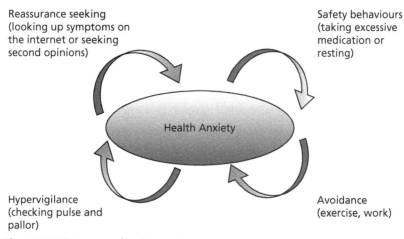

Reassurance seeking
(looking up symptoms on
the internet or seeking
second opinions)

Safety behaviours
(taking excessive
medication or
resting)

Health Anxiety

Hypervigilance
(checking pulse and
pallor)

Avoidance
(exercise, work)

Fig. 12.1 Maintenance of health anxiety.

John felt the formulation made sense and was willing to attempt to change some of his behaviours to move towards his goal of increasing his fitness to return to work.

John and his psychologist then devised a series of behavioural experiments to try out while following the advice of the cardiac rehabilitation programme. During the first session, John predicted that he would get breathless and tight chested and this might cause another heart attack, believing this to be 70% likely. When a heart attack did not occur, his belief dropped to 30%, and he was then willing to increase exercising.

Nevertheless, in spite of increasing his activity significantly, John continued to believe that if he did become very breathless, he would have another heart attack. John agreed to the next experiment with the cardiac nurse present, which was to get purposively breathless by climbing stairs and to observe the results. When he did so, John noticed some chest tightness, but also that it passed. As he continued, tightness then dissipated altogether, although he remained breathless. This time his belief dropped to 10% and he developed an alternative interpretation of his symptoms, that they indicated unfitness. He initially believed this 40% but it rose to 70% as he continued exercising over time, got fitter, and his breathlessness reduced. John then confidently planned a graded return to work.

Special issues here include the importance of checking medical issues. Working with other professionals such as cardiac nurses can be helpful to challenge excessive fears and help overcome avoidance.

Reducing disability and improving quality of life

Gladys, a 54-year-old ex-nurse, had been unemployed for 13 years and suffered chronic pain from a fall 30 years ago. She had undergone surgery, multiple other medical treatments, and was taking many painkillers from which she experienced little sustained relief. She reported that the pain affected all her activities: 'I can't cook or do housework, my family do everything—it's frustrating having to depend on others. I'm helpless'. Her mood was low and she obtained reduced pleasure from most activities. Her priorities in treatment were to manage more housework and to cook more.

The psychologist began by socializing Gladys to a self-management approach; the impact of pain on all her life, not just her body, was acknowledged, and therefore that a broad holistic approach to living with it was needed. Gladys's pain was validated: there was no doubting that the pain was real and physical and there was no implication of it being Gladys's fault to have been caught in a cycle of cure-seeking. The aim of the self-management approach was not to prevent Gladys from seeking a cure but rather to enable her to take a broader perspective and to focus on what enabled her to live currently as meaningful a life as possible.

The intervention started with addressing Gladys's 'all or nothing' tendency with activity (such as leaving ironing to accumulate for weeks and then tackling it all in one go, followed by increased pain and then going to bed), by using small specific goals with clear indicators of success (Gladys chose 20 minutes of ironing a week). Gladys developed skills in noticing the barriers that arose, many of which were psychological, such as guilt over not having done more and frustration at having to stop, unfinished. She asked herself 'which approach enables me to do more longer term?' She also clarified how much she valued being a nurturing mother to her children and wished to express this through cooking more. She then developed skills in approaching cooking tasks mindfully, that is, focusing on what her hands were doing, noticing where thoughts took her, and bringing herself back to the present moment, to her hands and the sensory aspects of cooking.

By the end of treatment, Gladys was ironing regularly and cooking for the whole family once a fortnight. She reported that she often felt tired and had increased pain afterwards, but it was worth it for the sense of achievement. She increased her open communication with her children about her capabilities and kept them involved in her goals, giving them the confidence to let her do more for herself.

This case illustrates the importance of clinical health psychologists recognizing the considerable limitations people may have in moving towards their goals, including being unable to work or not having money to do things. At times psychologists must be willing to sit with patients in their sadness and real losses, and resist jumping in to attempt to modify beliefs. Explorations of some of the valued qualities of activities that can be approached in another way are helpful, such as contributing by being a part of a social group.

12.7 Working within teams and organizations

A psychologist's role within a physical health care team is often to take a broader or meta-perspective on presenting issues, such as to consider contexts perhaps ignored by others such as family relationships, and past experiences, and to move beyond 'fire-fighting' problems to conceptualizing wider process issues. These might include how team members might feel 'pulled' to react in certain ways in particular situations. This is essential when developing psychological formulations within teams to help guide treatment decisions for individuals. Psychologists can also provide training about specific, tricky issues including breaking bad news; working with challenging behaviour that might impact on admission length; or how to provide information to maximize adherence. They can provide education on specific difficulties (e.g. PTSD) as well as clinical supervision.

At the organizational level, psychologists have roles in shaping future commissioning through ensuring the dissemination and use of efficacy research, and government guidelines concerning best practice with regards to psychological wellbeing.

12.8 Future directions and conclusion

Future work in clinical health psychology may involve extensions of the themes noted in the introduction to the chapter: for example, expert patients are likely to have a greater influence on service development and design than ever before, particularly when creating cross-culturally relevant services; and new technologies (e.g. smart-phones) may enable interventions to be both transportable and tailored to individuals' needs within their own environments. One key challenge for the profession is to be proactive and vigilant about retaining quality within psychological treatments as they are increasingly delivered by non-psychologists. Psychologists leading training, supervision, and dissemination of on-going outcome research can go some way toward achieving this.

The field started out as behavioural, and this is still in many ways at the heart of psychological approaches in this area. However, psychology has become more sophisticated, with moves towards clarifying values which provide *intrinsic* motivation for behaviour change. Improving illness management and lifestyle is not an end in itself; it must serve greater purposes as defined by the individual. Such work touches on core existential issues, including clarifying priorities in life, which resonate in all our lives.

Recent innovative approaches involving mindfulness and acceptance have made great strides by directly addressing restrictive psychological perspectives in society and indeed within our own profession: that is, the notion that the problems our clients face differ from our own, or that people need to get rid of or 'fix' their feelings, thoughts, and reactions before they can take steps toward achieving their goals or living according to their values. Working in this field inevitably engages psychologists in questioning assumptions about the enduring relevance and utility of societal messages about mind and body and about what a fulfilling life entails.

We hope we have succeeded in conveying what an exciting, varied, and challenging field physical health care is to work in. Although on some occasions, patients do have difficulty engaging with a psychological approach, this setting presents opportunities to work with people who have no prior involvement with mental health services, early in their difficulties, and to witness transformational change over short periods which can be extremely rewarding. Although working with people who have suffered serious injuries or have life-threatening health problems can be emotionally demanding, we feel it a privilege to work with people at the most vulnerable times of their lives, and we continue to find patients' courage and resilience in the face of exceptional circumstances, as well as their capacity to overcome difficulties, to be both inspiring and humbling.

References

Bray, D. (2009). Patient-centred care, Darzi and solution-focused approaches. In G. Latchford and J. Unwin (eds) *Division of Clinical Psychology, Clinical Psychology Forum, No. 199, July 2009 Special Issue*. British Psychological Society, Leicester.

Hayes, S.C., Luoma, J.B., Bond, F.W., Masuda, A., and Lillis, J. (2006). Acceptance and commitment therapy: model, processes and outcomes. *Behaviour Research and Therapy*, **44**, 1–25.

Hayes, S.C., Strosahl, K.D., and Wilson, K.G. (1999). *Acceptance and Commitment Therapy. An Experiential Approach to Behavior Change.* Guildford Press, New York.

Kabat-Zinn, J. (1990). *Full Catastrophe Living.* Delacorte, New York.

Kennedy, P., Duff, J., Evans, M., and Beedie, A. (2003). Coping effectiveness training reduces depression and anxiety following traumatic spinal cord injuries. *British Journal of Clinical Psychology*, **42**, 41–52.

Lazarus, R.S. and Folkman, S. (1984). *Stress, Appraisal and Coping.* Springer, New York.

McCracken, L.M. (2011). *Mindfulness and Acceptance in Behavioral Medicine. Current Theory and Practice.* Context Press, Reno.

Moorey, S. (1996). When bad things happen to rational people: cognitive therapy in aversive life circumstances. In P.M. Salvokskis (ed.) *Frontiers of Cognitive Therapy.* Guildford Press, New York.

Sage, N., Sowden, M., Chorlton, E., and Edeleanu, A. (2008). *CBT for Chronic Illness and Palliative Care. A Workbook and Tookit.* Wiley, Chichester.

de Shazer, S. (1994). *Words Were Originally Magic.* Norton, New York.

Tyrer, P., Cooper, S., Tyrer, H., *et al.* (2011). CHAMP: cognitive behaviour therapy for health anxiety in medical patients, a randomised controlled trial. *BMC Psychiatry*, **11**, 99.

White, C. (2001). *Cognitive Behaviour Therapy for Chronic Medical Problems. A Guide to Assessment and Treatment in Practice.* Wiley, Chichester.

Chapter 13

Working in clinical neuropsychology

Katherine Carpenter and Andy Tyerman

13.1 Introduction

Clinical neuropsychology is concerned with people whose thinking, behaviour, or emotions have become disrupted as a result of brain damage. Such neuropsychological changes often have a major effect on the person and their lifestyle, occupation, and family relationships.

Clinical neuropsychology has its own specialist knowledge base of neurology, neuroanatomy, and brain–behaviour relations. However, it still involves work with people with their own everyday life events and stresses who experience similar psychological problems to those in mental health settings, in addition to their specific neuropsychological changes.

The clinical neuropsychologist needs the expertise to make sense of what can be bizarre and frightening experiences for patients (such as their not being able to remember anything from one day to the next, or not being able to recognize their family by seeing their faces, but only on hearing their voices). However, sensitivity and understanding is also required to treat each patient with these problems as a whole person in a family and life context, not just as a dysfunctional brain. Over time the professional role may evolve from that of an expert assessor/advisor, to a trainer or guide in rehabilitation, to that of a mentor or facilitator in long-term personal and family adjustment.

Neuropsychological impairment

The term neuropsychological impairment encompasses an extremely wide range of difficulties in cognitive function, behavioural control, and emotional responsivity. Neuropsychological changes are often experienced alongside a range of other physical and sensory effects of neurological conditions such as weakness, loss of balance, and co-ordination, visual field deficits, loss of sensation, headaches, fatigue, and seizures.

The most common cognitive difficulties experienced after generalized damage to the brain are with attention, concentration, memory, and reduced speed of information processing. Following focal damage (such as stroke and tumour), specific deficits may be seen in motor skills, visual perception, spatial judgement, or language function. Disruption of executive function (i.e. higher level reasoning, planning, problem solving, self-awareness, and self-monitoring), which is particularly common after severe head injury, is of particular importance as it affects insight, understanding, use of compensatory strategies, and capacity for long-term adjustment. Experiencing such changes in cognitive skills can be bewildering and immensely frustrating for patients.

A wide range of behavioural and emotional effects may also be experienced, reflecting an interaction of primary neurological damage and secondary psychological reactions to neurological illness/injury and its effects. Common primary changes are of increased irritability, disinhibition, impulsivity, emotional lability, mood swings, and aggressive outbursts. A wide range of emotional reactions may also be experienced such as frustration and anger, fear and anxiety, depression, and loss of confidence and self-esteem.

There is a distinction between relatively circumscribed lesions such as those caused by a stroke (where a blockage or constriction of an artery results in loss of blood and oxygen to a particular area) or a penetrating missile injury, and diffuse brain injury caused by a closed head injury, a progressive neurodegenerative process, or a subarachnoid haemorrhage (in which an artery ruptures explosively, driving blood into the space around the brain and causing widespread damage). Neurological conditions differ markedly in both onset and course. Some conditions (such as anoxia, head injury, and stroke) are of sudden onset; infectious conditions (such as encephalitis and meningitis) may develop over a period of hours or days; whereas others conditions (such as tumours, movement disorders, or the dementias) evolve very gradually. Some conditions (such as head injury and anoxia) are single episodes followed by recovery and adjustment, others (such as epilepsy and multiple sclerosis) may be intermittent, while others are progressive (such as cerebral tumour and the dementias). As such, whilst some people require acute hospital care, followed by rehabilitation and community support, others may require limited input in the early stages of the condition, followed by increasing levels of medical, psychological, and social care as their condition progresses.

Neuropsychological services

In the UK, clinical psychologists specializing in work with people with a neurological condition and their carers can be based in a range of settings and may be at different stages in the pathway of care, from acute to community.

Neuropsychologists working with people at their first point of contact with services, either as outpatients or on admission to hospital, are usually located in hospital-based neurosciences centres. Much of the work carried out in such units involves emergency treatment or investigation of very sick or at-risk patients. As such, neuropsychologists work closely with medical and nursing staff but often need to see patients again as outpatients at a 'post-acute' stage, when many of the acute medical features have settled, and cognitive and emotional changes become much more relevant. Within rehabilitation settings clinical neuropsychologists typically work within inpatient or community neurorehabilitation teams or specialist community brain injury or stroke rehabilitation services. There are also a number of specialist services that focus specifically on the cognitive, behavioural, and/or vocational needs of people with brain injury.

The role of the clinical neuropsychologist varies markedly across settings. This chapter first outlines the acute neurological/neurosurgical setting and then moves on to the rehabilitation and community setting.

13.2 The acute neurology/neurosurgery setting

It is very helpful if psychologists have a good understanding of a number of distinctive features of the neuropsychological setting in which their work takes place, and of neuropsychological knowledge which informs clinical work.

The patients

Patients present at all ages and a good working knowledge of the developmental context is important. Detailed comprehensive assessment needs to take account of any sensory disturbance, motor problems, and episodes of altered awareness, as well as the more usual areas of pre-morbid medical/psychiatric history. This is important because neuro-logical disorders tend to present with a complex interplay of cognitive, emotional, behavioural, and physical features. These interact with each other and may affect assessment or measurement of any one component.

Medical context

New psychologists are often surprised by what can seem an intimidating medical-type environment in the acute setting. Neuropsychologists need to be flexible in switching between a medical model, which allows them to communicate rapidly with medical colleagues, and more eco-logically valid psychological models, which may have greater relevance when helping patients and their carers try to make sense of their experiences. Inpatient clinical work is often constrained both by competing demands (such as demand for beds, resulting in short hospital admissions) and by the general level of 'unwellness' of patients.

Parallel investigations

Clinical neuropsychology in an acute setting is only one of a number of several investigative approaches available to the neurologist or neurosurgeon co-ordinating care of the patient. Psychometric test results must be interpreted in the context of the overall formulation of the case and in the light of parallel investigations. History taking is central in neurological diagnosis, with many disorders being diagnosed on clinical grounds and investigations confirming information anticipated by the history. The progress in imaging techniques—computerized tomography (CT) and magnetic resonance imaging (MRI)—since the 1990s has radically altered the role of neuropsychology in relation to other specialties. CT and MRI now allow clinicians to look at neuroanatomy and pathology in the living brain, which means neuropsychological assessment is relied on much less for inferring localization of pathology. Cerebral blood flow and metabolism techniques—functional imaging (fMRI) and positron emission tomography (PET)—allow observation of the dynamic metabolism of the working brain. This is increasingly valuable for understanding brain–behaviour relations. Neurophysiology, which measures electrical brain activity using electroencephalographs (EEGs) and evoked potentials, is particularly important in the diagnosis of epilepsy.

Functional neuroanatomy

The human brain is the most fascinating and complex biological system and its anatomy is beyond the scope of this chapter. Feeling underconfident about neuroanatomy is one of the things that can put psychologists off working in the field; however, a basic working knowledge is adequate for many purposes.

Neuropsychological terminology

Somewhat impenetrable technical terminology for syndromes can be initially intimidating. Nevertheless, although unnecessary jargon should be avoided where possible, jargon is often useful shorthand between clinicians for what would otherwise be a complex phenomenon or concept to express.

Underlying concepts and assumptions

It is helpful to understand a few key tenets which underpin many of the ways neuropsychologists think. Cerebral dominance refers to lateralization such that either the right or the left side of the brain is specialized for a particular function. In the vast majority of right-handers (> 92%) and in a large proportion of left-handers (69%), speech, language, and verbal memory are represented in the left 'dominant' hemisphere. In contrast, the right hemisphere is predominant for tasks involving stimuli that cannot be easily put into words, such as visual memory function and interpretation of emotional expression. There is a subtle interplay between specialization and functional plasticity, whereby areas of the brain can sometimes take over functions for which they are not normally thought to be specialized. Making inferences about normal brain function from the study of brain-damaged patients assumes that a patient's brain was previously normal, and this may not always be the case (e.g. following early insult such as epilepsy). It also presupposes that we know what 'normal' is, whereas in fact there is considerable individual variation and there is evidence that the same lesion does not always lead to the same impairment in different patients.

Neuropsychological assessment

Clinical interview

Neuropsychological assessment usually involves an appointment lasting from 2–4 hours. With adults, a comprehensive semi-structured interview first reviews a wide range of factors relating to the patient's account (and those of close relatives) of the medical, social and educational/occupational background, presenting problem, and current symptomatology. As with any other interview, the psychologist is constantly developing a hypothesis and looking for disconfirming evidence, as well as making qualitative observations on aspects such as insight, comprehension, speech, and mental state.

Psychometric testing

A standard battery of tests can be administered. However, most neuropsychologists adopt a more flexible approach (Lezak *et al.*, 2012), often using certain core tests supplemented by other measures covering specific cognitive domains as and when appropriate. Neuropsychological tests are aimed at sampling behaviour in one or more cognitive domains, such as general intelligence, visuo-spatial perceptual ability, language, memory and concentration, attention, and higher-order skills such as planning and so-called executive function (Strauss *et al.*, 2006). As is common in many standard forms of measurement, the scores obtained by an individual on a test (measurement) of a particular psychological characteristic or process are compared with the average score obtained by a comparable group of individuals, usually the same age and from the same general population. The average of the comparable group is calculated and an individual score is expressed in terms of its departure from the group average (Crawford, 2012). This allows psychologists to take into account the fact that, for example, younger people tend to remember more than older people, and similarly that brighter individuals should remember more than those of more limited ability. An estimate is made of the patient's level of *pre-morbid* ability on the basis of both education and occupational attainments, as well as from their performance on more 'crystallized' components of cognitive performance (for example, knowledge of word meanings, which is more robust in the face of acquired damage). In addition to quantitative indices, qualitative observations on test performance are made. Standardized questionnaires may be included to assess health-related quality of life and mood.

A standard assessment normally includes a measure of pre-morbid function; a measure of general intelligence; orientation; verbal memory tests (including *immediate* and *delayed* recall of both narrative material and unrelated words); a non-verbal memory test; attentional and 'executive' tests as appropriate; and verbal fluency and additional language tests if needed.

Choice of test instruments obviously needs to take into account any sensory, motor, cultural, or linguistic constraints on the person. Many of the widely used tests (e.g. the Wechsler Adult Intelligence Scale IV) have been translated into other languages, but the proviso remains that in general the normative data on which they are based remain North American.

Testing is an area that can seem dry to the uninitiated. In fact this is far from the case. Cognitive evaluation involves what is effectively a series of monitored behavioural experiments in which as many variables as possible are controlled. A skilled neuropsychologist needs to be capable of developing and maintaining rapport with a patient while coaxing them through what can be an exacting set of tasks. Imagine being faced with a highly intelligent person, perhaps a company director or doctor, in the early stages of an insidious dementing process, and extracting the greatest amount of information possible from a minimum of testing, while protecting the dignity of the patient. This is an undoubted challenge. Quiet, well-lit surroundings without any undue distractions or interruptions are preferable to maximize the patient's performance; quite an opposite set of conditions are obviously required if one is assessing a patient's capability of returning to a stressful job in a busy open-plan environment.

Neuropsychological reports

A full written report is prepared following assessment and usually comprises sections on the medical background, personal history, clinical presentation, neuropsychological evaluation, and conclusions. Reports vary according to the audience for whom they are written. Internal reports in an acute neurology/neurosurgery setting tend to be succinct with cross referral to other medical reports. Rehabilitation reports may function as a contract between the patient, their carers, and the interdisciplinary rehabilitation team, and, as such, may use a goal-setting model. A good report will convey the clinical problem and its context, together with a detailed description of the test results and their interpretation, with a clear distinction being made between fact and observation, inference, and interpretation. A good report should also not be merely descriptive, but should provide a clinical opinion in relation to the underlying referral question.

Purpose of assessment

In the acute setting, the emphasis is on differential diagnosis, evaluation of the outcome of the intervention (e.g. drug treatment or operation), monitoring of change, and early identification of cognitive sequelae. All the information is taken together and interpreted in the light of the questions to be answered. These obviously vary from patient to patient but include the following: is there evidence that the patient's cognitive function has been adversely affected from a previously higher pre-morbid level? Is the pattern of deficits consistent with the known pathology and medical variables? Does the test profile reflect focal pathology or a generalized decline? What are this person's current strengths and weaknesses? Are their deficits likely to progress or improve? What is the likelihood of this person being able to return to their previous employment or academic study?

One common reason for carrying out an assessment is differential diagnosis between depression and dementia, which may present in similar ways. This is important because dementia is often caused by incurable disorders such as dementia of the Alzheimer's type or fronto-temporal dementia (Bozeat *et al.*, 2000), while pseudodementia due to depression can be treated. This latter patient group tends to show more concern and insight into their memory loss in addition to symptoms of depression. Depression and dementia are also by no means mutually exclusive since elderly patients often become depressed when they are beginning to lose their mental faculties.

Interventions

Intervention in the acute setting can be tantalizing and frustrating because the turnover of inpatients is high and because a specialist tertiary neuroscience centre may serve a population of 2–3 million, many of whom live some distance away. Most work is necessarily time-limited, post-acute, and carried out at outpatient follow-up.

Interventions generally comprise either neuropsychological rehabilitative procedures or cognitive or behavioural treatments derived from models widely applied in mental health work. Rehabilitation is not as fully developed in *acute* neurology/neurosurgery as it probably should be; detailed assessment of the problems forms the basis for goal planning, education, and information-giving, and the introduction of palliative coping strategies and techniques (such as mobile phones, tablet computers, sticky-backed notes, diary). Neurological/neurosurgical patients with emotional or behavioural problems may require a range of techniques, such as cognitive therapy for depression or anxiety (especially post-traumatic stress disorder), anger management, progressive muscle relaxation, sexual and relationship counselling, or management of pain.

Brain surgery is always a major life event. Sometimes the problems pre-date the neurological condition but are exacerbated by it or need tackling because they interfere with recovery; sometimes they are a direct result of an underlying neurological/neurosurgical condition (such as a frontal brain tumour or head injury). Either way they are often best dealt with by a neuropsychologist who is both experienced with the neurological context and familiar with the constraints of memory loss, language difficulty, dysexecutive symptoms, sensory and perceptual problems, or seizure activity.

Consultation, research, and audit

Neuropsychology cannot be useful clinically without liaison with parallel disciplines in the neurosciences. It is important, however, not to overestimate others' knowledge about neuropsychological variables: what often seems straightforward advice from a psychologist's viewpoint may actually be invaluable to the referrer. Liaison is particularly relevant in paediatric settings. It is crucial to understand that paediatric neuropsychology is not simply adult neuropsychology applied to children, and also that a thorough grounding in general paediatric psychology, within the developmental context and in cognitive development, is key (see Reed and Warner-Rogers, 2008).

Research in the acute setting is at the sharp end of clinical practice and in pressured hospital environments is predominantly aimed at evaluating outcome (cognitive status, functional disability, and health-related quality of life). The British Medical Research Council, for example, is concerned to enhance the quality of randomized clinical trials in the neurosciences; hence the potential future contribution of neuropsychologists in this area is considerable.

13.3 Rehabilitation/community settings

In rehabilitation and community settings, referrals may include a wide range of neurological conditions (e.g. head injury, multiple sclerosis, stroke) with contrasting patterns and course of disability. Onset peaks at different stages in the life cycle: typically, head injury affects the young single adult; multiple sclerosis the married person with a young family; and stroke the older adult with grown-up children. The impact on the person and the family is therefore very variable, depending upon the specific pattern of disability, individual coping resources, and personal, family, and social circumstances.

The complex array of neurological disability often has far-reaching effects upon the person, who may experience a wide range of emotional reactions including frustration and anger, fear and anxiety, depression, and loss of confidence or self-esteem. Whilst recovery and adaptation may continue over several years, many will be faced with restrictions in independent living, in returning to employment, in maintaining leisure interests and social relationships, and in contributing to family life. Neurological disability has a major impact on families, who are often left to cope with little support, especially where there are subtle changes in cognition and personality which are not apparent to extended family and friends. Many primary carers experience stress and distress, often amidst marked changes in family relationships, roles, and functioning. Spouses in particular may struggle to cope with the competing needs of work, home, and family amidst changes in the personal and sexual relationship with their partner.

The challenge for rehabilitation services is to ensure that people with a neurological condition achieve and maintain optimal independence and social participation. Clinical neuropsychologists play a vital role in meeting this challenge.

Assessment

The complex needs of people with neurological illness/injury require specialist and detailed assessment to clarify the nature of disability, and to plan rehabilitation. Whilst formal testing of cognitive function and emotional screening are undertaken routinely, more detailed assessment of emotional state and behaviour may also be required. The fundamental principles of neuropsychological assessment have already been described for the acute setting. However, in rehabilitation, the focus tends to be more functional: identifying strengths as well as weaknesses, clarifying rehabilitation needs and potential, and in monitoring recovery. The results of formal neuropsychological testing are considered alongside self and family reports, observations of nursing and rehabilitation staff, and any parallel assessments completed by other members of the multi-disciplinary rehabilitation team (e.g. medicine, occupational therapy, physiotherapy, speech and language therapy).

Feedback of complex neuropsychological test results to the person (who frequently lacks insight and may be distressed or defensive) and to the family (who may be understandably protective) is a highly skilled and challenging task (see Tyerman and King, 2012).

Interventions

The identified needs often require a broad range of psychological interventions including cognitive rehabilitation, behavioural management, neuropsychological counselling/psychological therapy, and specialist family interventions.

Cognitive rehabilitation

Core interventions are likely to start with an explanation of cognitive function and the person's specific cognitive impairment. This may be followed by re-orientation work (e.g. addressing key gaps in memory, restructuring of the environment) and on-going education and development of strategies to improve or compensate for specific cognitive difficulties, which increasingly include the use of electronic aids (e.g. smart phones and 'life-logging' cameras). Teaching about cognitive difficulties and related coping strategies can often be undertaken in group settings. In the longer term the focus often shifts to exploring alternative ways of organizing tasks and of limiting demands, for example in the work place. Regular reviews are vital to monitor progress, review rehabilitation strategies and goals, and guide on-going adjustments, especially a return to education or employment.

Behavioural management

Nursing and rehabilitation staff may require advice from clinical neuropsychologists about the management of agitated, disinhibited, or aggressive behaviour on the ward, sometimes in parallel with neuropsychiatric input. When major problems persist, a behaviour management programme may be required. In the community many people with a neurological condition and their relatives seek advice about the on-going nature and management of a wide range of behavioural difficulties (e.g. irritability, intolerance, impulsivity, disinhibition, and aggressive outbursts). In the longer term, further guidance may be sought about the on-going impact of behavioural difficulties on family and social relationships.

Neuropsychological counselling/psychological therapy

Neuropsychological counselling (e.g. provision of information, explanation, progress monitoring, promotion of insight/realistic expectations, and future planning) may serve a vital function in guiding and supporting the person through the challenging process of neurorehabilitation. This, combined with person-focused education, discussion, and/or support groups, will meet some of the emotional needs of people with a neurological condition. However, many may require some specific individual psychological therapy (e.g. anxiety or anger management, or help with mood swings or depression). Such interventions need to be adapted to take into account the person's cognitive difficulties and any neurologically based loss of emotional and behavioural control.

In the longer term, people with a neurological condition often need assistance in adjusting to their on-going disability, particularly when cognitive impairment has reduced the capacity for self-appraisal and problem solving. Psychotherapy, adapted to the neuropsychological constraints of the individual, can offer a structure within which to assist the person forward: in making sense of residual changes in themselves and their lives; in reviewing strengths and weaknesses; in identifying, clarifying, and prioritizing unresolved issues; and in finding a new direction through which to start to rebuild their lives.

Working with families

It is vital to include the family as fully as possible in the process of rehabilitation. A family member is commonly invited to initial interviews and assessment feedback sessions. This helps families to understand the nature and implications of difficulties and the rationale for proposed rehabilitation. Thereafter close liaison with the family is essential both to receive feedback about progress at home and to explain on-going rehabilitation strategies, which can then be reinforced at home. However, great care is required not to add to the stress on family members. The needs of families often warrant attention in their own right, as relatives may themselves be in need of specialist advice and support in coping with the impact upon both themselves and the family as a whole. Relatives often value highly the provision of specialist family services,

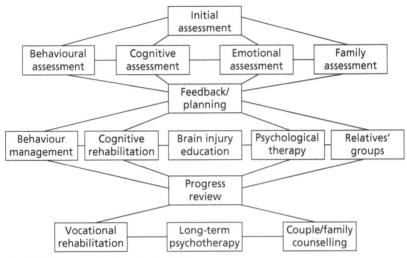

Fig. 13.1 Neuropsychological rehabilitation: a service example.

including individual advice and support, educational sessions, specialist couple/family therapy, and peer support (Tyerman and Barton, 2008).

Interventions in rehabilitation and the community are therefore many and varied, as illustrated for a well-developed community brain injury service in Aylesbury, UK (see Figure 13.1) and in the case example.

Case example

Jeremy, a professional man in his late 30s, was living with his wife and family when he incurred a very severe head injury in a road traffic accident. He remained in intensive care for over 2 weeks and in hospital for over 2 months.

Assessment

Jeremy was seen for initial assessment at 1 month post injury. At this early stage he was aware of some of his physical disability (fatigue, slurred speech, and reduced vision), cognitive difficulties (speed, memory, expressive language), and changes in emotional behaviour (irritability, frustration, aggression, disinhibition, mood swings, and depression). A neuropsychological assessment confirmed substantial cognitive impairment: reduced general intellectual ability, word finding difficulties, visuoperceptual difficulties, markedly reduced speed of information processing, and an impaired verbal memory. He also reported a low self-concept but no significant anxiety or depression.

Core neurorehabilitation

After feedback of assessment results, Jeremy commenced a rehabilitation programme 2 days per week, comprising psychological therapy, occupational therapy, physiotherapy, and a weekly cognitive rehabilitation group. Psychological therapy concentrated initially on emotional support and promoting engagement in his rehabilitation programme. As he progressed, the focus shifted to planning, organizational skills, and improving insight, awareness, and understanding. A neuropsychological reassessment at 7 months confirmed substantial progress, but his speed of information processing and psychomotor speed remained slow and marked impairment of verbal memory persisted. By 10 months he was becoming more aware of the range of his difficulties, but with increased insight came marked depression.

Vocational rehabilitation

As he was unable to return to his previous employment, Jeremy joined a brain injury vocational rehabilitation programme. He attended a weekly work preparation group, participated in two community vocational rehabilitation activities and individual project work, received neuropsychological counselling, and joined a weekly personal issues group. At 2 years post injury he started a voluntary work trial, but experienced marked frustration with his work restrictions and reduced role. At 3 years post injury he recognized that he was not able to cope with paid employment but continued with part-time voluntary work, started whilst on the programme.

Family work

During rehabilitation Jeremy's wife was supported regularly by a specialist social worker. At 1 year, the family situation was causing great concern. Jeremy was noted to be frustrated, unable to discuss family matters without getting irritated, and verbally aggressive if challenged or criticized. He was intolerant of noise and unable to cope with the pressures of a young family. His relationship with his older daughter was causing particular concern; he was, for example, struggling to cope with discipline and to support both her learning and her play. Over the next 2 years a clinical neuropsychologist and specialist social worker sought to guide and support the couple in understanding the family impact of the head injury, in managing his anger, in rebuilding his relationship with his older daughte,r and in facilitating marital communication. Specialist neuropsychological knowledge and skills were also used to help him to compensate for his cognitive difficulties in order to participate productively in couple counselling, since he found it difficult to appreciate others' views—tending to dominate discussions, interrupting frequently, and seeing issues categorically from his own perspective. Whilst the couple remained somewhat distant with little sharing at a personal level and limited physical intimacy, the couples work served to contain confrontation and to stabilize strained family relationships under the challenging circumstances.

Follow-up

When followed up at 4 years post injury, Jeremy had continued with his voluntary work and appeared more settled and relaxed. This was reported to have eased slightly the stress and friction within the family, although significant tension remained. He appeared at this stage to be resigning himself to his residual disability and associated restriction, although he did not take up the neuropsychologist's offer of further individual psychotherapy to assist in long-term personal, family, and social adjustment. Support for his wife continued on an infrequent basis for several more years.

The above example illustrates the wide range of psychological input that may be required, in this example working continuously to promote recovery and adjustment over many years. This included individual and group neuropsychological education and counselling, individual and group cognitive rehabilitation, anger management, family education and support, and couple counselling, within the context of interdisciplinary neurorehabilitation and specialist vocational programmes.

It is important to work in partnership with other health services (e.g. neuroscience centres, general hospitals, GPs, and mental health services) and with other community or voluntary agencies. This might include social services (regarding appropriate day, home, or residential care), job centres, education services, voluntary agencies, and carers' services. Working in partnership, neuropsychologists can assist many people with neurological disability and their families in their rehabilitation and adjustment.

13.4 **Conclusion**

Whilst sometimes seen as overly academic, clinical neuropsychology comprises a rich blend of specialist neuropsychological expertise and core clinical psychology skills. Hopefully this chapter has conveyed a flavour of this fascinating and challenging area and provided an insight into the complex pathways of care, from diagnosis and assessment in the acute setting, through rehabilitation, to the promotion of long-term adjustment in the community.

Whilst operating within a common neuropsychological framework, the nature of the work and core skills differ in emphasis across acute, rehabilitation, and community settings. As such, clinical neuropsychologists are a disparate group within different settings, attracting practitioners with contrasting interests and skills. A basic grounding in neuropsychology is provided in clinical psychology training, but practitioners normally need to develop their specialist expertise via further training and specialist supervision.

This is an exciting time in the neurosciences, with major technical advances, for example, in *in vivo* imaging, image-guided neurosurgery, and work on implants and neuronal plasticity. Computer technology and electronic devices also offer major potential benefits for those struggling to cope with neurological disability, but the challenge remains to make such advances accessible to all those with neuropsychological impairment. Advances in technology will hopefully extend the future range of medical treatment and rehabilitation options, which will further increase the need for, and contribution of, specialist neuropsychological expertise.

References

Bozeat, S., Gregory, C.A., Lambon-Ralph, M.A., and Hodges, J.R. (2000). Which neuropsychiatric and behavioural features distinguish frontal and temporal variants of fronto-temporal dementia from Alzheimer's disease? *Journal of Neurology and Neurosurgical Psychiatry*, **69**, 178–186.

Crawford, J.R. (2012). Quantitative aspects of neuropsychological assessment. In L.H. Goldstein and J.E. McNeil (eds), *Clinical Neuropsychology: A Practical Guide to Assessment and Management for Clinicians*, 2nd edn. Wiley-Blackwell, Chichester.

Lezak, M.D., Howieson, D.B., Bigler, E.D., and Tranel, D. (2012). *Neuropsychological Assessment*. Oxford University Press, New York.

Reed, J. and Warner-Rogers, J. (2008). *Child Neuropsychology: Concepts, Theory and Practice*. Wiley-Blackwell, Chichester.

Strauss, E., Sherman, E.M.S., and Spreen, O. (2006). *A Compendium of Neuropsychological Tests: Administration, Norms and Commentary*. Oxford University Press, New York.

Tyerman, A. and Barton, S. (2008). Working with families: a community service example. In A. Tyerman and N.S. King (eds), *Psychological Approaches to Rehabilitation after Traumatic Brain Injury*. BPS Blackwell, Oxford.

Tyerman, A. and King, N. (2012). Interventions for psychological problems after brain injury. In L.H. Goldstein and J. McNeil (eds), *Clinical Neuropsychology: A Practical Guide to Assessment and Management for Clinicians*, 2nd edn. Wiley-Blackwell, Chichester.

Further reading

Goldstein, L.H. and McNeil, J. (eds) (2012). *Clinical Neuropsychology: A Practical Guide to Assessment and Management for Clinicians*, 2nd Edn. Wiley-Blackwell, Chichester.

Gurd, J., Kischka, U., and Marshall, J.C. (eds) (2010). *Oxford Handbook of Clinical Neuropsychology*, 2nd edn. Oxford University Press, Oxford.

Larner, A.J. (2008). *Neuropsychological Neurology: The Neurocognitive Impairments of Neurological Disorders*. Cambridge University Press, New York.

Sacks, O. (2011). *The Man Who Mistook his Wife for a Hat*. Pan Macmillan Picador, London.

Wilson, B.A. (ed.) (2003). *Neuropsychological Rehabilitation: Theory and Practice*. Psychology Press, Hove.

Chapter 14

Clinical psychology in teams and leadership

Susan Llewelyn

14.1 Why are teams and leadership important?

Modern health care is complex, multi-faceted, and often provided by a variety of professional disciplines using different skills and competencies, based on a wide range of models and assumptions about people's health and wellbeing. The vast majority of health care professionals, including clinical psychologists, work in collaboration with others to meet the needs of their patients or clients (these terms are used interchangeably in this chapter). Most health care systems employ a surprising diversity of types of professional health care workers to provide input to patients, ranging from the largest groups such as doctors and nurses (many of whom also have specialist skills and post-qualification training) to smaller specialist groups such as dieticians or phlebotomists. The implications of this for patient care are that working *with* other professional groups, and the ability to function effectively within a team, are vital.

Furthermore, having a positive influence on the structure, process, and future priorities of the wider health care system is also crucial, as is the role of leadership. Indeed, leadership is now recognized as a key competence for clinical psychologists since it is recognized that this is essential for ensuring that psychological issues are at the heart of the provision of care for as many patients as possible. This chapter will review the importance of team working in the day-to-day work of clinical psychologists and explore opportunities to extend access to psychologically informed care to larger numbers of patients. It will also examine the role of leadership which not only is a key competence for psychologists in health care provision, but also potentially ensures the continued strength and self-determination of the profession itself.

14.2 **The importance of team work for clinical psychologists**

Most clinical psychologists are initially attracted to the profession because they wish to have a positive impact on the psychological wellbeing of patients. Traditionally the image held by many aspiring psychologists of exactly how this can be achieved is through the provision of one-to-one assessment and psychotherapy for individual clients; such personal individual contact is typically seen as the primary professional activity. Whilst this may be true some of the time, in fact the input of a psychologist is typically provided in collaboration with others, particularly in a team. Hence how the team communicates and works together has a huge impact on the quality and effectiveness of the psychological care provided.

Hugh, a clinical psychologist working in a mental health team, was asked to work psychologically with Peter, who had been recently admitted because of paranoid delusions and who was shortly to be discharged back into the community. Hugh recognized that any psychological work carried out with Peter would demand an understanding of not only Peter's current mood and behaviour but also the potential impact of any psychotropic medication prescribed, and knowledge of his domestic and employment situation. This required Hugh to liaise closely with the rest of the health care team about Peter's current and past situation, and to reach agreement over who would provide what aspects of Peter's treatment. Hugh also needed the co-operation of nursing staff who would provide emotional and practical support for Peter before and after therapy sessions, and throughout his stay in hospital. Hugh was aware that if other team members were not in sympathy with, or even aware of, his therapeutic work, there was a risk that it would become side-lined or undermined, or that information from the psychological work would not be integrated into the decision-making of the team regarding Peter's future.

Although seemingly stating the obvious, psychologists like Hugh need to establish good working relationships with all those around the patient, and to establish positive communication with key colleagues as well as with patients themselves, if the work is to make an on-going contribution both to specific individuals and to the future care of other patients.

The competencies needed to be a good 'team player' and communicator may also appear obvious, and perhaps because of this they may receive less attention and priority than other more apparently sophisticated competencies. Yet being a good listener, being respectful of the contributions of others, and being aware of the importance of diversity, as well as having the ability to hear and synthesize a range of perspectives whilst also establishing positive emotional contact with others, are all key abilities which promote the opportunity for psychologists to contribute to health care. Only a clinical psychologist who seeks to understand the perspective of others is likely to be received well by colleagues.

As already noted in Chapter 1, clinical psychology is a small discipline relative to some other health care professions and therefore makes up only a tiny proportion of the overall number of staff engaged in working to improve health. For example, in the UK, qualified clinical psychologists employed by the NHS (which is the largest health care provider in the world) comprise only around 0.08% of the workforce. This means that psychologists *must* work with, and through, others in order to have any impact on the care experienced by the vast majority of patients. Paradoxically, however, this can also place psychologists in a good position to influence health care provision; being in a minority, psychologists are often regarded as specialists, as well as having a somewhat tangential, expert role to contribute to routine care; hence psychologists are often invited to provide advice when standard approaches have not been successful. Rather like trouble shooters, psychologists in teams can sometimes suggest ideas that no-one else has yet thought of, and can map out ways of making progress that other staff members may not have contemplated. Standing outside the powerful hierarchies and long-established professional organizations of both medicine and nursing, psychologists can sometimes propose innovations and challenge existing approaches, precisely because they are placed somewhat external to the dominant systems. With an academic background and professional training that includes familiarity with a range of conceptual models, and a commitment to drawing on the evidence base, psychologists should be able to work flexibly with different staff groups, and offer alternative ways of solving clinical problems.

Anne, a newly qualified psychologist, wanted to design a programme to reduce the impact of challenging behaviour presented by a young woman living in a residential unit, which was staffed by a large number of care workers, some of whom were rather dismissive of the idea of a psychologist becoming involved. Anne realised that, no matter how elegantly designed her programme was, it would only have a hope of success if the staff were willing to implement it. This would depend, to a large extent, on her ability to engage the staff, and to design a plan that was feasible to deliver given staffing levels and the other competing demands and priorities for staff time. In order to achieve this Anne would need to take time to understand the staff as well as the resident, and to initiate and maintain good communication. She therefore made time to sit down with staff, sharing cups of tea or coffee on several occasions, to discuss shared concerns and explain the programme carefully. In doing so Anne showed a willingness to work flexibly and collaboratively, rather than simply instructing the staff in how to implement the programme, and leaving them to it.

Although the points raised by Anne's approach may be readily apparent, the importance of people skills, of willingness to work as part of a team, and of carefully respecting the contribution of others are often under-recognized to the detriment of clinical psychologists' potential contribution, both individually and as a profession.

14.3 The importance of team work for health care

Given that most modern health care is provided by teams, and that teams are effectively the vehicles by which the skills of practitioners are delivered to meet the needs of patients, it is perhaps surprising that until recently little attention had been paid to exactly how that vehicle impacts on the quality of care provided. However, research by West and colleagues (e.g. West, 2004) has clearly demonstrated that the effectiveness of team work significantly affects a whole range of outcomes, including the health and wellbeing of both staff and patients. Working in a variety of health care settings, including acute care, long-stay hospitals, community mental health teams, and primary care, West's research group has shown that where teams work well together, the quality of patient care is higher, and that good team working actually prevents deaths, as well as reducing illness and patient distress. A range of studies, across both huge national samples and smaller intensive investigations, have shown that where there is good team working patients are more satisfied with the health care they receive, and staff are happier in their jobs. Furthermore, error rates, incidence of violence from patients or staff, and allegations of bullying and harassment are all significantly lower where team working is good. This is not really surprising: if a member of staff likes and feels able to trust their colleagues, they will feel more relaxed and confident at work, which will be conveyed to patients through more focused working. Staff will also feel more able to call for help when needed, resulting in fewer staff injuries and more open discussion of errors, in turn leading to safer work places and a more open learning culture.

The key questions then are, what constitutes good team work, and how can clinical psychologists help to establish this?

Drawing on evidence reported by West and co-researchers, Kelly, an experienced clinical psychologist working in a community mental health team, facilitated an away-day designed to increase her team's effectiveness. She made use of West's definition of a 'real team', i.e. a small group who have clear objectives, work closely together to achieve those objectives, and meet regularly to review their effectiveness to see how to improve their work. Kelly was aware that teams also need to be clear about their vision, what exactly they are there for, and who constitutes the team. She discovered that, as is unfortunately typical of many teams, there was confusion about the team purpose, a lack of objectives, muddle between different interpretations of what the team was supposed to be doing, and lack of an agreed vision.

Kelly first agreed with the team that they needed to establish some clarity about their overall purpose, and then to develop focused team objectives to describe the specific and realistic ways in which the team purpose could be delivered within an agreed time frame. After much debate, Kelly's team agreed that its purpose was 'to provide a range of responsive community-based services for adults of working age living locally, using evidence-based treatments and a multi-disciplinary approach, in order to promote recovery and to prevent relapse'. From this, specific and achievable team objectives were articulated, including 'to develop an assessment protocol so that all referred patients have a care plan agreed within 4 weeks of referral' and 'to implement the revised on-call rota within 6 months to improve liaison with crisis services'. Having agreed the team's purpose and objectives, Kelly then encouraged individual members to clarify their own roles within it, and to agree the team's operating principles, including what meetings would be held, how decisions should be reached, and what review procedures were in place. With structural issues such as these agreed, Kelly was then able to assist her team to establish more effective processes, including functional and clear communication systems, and how to benefit from the diverse range of experiences and skills existing amongst the team members.

In some teams, existing team managers or leaders (often from a nursing or medical background) already possess some of the competencies needed to support the development of effective team processes, but some do not, and the consequences for patient care and staff morale are highly negative. Psychologists like Kelly are potentially well placed to promote the development of more effective processes, usually by using their knowledge of systems rather than by using positions of formal authority. Again this requires effective communication skills and convincing application of psychological knowledge in order to achieve such influence. Health care organizations, like all organizations, can unwittingly become mired in poor practice without really being aware of how it developed; the result can be troubled teams, unhappy staff, and poorly served patients.

In working with a troubled team it is easy to attribute the problem to the personality of one or more individual team members. However, all too often this is an example of the 'fundamental attribution error': the pervasive human but mistaken tendency to locate causes in individuals, rather than in structures or processes. Instead psychologists should attempt to assess structural, process, and individual sources of the conflict, in the knowledge that many team problems develop from poor structures and procedures rather than from particularly difficult or disruptive individuals. Building the power and influence of enabling systems is normally much more successful than attempting to decrease the power and influence of inhibiting forces, or attempting to 'sort out' difficult colleagues who seem to be almost inevitably present in many teams. As we know from elsewhere in psychology, supporting and encouraging the positive usually works much better than focusing on the negative.

14.4 **Building psychologically informed care through consultancy**

An alternative, and growing, role for clinical psychologists working in teams is the provision of consultation to colleagues who are working with demanding individuals or in very challenging situations, for example for those working in palliative care or forensic services, or in services for people diagnosed with personality disorder. Here the clinical psychologist works as either a facilitator for team discussions or a consultant in the development of new ways of approaching the clinical problem. Consultancy can be formal (after an agreement is made regarding who will provide exactly what form of help for whom for how long), or informal, whereby advice is provided ad hoc as required, for example by adding helpful comments or reflections to team discussions or meetings. In either case, the psychologist uses their specialist skills and knowledge to help others to fulfil their specific clinical tasks.

Ian, working as a psychologist in a harm minimization team, wanted to help his team to respond more positively to some particularly challenging behaviour presented by Holly, a young woman with alcohol dependence. Ian's aim was to help team members respond constructively to Holly, rather than to act punitively or withdraw from engagement with her. Ian asked the team to note down, and reflect on, their interpretations of Holly's behaviour and the feelings it evoked. Team members expressed great frustration towards Holly, and their interpretations were that she was 'manipulating' the team and 'testing their boundaries'. They saw their responses as necessary in order to 'show her who's in charge'. After they had expressed their frustrations, Ian respectfully introduced new ways of thinking about Holly developed from a psychological formulation which linked her behaviour to a core belief that she is unlovable, and a consequent tendency to reject others before they reject her. Based on this new understanding, the team started to feel greater empathy towards Holly, reduced their attributions of blame, and began to find a way forward in resolving the problem.

   Anna worked with nursing staff in an inpatient rehabilitation unit for people who have had a spinal injury. Anna noticed that the staff were in constant disagreement and effectively split between some of the staff who felt very sympathetically towards a particular patient, Bill, whilst other members of staff were convinced that he was making more of his injuries than was necessary and felt irritated by his requests for apparently special treatment and privileges. It emerged that Bill had a particularly difficult family background prior to his injury, in part leading to his sense of deprivation and abandonment in the present crisis. By listening to these accounts and trying to draw up a comprehensive formulation, Anna, acting as a consultant, enabled staff to see how they had inadvertently recreated in the unit an unhelpful opportunity for Bill to distract himself from his need to face up to changes that would become necessary in his life given his injury, by apparently forging close relationships with some staff and disparaging others. This had been a long-standing unhelpful pattern in Bill's life prior to the injury, exacerbated by his current high levels of anxiety and depression.

Ian's example demonstrates how psychological formulation can help to illuminate a way forward (why Holly was acting as she was), and to encourage the team to move away from simply labelling her behaviour or potentially adding to her problems by misunderstanding or inadvertently reinforcing her dysfunctional reactions. Similarly, by enabling the staff to understand the behaviour through a psychological formulation, Anna helped staff to work together to address Bill's psychological needs, rather than ignoring, or even worsening, them.

14.5 **The contribution of supervision**

Psychologists may also take on the role of clinical supervisor to staff from a variety of professional groups, thereby enabling greater numbers of patients to benefit from psychologically informed treatment. Supervision has a primary educational function, but it also enhances services to clients by improving supervisee competence and providing an opportunity for restorative support for the clinician, that is, giving the supervisee encouragement and a chance to off-load emotions. Good clinical supervision (which should be distinguished from consultancy) requires the establishment of a trusting and reliable supervisory relationship, just as good psychotherapy requires the existence of a positive therapeutic alliance. Although they are different processes, supervision and psychotherapy have key professional skills in common, such as the ability to focus on the needs of the patient/supervisee, establish boundaries, provide an opportunity for reflection, suggest a framework (but not take over), contribute to learning and confidence, and ensure the wellbeing of the patient. Supervision may be provided in groups or individually, with the central aim of supporting the quality of each supervisee's work. Some models of supervision focus on the development of specific techniques for use with a specific client, such as how to ask Socratic questions or set homework tasks in a specific case, while others focus more on needs expressed by the supervisee, and on the development of confidence or the provision of appropriate personal support when undertaking emotionally demanding work.

Almost all clinical professional groups now require practitioners at all levels to participate in on-going supervision, although different professions have different requirements, so some flexibility is needed. A related role is mentoring or coaching, which involves, for example, a senior psychologist providing the time and opportunity for a more junior psychologist or health care practitioner to discuss and think through difficulties at work and to explore options. Whatever the model, provision of supervision and mentoring gives an opportunity for psychologists to increase psychological awareness and to promote psychologically informed ways of working across a large number of staff or patients, which in numerical terms should have a greater impact than providing one-to-one clinical work would ever be able to accomplish.

14.6 **Leadership in clinical psychology**

Effective organizations need effective leaders, although this does not imply there has to be just one leader or that leaders should hold the sole responsibility for organizational effectiveness. The days are thankfully gone where leadership was considered an in-born quality, normally reserved for the first-born sons of the upper classes (or, in a health care context, for senior doctors), whose role it was to tell others, from a position of unquestioned authority, how to conduct their lives or work. Modern concepts of leadership recognize the importance of situation and relationships, and that leadership styles need to change in changing contexts. More importantly, leaders now tend to acknowledge the importance of followers, seeing that leaders and followers need to work closely together to meet their shared objectives. Leadership should also be distinguished from management, although the two are often interdependent and may co-exist in one person. At its simplest, leadership involves setting the direction of an organization and ensures commitment to its vision, while management ensures that processes and structures are in place to deliver that vision: 'Management is efficiency in climbing the ladder of success; leadership determines whether the ladder is leaning against the right wall' (Covey, 1994, p. 101).

Within clinical psychology it is possible to distinguish two mains forms of leadership: *clinical leadership*, which concerns the ability of psychologists to influence the care provided for patients and the achievement of positive clinical outcomes; and *organizational leadership*, which concerns the effective organization of services and functions within health care services, and which aims to shape the organization's future direction. A primary aim of clinical leadership is to improve patient outcomes, and it involves the psychologist in helping other staff members to develop their skills and knowledge when working with patients, as well as in shaping services to improve the quality of clinical work provided. Therefore, all psychologists who work in clinical teams have a role to play in providing *clinical leadership* to a greater or lesser extent, by promoting the value and importance of considering psychological issues in the formulation and treatment of service users, by contributing to team discussions and plans, or by carrying out audits and research that highlight (for example) the need for improved services for particular groups of people. Clinical leadership shares psychological ideas so that more patients can benefit, and it can be provided through clinical supervision, team discussions, consultation, or mentoring, as described in other chapters of this text. The skills needed to provide such leadership are, first, competence in the tasks required; second, the skills to persuade others of the value of the new way of thinking or behaving; and third, the capacity to enable others to develop competence and confidence themselves.

As they become more experienced, clinical psychologists are also increasingly likely to be in positions that involve providing *organizational leadership*, for example by taking senior roles in a multi-disciplinary team, or by leading a group of psychologists within a larger organization. Organizational leadership is about setting direction and strategy, and is likely to involve a formal position of authority. Not all psychologists wish to take on formal leadership roles, but the risks of not doing so are that other professional groups will assume greater responsibility for determining the future of health care provision, as well as for the development of the profession itself, which may well have a negative impact on the quality of care provided, as well as on the future opportunity of psychologists to develop professionally.

Whether it is clinical or organizational leadership, one helpful definition that reflects how many people, including clinical psychologists, currently understand the concept of leadership, is that provided by Yukl (2002): '*the process of influencing others to understand and agree about what needs to be done and how it can be done effectively, and the process of facilitating individual and collective efforts to accomplish the shared objectives*' (p. 7). Another current definition is that it involves taking responsibility for enabling others to achieve shared purpose in the face of uncertainty (Gantz, 2011). A related concept is that of the 'authentic leader', who has self-awareness, maximizes their strengths, and understands their weaknesses, to help others to see the big picture (George, 2003).

As all these definitions show, the ability to work collaboratively and from a shared value base is implicit and central to leadership, as is the intention to work closely with others towards the establishment of a shared goal or vision. There are a number of skills and competencies required for effective performance of such a role, including the ability to form effective relationships, the willingness to take opportunities to develop ideas and establish priorities, and the confidence to take action to achieve results. An additional competence is the ability to facilitate the development of others, and to motivate others in making changes despite anxiety or resistance. This is a far cry from the notion of leader as autocrat, which would understandably be off-putting to many psychologists whose values strongly tend towards collaboration and respect for others. Instead these competencies clearly overlap and build on those already held by clinical psychologists. The ability to 'understand and agree about what needs to be done and how it can be done effectively, and the process of facilitating individual and collective efforts to accomplish the shared objectives' is, of course, a core psychotherapeutic skill, together with the ability to think clearly, prioritize, and problem solve.

Having said that, organizational leadership additionally involves an ability to address systemic and organizational issues, to address and use power, and to work effectively with colleagues from other disciplines in committees or in project groups. This, in turn, tends to require an ability to engage with the practical demands of running any organization, including attendance at or chairing committee meetings, speaking up and standing behind decisions, understanding budgets, grappling with operational issues, and developing strategy. To thrive in such positions the psychologist needs to develop a certain degree of political astuteness and organizational sophistication (sometimes defined as the ability to rock the boat without falling out of it) and this can best be developed through experience, observation, and help from a mentor. Political astuteness means, as far as possible, developing the ability to identify the power holders who can make the important decisions within the organization, understanding their position, working out how your views fit in with their position, finding allies, planning, and being clear about strategy and tactics. It also requires self-awareness and energy, as well as commitment to a clear vision of what all this work is aiming to achieve.

No psychologist should ever attempt to work in organizations in isolation, since bringing about change is demanding and potentially demoralizing. It is vital not to fall for what Georgiades and Phillimore (1975) ingeniously called 'the myth of the hero-innovator'. This is someone who, fired up with good intentions and beliefs, charges enthusiastically into an organization, trying to bring about instant improvements, but is immediately and unceremoniously rejected, since, as Georgiades and Phillimore say: 'organisations such as schools and hospitals will, like dragons, eat hero-innovators for breakfast' (p. 315). Instead psychologists need to think and assess systemically and carefully, ensure adequate timescales for any change to become embedded (which can take many years in some instances), always work with support and never alone, and aim to protect other people who are also trying to bring about positive changes.

Both the Division of Clinical Psychology (DCP) of the British Psychological Society and the NHS Institute for Innovation and Improvement have drawn up frameworks in order to support and promote the development of effective health care leadership. These include the following:

- Demonstrating personal qualities (e.g. developing self-awareness, integrity, and the ability to recognize the impact of oneself on others).

- Working with others (e.g. developing networks and working with teams).

- Managing services (e.g. planning and managing the performance of others towards agreed goals).

- Improving services (e.g. assessing and making sure as a minimum that services ensure patient safety, as well as evaluating the effectiveness of any services provided).

Achieving all of this is obviously not a task for clinical psychologists in the very early stages of their career. Nonetheless it is heartening to see that the notion of leadership espoused here is strongly influenced by psychological concepts, includes integrity and sensitivity to others, and prioritizes the need for values-based work.

The DCP framework (2010) also provides guidance on the leadership competencies to be expected at different stages of the psychologist's career, and point to the usefulness of psychological theory or concepts for aspiring leaders. Leadership tasks for a newly qualified psychologist, for example, include promoting psychological approaches in teams and care settings, being a role model, providing supervision, mentoring peers and others, undertaking leadership or research projects, identifying opportunities for service development, developing political and organizational awareness, and understanding the impact of self on the wider system.

14.7 **Conclusion**

Much good psychological work takes place indirectly through collaboration with others. It is therefore vital to take time to build relationships and understand the wider system, even when there are pressures to treat or assess more individual patients, either in order to meet targets set by others or to satisfy personal interests. Applications of psychological theory and knowledge can contribute enormously to the quality of services experienced by patients, and it is therefore essential that psychologists develop good team working and leadership competencies. Only then can clinical psychologists truly make a substantial contribution to health care, as well as being assured of the healthy long-term future of the profession.

References

Covey, S. (1994). *The Seven Habits of Highly Effective People: Powerful Lessons in Personal Change*. Simon & Schuster, London.

Division of Clinical Psychology (2010). *Leading Psychological Services*. British Psychological Society, Leicester.

Gantz, M. (2011). Leading change: leadership, organisation and social movements. In N. Nohria and R. Khurana (eds), *Handbook of Leadership Theory and Practice*, pp. 527–586. Harvard Business School Press, Boston.

George, B. (2003). *Authentic Leadership*. Jossey Bass, San Fransisco.

Georgiades, N.H. and Phillimore, L. (1975). The myth of the hero innovator and alternative strategies for organisational change. In C.C. Kiernan and F.P. Woodford (eds), *Behaviour Modification with the Severely Retarded*. Associated Scientific Publishers, Amsterdam.

West, M.A. (2004). *Effective Teamwork: Practical Lessons from Organizational Research*. BPS Blackwell, Leicester.

Yukl, G. (2002). *Leadership in Organisations*, 5th edn. N.J. Prentice Hall, Englewood Cliffs.

Chapter 15

Working with cultural diversity

Kamel Chahal

15.1 Introduction

'We see as the basis of our humanity the fact that we are all ultimately the same. We are vulnerable. We are embodied creatures. We feel hunger, thirst, fear, pain. We reason, hope, dream and aspire. These things are all true and important. But we are also different. Each landscape, language, culture, community is unique. Our very dignity as persons is rooted in the fact that none of us—not even genetically identical twins—is exactly like any other.' (Jonathan Sacks, 2002, p. 47.)

15.2 Race, ethnicity, culture, and diversity

The terms race, ethnicity, and culture are often used interchangeably, although their meanings are significantly different. The Oxford English Dictionary defines race as *'A large group of people with common ancestry and inherited physical characteristics'*. Race is now accepted to be a redundant concept due to the faulty assumption that racial groupings remain static.

Ethnicity derives from the Greek word 'ethnos' meaning 'a people' and defines a person as belonging to a group with a certain shared set of characteristics, including ancestral and geographical origins, social and cultural traditions, religion, languages, and history. Ethnic groups are perceived as transactional, shifting, and essentially impermanent, implying a degree of choice which 'race' precludes. Ethnicity is essentially self-defined, reflecting how a person perceives him/herself and captures the diversity of their subjective position, experiences, and history.

Culture is a social construct that profoundly impacts the way people perceive and make sense of the prominent social world(s) they experience and inhabit. It is situational, flexible, and continually evolving in response to the demands and pressures both of its own internal process-es and through its contact with the varieties of other social worlds indi-viduals also encounter. Culture is all-pervasive, it being communicated both verbally and symbolically and encompassing the everyday as well as the esoteric. All cultures have their own health beliefs and patterns of help-seeking behaviour, which may be historically linked to particular religious or philosophical views of personhood and the body.

Diversity as a concept sets out to respect qualities and conditions that are different from one's own and are outside the group(s) to which one belongs, yet pertain in other individuals and groups. These include age, ethnicity, class, gender, physical abilities, race, sexual orientation, reli-gious status, gender expression, educational background, geographical location, income, marital status, parental status, and work experiences. These categories of difference can be fluid and are therefore always best self-identified.

15.3 Social contexts: individualistic and collectivistic societies

Individualism predominates in the Western world. Individualism views the individual as the primary unit of reality and of ultimate importance, each person being influenced by other individuals and co-operating with them, building on their ideas and achievements, but with the emphasis always on the person themselves holding the most signifi-cance. As such, individualism sees society as a collection of individuals, rather than something over and above them. The 'self' is conceptualized as the thinking, feeling, and observing originator, controller, and creator of behaviour with full responsibility for self, and, as such, is expected to be autonomous. Relationships are seen as the interaction of individu-als within larger social units that exist primarily to meet the needs of the individual. Biological explanations for psychological and physical health predominate (e.g. genetic predispositions, organic deficits, and chemical imbalances), the origin of which is always within the individ-ual who is thus largely held personally responsible for whatever does not function. The belief that one's behaviour is controlled by something or someone else is often defined as psychopathology and understood to occur through projection, irresponsibility, externalization, and/or as delusional.

Collectivism predominates in the non-Western world and maintains that the social group is an entity in its own right, acting upon people through group influences. The emphasis is on stringent co-operation and adherence to the norms and expectations of the group, community, and/or nation, which are seen as the primary unit of reality. This view does not deny the reality of the individual but rather sees individual identity as essentially constituted through relationships with others in the group. Illness in collectivist thinking is often attributed to combinations and interactions between various worlds, with a higher degree of fluidity accepted between the supernatural and the social. Models of explanation for ill health include others being held responsible for illness due to interpersonal malice (e.g. evil eye, witchcraft) with a possibility of supernatural causality, in which illness may be a divine punishment from spirits and gods for neglecting religion or participating in immoral behaviour. On this basis, neither Western remedies nor herbal cures are considered effective, actual cure involving atonement and acknowledgement of sin, often through processes that involve ritualized cleansing.

15.4 **A rapidly changing world**

Global mobility has increased dramatically over recent decades, driven by factors ranging from escaping conflict and persecution to ease of travel between countries allowing people to seek more favourable economic conditions elsewhere. As a result, many countries have and continue to become increasingly diverse in their ethnic and cultural composition.

This is well illustrated by the England and Wales census data (Office for National Statistics, 2011) which reported that a fifth of the population now have an ethnicity that is not white British; 13% of the population having been born outside of the UK, with nearly half of this number having arrived within the last 10 years. Ethnic minority populations have typically been located in more densely populated urban areas; over half the population of London defining their ethnicity as other than white British, a third of whom are born outside the UK. Ethnically mixed relationships have increased by 47% since 2001; two million households now consist of complex and multiple shared identities, thus illustrating the complexity of changing allegiances between groups and cultures as migrants increasingly intermix.

15.5 **Refugees and asylum seekers**

Whilst there is a great deal of diversity amongst migrants, refugees, and asylum seekers in the UK and around the world, they also share a range of common experiences. These populations are especially vulnerable to developing mental health problems due to the range of traumatic events experienced as a consequence of famine, war, and/or persecution in their home country. The loss of homeland, family, friends, and personal identity are all significant precipitants for the development of mental health problems, including symptoms of post-traumatic stress disorder (PTSD) and depression. Adapting to a host society that may be hostile or indifferent, with very different values, culture, religion, and language, can result in an increasing sense of isolation and marginalization, which further impacts on mental health.

15.6 **Racism**

'Racism is a system of dominance, power and privilege based on racial group designations; rooted in the historical oppression of a group defined or perceived by dominant group members as inferior, deviant, or undesirable and occurring in circumstances where members of the dominant group create or accept their societal privilege by maintaining structures, ideologies, values and behaviour that have the intent or effect of leaving the non-dominant group members relatively excluded from power, esteem, status, and/or equal access to societal resources.' (Harrell, 2000, p. 43.)

The Macpherson Report (1999) investigated the persistent lack of appropriate police response to the murder of the black teenager Stephen Lawrence in London in 1993. It became a watershed moment in the UK due to its identification of institutional racism as an extensive problem within all British public services. Macpherson's report defined institutional racism as: 'The collective failure of an organisation to provide an appropriate and professional service to people because of their colour, *culture or ethnic origin. It can be seen or detected in processes, attitudes and behaviour which amount to discrimination through unwitting prejudice, ignorance, thoughtlessness and racial stereotyping.'* (p. 28.)

15.7 **Ethnicity and mental health services**

Research in the UK over the past two decades has identified consistent differences in the pathways to care between the white British population and those from diverse black and minority ethnic (BME) backgrounds. African Caribbean individuals have been recognized to be four times more likely than their white British counterparts to be subject to compulsory psychiatric detention, often following contact with the police; they receive higher doses of medication and are often managed through the use of physical restraint and seclusion whilst in hospital. In contrast, white British patients are more likely to access mental health services via their GP and to be offered psychological therapies as part of subsequent care (Fernando, 2003).

The results of the final annual 'Count me in' census conducted in March 2010 across England and Wales (Care Quality Commission and National Mental Health Development Unit, 2011) identified that 23% of the people receiving inpatient care were of BME origin, although BME communities comprise less than 9% of the population. Black mental health service users have described their experiences within mental health services as *'inhumane, unhelpful and inappropriate'*, stating that they have been treated with a lack of respect by services that are *'not accessible, welcoming, relevant or well integrated into the community'* (Keating *et al.*, 2002, p. 9). Stereotypical perceptions of black people were identified by service users to be a consequence of racism, cultural ignorance, stigma, and anxieties associated with mental illness, all of which act to undermine the way in which mental health services assessed and responded to the needs of these communities.

Extensive research in both the UK and USA has shown that BME groups are generally excluded from, marginalized, and either unable or unwilling to access mainstream clinical psychology services. The issues of accessibility and acceptability of psychological services for these communities have been recognized to be complex and interrelated.

15.8 **Accessibility of psychological services**

One of the fundamental principles of the British NHS is that services are equally accessible and available to all members of the community, yet service users from BME communities are significantly more likely than their white peers to be prescribed medication rather than to be offered talking therapies. GPs are less likely to refer African-Caribbean adults to secondary mental health services unless they are at crisis point, despite frequent GP attendances, resulting in common mental health problems going underdiagnosed, with ramifications for their longer-term mental health. Although recommendations since 1995 have been made for psychological therapies to become more accessible and culturally acceptable, problems of accessibility are still known to exist within all levels of mental health care. Language barriers and stereotypes of BME people as not being 'psychologically minded' are also significant factors in hindering access to psychological services.

BME communities themselves remain sceptical about the use of psychology services due to their perception that these services are unable to adequately understand and work with issues that frequently affect them, such as racism, disadvantage, discrimination, oppression, and experiences of social isolation. This 'cultural mistrust' relates to concerns that psychological distress may be misunderstood, misconstrued, and/or pathologized, with the individuals' own beliefs severely compromised or undermined. Negative past experiences, an insufficient awareness of existing services and what they offer, together with fears that confidentiality may be compromised are all known to play a significant role in determining the effective accessibility of services.

15.9 **Acceptability of psychological services**

Acceptability of psychological services refers to the extent to which interventions offered actually meet the needs of individuals and communities in a way that is experienced as congruent with their culture, and with which they are able to effectively engage.

Western models of therapy privilege ideas of independence and self-actualization as being indicative of good mental health, the focus being on the individual as the most important unit, reflecting the values and norms held within Western individualistic societies. In contrast, non-Western collectivist cultures focus more on notions of spirituality and communality, seeing the individual as secondary to family and community. For psychological therapy to be culturally appropriate it has to understand and incorporate service users' culture-bound notions of mental health into assessment, formulation, and intervention.

15.10 Cultural context of mainstream psychology

As described in Chapter 1, the roots of psychology, as both a distinct scientific discipline and a field of practice, derive from Western Europe and North America and as a consequence are deeply imbued with Western discourse. Mainstream psychology has been criticized for employing categories and models based on research with an assumed set of valid universal norms, although these norms are actually derived from very limited segments of unrepresentative populations' (e.g. American undergraduates). These universalist assumptions have been justified through the belief that we as humans are all fundamentally alike in our significant psychological functions, and that cultural and social contexts do not affect the 'deep' or 'hardwired' structures of the mind. Hence these categories and standards have been seen as suitable for 'measuring', understanding, and evaluating the characteristics of other diverse populations. This knowledge is then applied to wider diverse populations with 'hypotheses' being tested and 'instruments validated', on the presumption that they are able to measure universal social and psychological characteristics, even though the methods and standards are derived primarily from selective Western populations.

15.11 What about clinical psychology?

Clinicians who have not yet examined their personal biases regarding difference may collude unintentionally with a 'culture-blind'/colour-blind approach to clinical practice. This culture and colour blindness results in unexplored cultural biases through the denial, distortion, and minimization of the impact of cultural factors, prejudice, and racism on the person's psychological and mental health (Constantine and Wing, 2007).

Clinical psychology can be criticized for the dominance of a 'one-size-fits-all' linear dualistic deficit model, lacking in multi-cultural perspectives. Issues related to diversity and social inequalities have often been inadequately addressed especially in research, where categories are imposed without an understanding of what the pertinent issues are for the communities being investigated. This exclusion of diversity in favour of homogeneity and conformity to the accepted norms of Euro-centric societies results in the maintenance of a status quo, and is illustrative of wider social control thorough the reproduction and amplification of discriminatory practices which are institutionally racist.

15.12 Cultural competency: what actually is it?

Working collaboratively with clients requires the ability to remain curious and not make assumptions, through recognition and owning of one's own biases, prejudices, and stereotypes. Cultural competency involves also understanding the impact of one's own value base and culture by appreciating the power imbalances that arise due to pre-existing societal inequalities. Through an understanding of these issues and how they impact on therapeutic encounters, clinical psychologists can become more consciously aware of their own levels of understanding and effectively manage and further develop their cultural competency within supervision.

Since the emotional impact of clinical practice and the learning required to achieve cultural competency can feel both immense and threatening, there can often arise an unconscious tendency to avoid the need for cultural competency. Consequently little importance may be placed on working with cultural difference, resulting in culturally blind ways of working which actively disregard the importance of the clients' perspective on their own beliefs and lived experience.

Cultural competency is therefore not about having as much detailed information about a particular culture or people as possible, but is rather about acquiring a full understanding of the person free from misconceptions that may result from one's own ethnocentricity, assumptions, and stereotypes. It requires appreciation, and effective management of, the impact of the unequal distribution of power held within the therapeutic relationship which invariably accompanies the professional status held by clinical psychologists, since these can parallel the social inequalities that exist in the wider environment.

Irena Papadopoulos and colleagues' (1998) comprehensive model for the development of cultural competency in health professionals consists of four stages:

1 Awareness: an examination of the clinician's own personal value base and beliefs in order to understand the nature and construction of their own cultural identity, and its influence on their own health beliefs and practices.

2 Knowledge: an understanding of health beliefs and behaviours, often enhanced through meaningful contact with people from diverse communities, thus providing an increased appreciation of the problems they may experience as well as their similarities and differences. Inequalities in health that exist within and between cultural groups are often the result of structural forces in society. The power of health care professionals and the role of medicine in contributing to these structural forces, and hence to social control, need to be far better appreciated and acknowledged.

3 Sensitivity: how clinicians view the people they help. Truly collaborative partnerships are an essential component of culturally sensitive practice since they reduce the use of oppressive forms of power. Clients can be enabled to challenge power and have real choices made available to them through a process of facilitation, advocacy, and negotiation, all of which can only be achieved on a foundation of trust, respect, and empathy.

4 Competence: this final stage requires the synthesis and application of previously gained awareness, knowledge, and sensitivity within the practical skills of assessment and clinical diagnosis. The most important component here is the ability to recognize and challenge overt and covert racism and other forms of discriminatory and oppressive practice.

15.13 **Context analysis**

A 'culturally blind' approach can result in potentially complex problems, this lack of awareness and understanding of differences in cultural contexts being particularly problematic when psychologists from individualistic backgrounds are working with clients from collectivist communities. For example, when viewed through an individualistic lens, the interdependence with others that is fundamentally the central premises of a collective culture can easily be perceived and pathologized as enmeshment, overinvolvement, and dependency. Similarly a lack of language to describe emotional states and a disregard for the self can easily be misjudged as a lack of 'insight' or not being 'psychologically minded', whilst the concept of enduring suffering and a sense of fatalism that can be an accepted part of the collective mindset can be misinterpreted as passivity, helplessness, and hopelessness.

Context analysis sets out to understand the cultural construction of social and personal meanings without pre-assuming knowledge of the similarities and differences that exist. It proposes three dynamic and complex interrelated systems that are mutually formed and co-created within a set of circular relationships:

1 The individual with their distinctive biological make-up and unique history of experiences, constituted in part by their roles and statuses within one or more social systems from which they derive their personal meanings and identity.

2 Immediate social structures consisting of the family and other institutions within the culture (e.g. religious organizations) which specify the ideal of appropriate relationships, roles, privileges, and associated expectations. Codes of expected conduct, such as those between various categories of family members, exist in all cultures and are often based on hierarchical relationships with recognized obligations, privileges, constraints, and prescribed patterns of communication, all of which impact on individual development.

3 Culture in its symbolic sense. A person throughout their development participates in social structures that are deeply embedded with culturally based symbols and values from which he/she derives their

personal meanings. Through interaction with others from birth, a person becomes the carrier and exemplar of cultural meaning, ensuring that their engagement with cultural symbols and systems remains continuous, intimate, and involved. This results in various roles and locations within social systems with attached contingencies, resources, obligations, opportunities, and constraints. All diverse cultures have their own local theories about social thought, psychology, and emotion, developmental psychology, child rearing, and cognitions, which can go unrecognized by Western-based social or natural sciences. These differences are frequently related to gender, age, kin, and close relationships and are held as common knowledge; accepted as obvious to the person and family, but often opaque to outsiders.

15.14 Community psychology

Community psychology is a framework of psychological intervention that views psychological problems within their social and political contexts, rather than simply as individualized forms of distress. It aims to intervene at a community level by employing strategies that empower community members to work together and develop social relations that have productive benefits and to actively reduce the individual's sense of isolation and helplessness within their lived situation. As such, community psychology is an approach that can successfully begin to overcome the issues of accessibility and acceptability of psychological services by engaging diverse communities more collectively. Developing partnerships with voluntary sector organizations that have a social inclusion agenda and recognize the impact of social inequalities often provides a sound framework for such work.

15.15 Use of interpreters

The use of interpreters can allow clinical psychologists to overcome language barriers between themselves and clients. Interpreters have complex roles within mental health services; they are required to elicit information, simplify messages, and translate language, including culturally based metaphors, psychiatric terms, and non-verbal communication. Interpreters are often expected to introduce information on service context as well as on the service user's cultural context, whilst clarifying messages, and elaborating on and explaining roles and norms of the interaction, organization, and community. Inevitably they selectively filter out and translate information in order to maximize how much is correctly understood by all involved. Prior knowledge of mental health and psychology is important, since psychiatric terms, due to their origins within Western science, may not actually exist in the language and culture into which they require translation. Interpreters' roles may additionally expand to that of cultural advisors and brokers; they may effectively become advocates on behalf of service users, and at times the facilitators of important policy-making decisions through link-work with communities. As such, services employing interpreters need to appreciate their prior experience, expertise, and levels of training (Tribe and Ravel, 2003).

15.16 **Religion and spirituality**

Religious practices and spirituality are normally deeply rooted in diverse and collective cultures and can be central to many people's daily lives. Psychologists exploring religious beliefs need to remain open-minded and curious about the relationships people have with God and spirituality. This requires a conscious awareness of one's own belief system whilst displaying a genuine willingness to want to learn and reflect on clients' self-perception in relation to aspects of faith and spirit. Illness can negatively affect faith, which in itself might be very important to the person's healing. It is often useful to link with spiritual leaders such as Imams and priests who also have knowledge of mental health issues.

15.17 **Case example**

Rabina, a 22-year-old, recently married Muslim woman, was admitted to an acute psychiatric ward. She was diagnosed with psychotic depression after presenting as very tearful, isolated, guarded, and paranoid. Rabina had migrated from Pakistan the previous year to live with her new husband and his family; she spoke limited English. Rabina believed her problems had resulted from 'nazar' (the evil eye), whilst her family believed that she had been possessed by a 'jinn' (a spirit) and had consulted a religious leader about her prior to her admission. Staff reported that her daily contact with her in-laws was problematic since she would only communicate through them and would only eat food that they bought in. Staff were concerned that, on discharge, she would return to what they viewed as an 'enmeshed and over-involved' family and therefore advised Rabina and her husband to move away from the parental home.

The team clinical psychologist constructed a context analysis with Rabina and her sister-in-law via an Urdu interpreter. Questions included:

- What are your health beliefs and cultural explanations regarding the effects of 'nazar' and 'jinn' on both physical and mental health?

- What are the similarities and differences in the expected codes of conduct for recently married woman with regard to roles, responsibilities, and behaviours among rural Pakistani families compared to your family's expectations in the UK?

- What are the issues related to stigma and shame that Rabina and the family have concerns about?

Rabina shared her experiences of dislocation following her move from rural Pakistan to England following her arranged marriage to the family's only son, whom she had met only briefly before the wedding. He was the youngest of five siblings, all of whom were bilingual and born in Britain. Rabina's parents, siblings, and extended family all still lived in Pakistan. Rabina stated that she expected to live with her husband's family for her entire married life whilst dutifully caring for his parents in their old age. She explained that, at present, her speech and demeanour were expected to be the most constrained in the family or she risked being seen as 'ill-bred' by both the family and community. However, she explained that as she got older and had children she expected to gain an increased status within the family, accompanied by more social freedoms.

Rabina recognized she had become psychologically vulnerable to depression when she had left behind her close-knit family, friends, and rural culture. Although Rabina described her new family as loving and supportive, she had experienced a considerable level of cultural dissonance as a consequence of family members' varying adherence to both Pakistani and British norms. She described their reactions and comments as difficult to understand and predict at times, and that this had left her feeling confused and emotionally isolated. After several sessions Rabina disclosed that she had "failed to carry a baby" as a consequence of 'nazar' which had been maliciously cast upon her. She had remained determined to keep her miscarriage a secret from the family, who had been unaware of her pregnancy. She held a deep-seated fear that were they to discover what had happened, she would be rejected as an inadequate daughter-in-law and wife and sent back to Pakistan so her husband could remarry. She had become very distressed and hostile when her husband had insisted that the family be informed of her miscarriage, and had accepted their conviction that she was possessed by a jinn as an explanation of her culturally unacceptable behaviour.

Given this context analysis, the explanations of 'jinn' and 'nazar', which had been labelled delusional by ward staff, were hence recognized to be culturally normative conceptualizations by Rabina and her family. Rabina also feared loss of the family 'izzat' (honour) as a consequence of community gossip about her difficulties and subsequent admission. The Urdu interpreter therefore reassured her prior to each session that all her health details would remain fully confidential.

Rabina eventually agreed to her formulation being shared with ward staff. The clinical psychologist, interpreter, and sister-in-law also met with ward staff and reflected on their understanding, assumptions, and expectations of the differences between British and Pakistani culture (e.g. arranged marriage and superstitious beliefs). Key questions designed to elicit changes in staff practice were:

- How could staff better understand, respect, and support the cultural strengths of Rabina and her family?
- How could staff overcome the fears and mistrust that Rabina and her family had of the ward and mental health services in general?
- How could any discriminatory and oppressive attitudes that had developed towards the family be acknowledged and challenged?

Staff were informed that families in Pakistan were expected to provide food for those in hospital and this culturally embedded practice was being used by the family to nurture and re-establish their relationships with Rabina.

Rabina reported that the psychologist's work was very helpful, in that it provided a reflective non-judgemental space within which she could openly explore the impact of her migration, the associated losses, her miscarriage, and her subsequent fears. She gained strength by reciting prayers and started to accept her miscarriage as God's will. 'Skype' contact was organized with Rabina's sister in Pakistan in whom she confided all of her emotional distress, including difficulties adjusting to life within a family acculturalized to British norms, and her subsequent fears of being rejected as not good enough after the miscarriage. As the medication improved her sleep, and following meetings with her husband and sisters-in-law, she started to emotionally process her loss without fear of being rejected or ostracised. Rabina also confided in her sister-in-law, who subsequently shared her own experience of miscarriage and reassured Rabina that her husband and family would accept and support her through her grief, and that the wider community would be sympathetic.

15.18 **Conclusion**

The experiences of psychological and mental health care are considerably different and frequently negative for diverse populations when compared to those of host communities. Clinical psychologists must take a culturally competent approach in their work with diverse populations in order to both develop their own individual practice and increase the accessibility and acceptability of psychological services to these communities.

References

Care Quality Commission and National Mental Health Development Unit (2011). *Count me in 2010* (<www.cqc.org.uk/sites/default/files/media/documents/count_me_in_2010_final_tagged.pdf>).

Constantine, G.C. and Wing, D.W. (2007). *Addressing Racism: Facilitating Cultural Competence in Mental Health and Educational Settings*. Wiley, New York.

Office for National Statistics (2011). *England and Wales Census* (<http://www.ons.gov.uk/ons/taxonomy/index.html?nscl=population>).

Fernando, S. (2003). *Cultural Diversity, Mental Health and Psychiatry: The Struggle Against Racism.* Brunner-Routledge, London.

Harrell, S.P. (2000). A multidimensional conceptualization of racism-related stress: implications for the well-being of people of colour. *American Journal of Orthopsychiatry,* **70** (1), 42–57.

Keating, F., Robertson, D., Francis, F., and McCulloch, A. (2002). *Breaking the Circles of Fear: A Review of the Relationship Between Mental Health Services and African and Caribbean Communities.* The Sainsbury Centre for Mental Health, London.

Macpherson, W. (1999). *The Stephen Lawrence Inquiry .* The Stationery Office, London.

Papadopoulos, I., Tilki, M., and Taylor, G. (1998). *Transcultural Care: Issues for Health Professionals.* Quay Books, Mark Allen, London.

Sacks, J. (2002). *The Dignity of Difference: How to Avoid the Clash of Civilizations.* Continuum, London.

Tribe, R. and Raval, H. (2003). *Working with Interpreters in Mental Health.* Brunner-Routledge, London.

Further reading

Lago, C. (2006). *Race, Culture and Counselling: The Ongoing Challenge,* 2nd edn. Open University Press, Maidenhead.

Chapter 16

The future of clinical psychology

David Murphy and Susan Llewelyn

16.1 Introduction

In this concluding chapter, we as Editors would like to offer some reflections on the future of clinical psychology as a profession, especially regarding its likely overall contribution to healthcare and its scope for further development. In doing so, we draw on the contents of the preceding chapters and on other recent literature from both within the discipline and elsewhere.

When discussing the potential future trajectory of clinical psychology as a discipline, it is perhaps helpful to start by considering how far it has come in a relatively short period. Clinical psychology has only existed as a distinct branch of psychology for just over a century. Moreover, in the UK, clinical psychology has only been officially recognized for about half that time; and in many other countries, for example Sri Lanka and Japan, it is still struggling to become established as an independent profession in its own right (De Zoysa, 2012; Shimoyama, 2011). Considered in this light, the development of the profession that has occurred across many countries, even since the first edition of this book was published in 1987, and the diversification in the range of areas illustrated in the chapters of this text, is nothing short of remarkable. Clinical psychology has become an accepted and indeed *expected* component of the system of care, for difficulties ranging from psychosis to chronic pain and throughout the lifespan, from neonates to those receiving palliative care. This fact is testament to the value that can be brought to bear by the practical application in clinical settings of empirically based psychological principles and methods. This is the same intrinsic value that the first clinical psychologists originally brought to clinical settings over one hundred years ago. Thus, Helen, Chris, Jana, and Alice, whose roles were described in Chapter 1, can be seen as extending the process of applying psychological principles to overcome psychological difficulties that Lightner Witmer began when helping children overcome specific language difficulties in Philadelphia, and which was continued later by Monte Shapiro's careful, scientific hypothesis-driven approach to assessment and treatment of a patient with social anxiety at the Maudsley Hospital, London.

Moreover, the potential value of applying psychological understanding to clinical situations has increased over the intervening years as the underlying explanatory models have evolved and new forms of psychological application have been developed. Figure 16.1 shows the dramatic rise over this time in the number of published scientific papers containing the term 'psychological'. This process is by no means at its end; indeed relative to the developments in medicine, our understanding of both the psychological mechanisms underlying clinical problems and the most effective approaches to intervention are still in their infancy. There remains therefore huge potential for further new advances and the extension of psychological approaches to novel domains of practice.

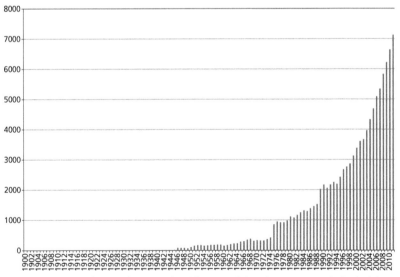

Fig. 16.1 Number of scientific journal articles containing the term 'psychological' in the title or abstract. (Data reproduced from The National Library of Medicine.)

It is, however, also important to recognize that the future course of clinical psychology as a profession will be dependent on the development of the wider health system within which it is based. Nowhere is this truer than in the UK where the birth of the profession was closely linked to the development of the National Health Service (NHS), in the immediate aftermath of the Second World War. Subsequently the major period of growth in clinical psychology also coincided with the period of the largest increase in health care spending in the history of the NHS, which in turn coincided with a period of sustained increase in gross domestic product (GDP) (see Figure 16.2).

Thus it seems highly probable that the development of the profession over the coming years will also be influenced by the wider social and political context, which includes changes in the global economic climate and a growing reluctance to pay tax. It is relevant here to note that public spending in most economies (including the UK) has recently

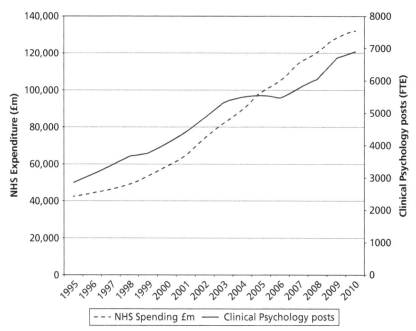

Fig. 16.2 Clinical psychology posts in the NHS (full-time equivalent) and total NHS expenditure (£ million). (Data reproduced from the NHS Census and Office of Health Economics.)

been significantly constrained relative to the substantial growth seen in earlier years, and that this is also likely to impact on the medium- and long-term evolution of the profession.

16.2 Likely future themes

During 2012, the World Economic Forum, in collaboration with McKinsey & Company, worked with a large sample of health system leaders, experts, and policy makers to envision what health care systems around the world would look like in 2040 (World Economic Forum, 2013). Their conclusions also have important implications for the future of clinical psychology. First, the report predicts that, despite constraints on finances, health care expenditure will continue to rise steadily over the coming years. The increase is predicted to result from proliferating demand on health care systems resulting from an ageing population, expansion of the number of those with long-term conditions, increasing public expectation, and lack of 'value-consciousness' among consumers. Second, the report predicts that this increase in demand on the system will be coupled with a continuing rise in unit costs of health care and sub-optimal allocation of resources, to create a major upward pressure on health care spending. Thus, for instance, predictions of required health care spending in the UK as a proportion of GDP range up to 14%, which represents a 50% increase from current levels. However, this is dwarfed by estimates for many other European countries, and in particular the USA, where estimates of health spending as a proportion of GDP range from 24% to 27%. It is clear that putting these predictions of demand for health care expenditure in the context of the prolonged period of slow economic growth that is forecast has very serious implications. Indeed, even where health care is considered a priority area and protected from cuts relative to other areas of spending, there will still be considerable financial pressure on health care systems for many years to come.

Next, the World Economic Forum report details the proposed response to this pressure from individual countries, and interestingly there is consensus from a range of different countries and health care systems about the four common themes that emerge:

1 Investing in *prevention*, particularly early interventions in child-hood and on behaviour change in adults to reduce demand from long-term health conditions.

2 *Efficient delivery* of health care, shifting health care out of hospitals into communities and utilizing skill mix in delivery.

3 *Increasing innovation* to increase efficiency by various means including increased competition.

4 Increasing focus on *outcome measurement* to permit focus of expenditure on maximizing value.

If correct, this analysis requires a major shift in orientation from all health care professions to respond effectively, and will present significant challenges, but also, we argue, considerable opportunities for the profession of clinical psychology.

Another important theme which must be noted is that, unlike some other areas of health care, the current availability of psychosocial interventions for those who are in need remains very limited indeed. Despite measures being taken in a variety of countries to increase access to mental health services, it is still the case that even in the most developed health systems, only a minority of people with diagnosable mental health problems currently receive any treatment at all. For instance, the 2007 Psychiatric Morbidity Survey in England (NHS Information Centre for Health and Social Care, 2007) found that only 24% of people with the most common mental health problems (anxiety and depression) were receiving any treatment. Moreover, of the minority who were receiving treatment, less than half were receiving any form of psychological intervention, and only a very small proportion of these appeared to be receiving input from clinical psychologists. Subsequently Kazdin and Rabbitt (2013) highlighted that, although the number of trained mental health professionals such as clinical psychologists has increased significantly in recent years, this number remains dwarfed by the numbers of the population who experience mental health problems. Large-scale prevalence studies, such as the National Co-Morbidity Study in the USA, have consistently shown that approximately 30% of the population meet the diagnostic criteria for at least one mental health problem in a

12-month period. This equates in the UK to nearly 19 million people with diagnosable mental health problems, whereas the total number of registered clinical psychologists in the UK is only 10,500 (source: Health and Care Professions Council (HCPC) registration statistics November 2012), equating to only one clinical psychologist for every 1,800 people with a mental health problem.

Moreover, even this limited access is markedly uneven across the population, and is often influenced by social-economic and ethnic characteristics, as discussed by Kamel Chahal in Chapter 15. How can clinical psychology respond to the demands of meeting population needs in the context of huge financial pressure on health systems? There is no doubt that this represents a significant challenge, and that traditional models of service delivery will be simply insufficient in the future.

16.3 Implications for clinical psychologists

In recent years a number of psychologists have attempted to begin to address such questions, and many of the chapters in this book include references to preliminary attempts to identify sustainable ways of working for the future. The following section of this chapter will consider how far clinical psychologists have been able to develop thoughtful responses to the issues identified here and how far we have yet to travel.

Prevention and early intervention

The role of clinical psychologists in prevention and early intervention is a theme that has been picked up in many of the chapters of this text. For example, Duncan Law in Chapter 4 highlights the benefits of early interventions with children in terms of both preventing suffering for affected individuals later in their lives and reducing the economic burden on society. Kessler *et al.* (2007) writing in a psychiatric journal also report that approximately 50% of all lifetime mental disorders have their onset by the mid-teens, and up to 75% by the mid-20s: many clinical psychologists have taken good heed of these types of data. The preventative theme is also evident in the work of psychologists providing psychological interventions for patients with long-term physical conditions such as diabetes or spinal injury. As described by Elenor McLaren and

David Murphy in Chapter 12, focusing on enhancing self-management can reduce deterioration in physical health later in life, resulting in not just maintenance of quality of life for the individual, but also reduced demand on the health system overall.

It should be noted that the areas of prevention and early intervention have been domains to which clinical psychologists have contributed from the very early days of applied psychological practice, and the profession should therefore be particularly well placed to respond to this challenge.

Efficient delivery/skills mix

In their conclusion to Chapter 3, John Cape and Yvonne Millar highlight the dilemma of psychologists in primary care in finding a balance between direct and indirect work. On the one hand, complex problems generally require an individualized formulation to be developed, based on careful assessment that is informed by multiple perspectives followed by a multi-modal approach to therapy, possibly delivered by a highly trained practitioner such as a clinical psychologist. On the other hand, the impact of a highly trained clinical psychologist may be greater if they are able to guide and support other staff to either deliver psychological interventions or utilize psychological principles in their own interactions with patients. This is well illustrated by Cape and Millar's example of consultation with a general practitioner regarding a patient with health anxiety, and is also demonstrated by studies on team working and supervision described in Chapter 14 by Susan Llewelyn. It is likely that demand for this kind of input from clinical psychologists will increase in the future.

The broader issue of what level of training and skills is required in the psychological workforce also runs through many of the other chapters, particularly those that describe England's Improving Access to Psychological Therapies (IAPT) programme. IAPT rests on the foundation of a stepped care approach, underpinned by a workforce comprising practitioners with a range of levels of training including psychological wellbeing practitioners, high-intensity therapists trained to deliver primarily CBT, and clinical psychologists. Highly trained clinical psychologists are an expensive resource in a health system and, if more people can be treated effectively by innovative approaches utilizing stepped care and a skill mix, then such approaches must be carefully considered, particularly in times of economic austerity.

Innovative approaches

The history of clinical psychology has demonstrated that developing new ways of assessing and treating people has had a major impact on improving the experience of many people with psychological distress. The revolution in our understanding of psychotic symptoms, for example, as described by John Hanna and Alison Brabban in Chapter 5, shows how painstaking theoretically based *psychological* thought about distress can lead to important innovations about how people are treated in practice. The major changes forecast for the future delivery of health care mean that innovative thought will become even more important.

Mary Jane Rotheram-Borus and colleagues (2012) at the University of California have recently highlighted the potential of 'disruptive innovation' in the delivery of psychological interventions. In contrast to traditional services which are designed to 'satisfy the full range of needs of the most demanding consumers', disruptive innovation, they state, 'provides a simple and less expensive alternative that meets most of the same needs for the *majority* of consumers' (p. 467). They argue that such services are more accessible, scalable, replicable, and sustainable. Examples of disruptive innovations in other sectors are the introduction of cash machines in the banking industry and mass distribution of generic reading glasses; such solutions meet the needs of the majority of consumers in most circumstances. Examples of disruptive innovation in psychological interventions might include use of brief self-management interventions, 'task shifting' from highly trained mental health professionals to paraprofessional workers, or 'task sharing' between different professionals, as well as increased use of technology and multi-media, e.g. web, mobile phone, to deliver interventions. Within this text, Chapter 13 by Katherine Carpenter and Andy Tyerman note the possibilities of utilizing new technology in neurorehabilitation, whilst in

Chapter 11, Nick Grey and Sue Clohessy outline novel ways of treating PTSD using computer games. The application of this type of thinking to clinical psychology is challenging and indeed potentially anxiety provoking; however, innovations that allow for a much greater reach of psychological services to a higher proportion of the general population also provide opportunities for clinical psychologists to utilize the full range of their competencies, and hence to play a leading role in integrated and comprehensive services within mental and physical health care in the future.

Improved measurement of outcomes and psychological wellbeing

The development of efficient, innovative, and accessible methods for the prevention and treatment of psychological distress rests both on the ability to accurately assess the outcomes of interventions in clinical practice and on the capacity to measure changes in the prevalence of psychological difficulties and their burden in the general population. We would argue that doing this in psychologically sophisticated ways is vital. In routine practice, valid standardized measures need to be employed consistently in order to monitor outcomes; for instance, analysis of outcomes from the IAPT programme in England clearly demonstrates that outcome assessment relying on conventional monitoring systems (e.g. at intake and discharge) as opposed to a session-by-session monitoring system is very likely to lead to overestimation of effectiveness, since people who terminate treatment prematurely generally have poorer than average outcomes.

Furthermore, if the long-term aim is to decrease the incidence and prevalence of psychological difficulties in the general population, there must be methods of measuring this directly. In their challenging paper 'Rebooting psychotherapy research and practice to reduce the burden of mental illness', American psychologists Kazdin and Blase (2011) argue that 'a national database is a fundamental step for decreasing the burden of mental illness because it provides a baseline to better establish the extent of the burden and whether there are any changes over time' (p. 29). In the UK there have been a number of developments that do contribute towards this, such as the Adult Psychiatric Morbidity Survey conducted in 1993, 2000, and 2007 by government agencies. These studies provide valuable information on the mental health of the nation but are, of course, subject to the limitations of the psychiatric diagnostic classification model, the drawbacks of which have been highlighted by clinical psychologists (e.g. the British Psychological Society (BPS) Division of Clinical Psychology, 2013). The 2011 Office for National Statistics survey for the first time included questions on wellbeing, including self-rated happiness and anxiety, while the UK Household Longitudinal Study of 40,000 UK households included measures of psychological health. Clinical psychologists, with their high-level training and competencies in research methods and psychometrics, are ideally placed to contribute to local, regional, and national assessment of psychological outcomes of this sort, which will likely play a crucial role in shaping health care delivery in the future. Until quite recently, however, clinical psychologists have tended not to see this type of work to be of major concern to them. We would suggest that this needs to change.

16.4 Clinical psychology practice and academic psychological science

The foundation of clinical psychology practice is, of course, the academic discipline of psychology, particularly its empirical emphasis. An undergraduate qualification in psychology is a prerequisite for clinical training, since both the knowledge base (for example in cognitive psychology, child development, and social psychology) and the epistemological base (the reliance on the empirical evidence base and the use of theory) together provide the underpinning and legitimacy for the profession's successes and steady growth in numbers over the past century. Indeed there is an on-going and integral need for the development of the science base of clinical psychology. There is always a risk that practitioners will become overintrigued by the art of therapy, for example, and will neglect measurement of outcomes. History has, however, clearly demonstrated that this, and separation from the discipline's empirical foundations, is likely to lead to a diminution of effectiveness and innovation, to the likely detriment of the profession and its users alike.

Yet the balance between science and practice has been questioned in recent years, particularly in the USA where a degree of tension has developed between the applied and the academic wings of the discipline. Indeed, in 2008 the Association of Psychological Science launched an alternative training accreditation scheme (to rival that run by the American Psychological Association (APA)) with the stated aim to '*promote high-quality, science-centred education and training in clinical psychology*' (Psychological Clinical Science Accreditation System (PCSAS) website). Currently over 60 training programmes, including Harvard and University of California, Los Angeles (UCLA), are accredited through this scheme. In his 2012 Monte Shapiro Award Lecture (BPS, 2012), Professor Graham Turpin, past chair of the Division of Clinical Psychology in the UK, argued that a gulf has also developed in the UK between the academic discipline of psychology and both the profession of clinical psychology as a whole and the clinical psychology training community. He argued for a reintegration of clinical psychology with its parent discipline, a more developed clinical-academic career pathway, and the collaborative development of clinically focused master's-level programmes which could prepare graduates for assistant psychologist roles within health care settings. This debate is currently ongoing.

Over recent years, there has also been controversy concerning both the necessity of research competencies featuring so prominently in clinical training, and the requirement for the entry-level qualification to be a doctorate. However, the fact that so many improvements in our understanding of psychological disorders and their treatment have arisen from research carried out by clinical psychologists, even since the last edition was published in 2006, must be testament to the relevance of research competencies. Whilst many clinical psychologists do not themselves undertake formal large-scale research after completing their training, they almost certainly play a key role in research and audit projects that are carried out in clinical services, as has been highlighted by many of the chapter authors of this book. Moreover, it is clear that in such a rapidly developing field, the skills needed to critically evaluate new findings, integrate them with extant theory and evidence, and apply them to clinical practice together make a crucial contribution to all clinical settings.

In addition, the generic base of clinical training has also been questioned. But while there may be some scope for specialization, there is a strong argument that in order to deliver and sustain effective clinical psychology practice and research across a career, psychologists must possess generic clinical knowledge and skills. We argue that current training provision is well equipped to deliver this, although how this question will be resolved in future is yet to be seen.

Finally, although psychologists' academic training highlights the impact of many complex factors on behaviour (from reinforcement schedules, to the effect of conformity, to the impact of child rearing practices and neuropsychology), we also need to understand the macro causes of behaviour (such as poverty and racism) and how we can best use this understanding to make sense of distress in our clients' lives and in health care itself. Examples of psychologists working to support clients in the face of ageism or racism have been included here (see Chapter 6 by Cath Burley and Chapter 15 by Kamel Chahal, respectively), and show how important it is that we do not practice in a vacuum, out of contact with the powerful social contexts that shape so many of the experiences of our clients and colleagues.

16.5 Ethics and values

Although we have argued for the importance of responding creatively to likely future needs, clinical psychologists must also keep in close touch with their essential value base. The fundamental ethical stance of the profession, that each unique individual has value and worth, underpins the nature of all interactions with others, as well as determining priorities. For example, the contributions made by clinical psychologists working with psychosis, as outlined by John Hanna and Alison Brabban (see Chapter 5), or with sex offenders, as outlined by Jeremy Tudway and Matthew Lister (see Chapter 9), demonstrate the importance of making close, respectful relationships with others. This is an aspect of clinical work where the input of psychologists has often been especially valued by service users. Likewise the emphasis by Steve Carnaby in Chapter 8 on working collaboratively and attentively with people with learning disabilities illustrates the profound conviction that paying close and respectful attention to each person is the key to good clinical outcomes, as well as being ethically the right thing to do. The reflective capacities of psychologists are also crucial here, ensuring that interventions are based on a thoughtful understanding of both self and the recipient of services, each within their particular social context.

16.6 Organizational skills and leadership

This chapter has argued that the challenges likely to face all healthcare providers in the future will be considerable and potentially radical. We will need good organizational and professional skills to navigate our place within the wider social context, and to ensure that members of the profession can simultaneously work effectively as clinicians to resolve human distress as required by their employing organizations, whist also maintaining their independence and critical capacity, for example by questioning the structures and conventions that contribute to the mental health problems experienced by members of that society. In many counties including the USA and the UK, for instance, choices about what therapies should be used for what condition are increasingly being made by public committees, not by independent professionals. In the USA, the government has contributed significantly to the debate over whether or not psychologists should have prescribing privileges, while in the UK, the state has played a growing role, such as determining whether or not psychologists can act as expert witnesses in Court. More importantly, in many countries, the state requires professionally qualified practitioners to register in order to make use of the title 'Clinical Psychologist', and thereby exerts a significant influence over the content and structure of training. This extension of control by others external to the profession seems likely to continue, so psychologists need to be both watchful and responsive. As argued by Susan Llewelyn in Chapter 14, what this also means is that there needs to be good leadership and political expediency, and a clear awareness of the advisability of making and nurturing allegiances with other professional groups such as medicine, nursing, and management.

16.7 **Conclusion**

In the words of the well-known management writer and lecturer Peter Drucker, '*The only thing we know about the future is that it is going to be different*'. It is, of course, inherently problematic to attempt to predict the future in any sphere and certainly clinical psychology is no different. However, it is possible to discern some clear currents that will influence the profession over the coming years.

First, the remarkable success of clinical psychology has been built on the application of empirically based psychological theories and methods to the assessment and management of clinical problems. As the underlying psychological knowledge base continues to develop, there will be increasing opportunities to innovate and refine the application of clinical psychology to existing and novel areas. However, the development of the profession cannot be seen in isolation from the health care system as a whole, whether this be publically funded (as in the UK's NHS) or insurance-based or self-funded as in other countries. There are clear challenges ahead for all health systems in the coming decades and these will inevitably impact on clinical psychology. There will be an increasing demand for services whilst overall resources, including workforce numbers, will remain broadly static in most developed economies; this will result in an increased drive for efficient and innovative delivery. In the UK, numbers of posts in the public health system will not increase in the way that they did in the 1990s and the early 2000s, which in turn will inevitably have some impact on training programmes.

Second, the overall current state of health care provision in relation to the vast extent of psychological need is relevant, whereby most people with mental health problems still do not access professional help. Moreover, the potential benefits of evidence-based treatments and the potential for prevention and early intervention to reduce later suffering is still very far from being realized, with detrimental effects for the individual and society as a whole. Thus we predict that there will inevitably be a continuing drive to 'upscale' the delivery of prevention and interventions for psychological difficulties.

Third, academic psychology, together with neuroscience, is currently making huge strides in improving our understanding of human behaviour and experience. Working in the 'messy', uncontrolled world of clinical application, clinical psychology has the task of assimilating and applying that knowledge in ways that are ethically based and which will both enrich the users of services and inform the basic science that is the foundation of the discipline.

It is possibly not too much of a leap to 'join the dots' of these converging influences to see that the role of clinical psychologists in the future will, and indeed must, develop accordingly. The days when clinical psychologists were located in uni-professional departments and could offer non-time-limited, one-to-one psychotherapy to a small number of referred clients are no more. The future is clearly one in which clinical psychologists will be part of an integrated system of delivery of interventions of varying intensities, by a team of staff with a range of levels of training, and through a variety of media including electronic and in some instances by using minimal personal contact. Services in the UK are likely to be increasingly offered via a range of providers including private, public, and third sector organizations, and psychologists are going to need good organizational understanding and skills, as well as adaptability and flexibility, to navigate these.

Although this is a challenging picture and may appear somewhat uncomfortable at first, in fact the competencies required to function within such a system map very well onto those of clinical psychology, particularly training in multiple models of therapy, team working, research, and evaluation skills. An emphasis on the quality of what clinical psychologists can uniquely contribute, through an integration of psychological theory and practice, will be crucial. Increasingly clinical psychologists will be required to develop and utilize broader leadership and clinical management skills within health systems, and clinical psychology trainers will have to be well equipped to foster these skills in the high-calibre psychology graduates entering their programmes.

Therefore, and in conclusion, we expect that those entering the profession of clinical psychology now and in the future will pursue careers that will be as rewarding and fascinating as those pursued by their predecessors, and which will focus on providing high quality innovative services for the future. These newly qualified clinical psychologists will likely be working in a diverse range of settings, as described in the chapters of this book, and in many new settings, as yet undeveloped, that may well feature in any subsequent editions. The future will undoubtedly present many challenges, but it will also provide opportunities for clinical psychologists to apply new theoretical insights and psychological methods to a broad range of clinical problems, in order to improve the quality of life for those using their services.

References

British Psychological Society (2012). DCP Annual Conference Monte Shapiro Lecture 'The next sixty years: dilemmas and future milestones' (<http://www.youtube.com/watch?v=SbJblXFdhnY>).

British Psychological Society Division of Clinical Psychology (2013). Position Statement on the Classification of Behaviour and Experience in Relation to Functional Psychiatric Diagnoses—Time for a Paradigm Shift (<http://dcp.bps.org.uk/dcp/the_dcp/news/dcp-position-statement-on-classification.cfm>).

De Zoysa, P. (2012). Practice of clinical psychology in a medical setting in Sri Lanka: trials and tribulations. International Journal of Psychology, 47, 643.

Kazdin, A.E. and Blase, S.L. (2011). Rebooting psychotherapy research and practice to reduce the burden of mental illness. Perspectives on Psychological Science, 6 (1), 21–37.

Kazdin, A.E. and Rabbitt, S.M. (2013). New models for delivering mental health services and reducing the burdens of mental illness. Clinical Psychological Science, 1 (2), 170–191.

Kessler, R.C., Amminger, G.P, Aquiliar-Gaxiola, S., Alsonso, J., Lee, S., and Ustun, T.B. (2007). Age of onset of mental disorders: a review of recent literature. Current Opinion in Psychiatry, 20 (4), 359–364.

NHS Information Centre for Health and Social Care (2007). Adult Psychiatric Morbidity in England, 2007: Results of a Household Survey (<http://www.hscic.gov.uk/pubs/psychiatricmorbidity07>).

Psychological Clinical Science Accreditation System (<http://www.pcsas.org/history.php>, accessed 12.05.2013>).

Rotheram-Borus, M.J., Swendeman, D., and Chorpita, B.F. (2012). Disruptive innovations for designing and diffusing evidence-based interventions. American Psychologist, 67 (6), 463–476.

Shimoyama, H. (2011). An international Comparison of Clinical Psychology in Practice: West Meets East. Kazama Shobo, Tokyo.

World Economic Forum (2013). Sustainable Health Systems: Visions, Strategies, Critical Uncertainties and Scenarios. WEF, Geneva.

Becoming registered as a clinical psychologist in the UK

Training in clinical psychology in the UK involves undertaking a 3-year full-time clinical doctoral programme that is approved by the Health and Social Care Professions Council (HCPC). Prior to entry, all doctoral training programmes require entrants to have attained a good honours degree in psychology. Over the course of the programme, trainees develop academic, research, and clinical competencies in clinical psychology, together with professional and personal competencies which enable them to become registered with the HCPC as clinical psychologists and subsequently to find employment in health and social care organizations. Successful graduates also become eligible to apply for Chartered Status with the British Psychological Society.

There are currently 32 university-based programmes in the UK which all provide postgraduate training in close collaboration with the NHS. Applications for all but one of the programmes in mainland UK are processed though the Clearing House for Postgraduate Courses in Clinical Psychology based at Leeds University (applications for the programme in Northern Ireland are taken directly, and the University of Hull operates a combined undergraduate/doctoral programme). Candidates are able to apply to up to four programmes using an online application form provided by the Clearing House at Leeds, copies of which are then distributed, together with confidential references (supplied independently from referees nominated by the applicant) to their nominated four universities. A standard fee is payable to the Clearing House for online access to an information Handbook and the application forms, and for processing all forms on behalf of candidates and universities. Information on all programmes, including selection procedures, details of programme staff, curriculum, entrance requirements, and other relevant details, is provided in the Handbook, and candidates are recommended to read this carefully before making applications. Further information is available from the Clearing House (see <www.leeds.ac.uk/chpccp>). The website provides helpful information including answers to frequently asked questions. There is also an 'Alternative Handbook', produced by the Pre-Qualification Group of the British Psychological Society (BPS) Division of Clinical Psychology (DCP). This provides very detailed views about various aspects of each programme that have been gathered from a survey of current trainees. The Alternative Handbook is available from the DCP affiliates group webpage (<http://dcp-prequal.bps.org.uk/dcp-prequal>) and is currently free to members.

Obtaining a place on a training programme is challenging, and there are a large number of applicants for each place (on average in 2012 there were over six applicants for each place). Given that all training is run, and largely funded by, the NHS, candidates should be aware that programmes are required to select candidates who can demonstrate a commitment to continuing to work in the NHS after qualification. Candidates from outside the European Economic Area (EEA) are also required to have a work permit or equivalent throughout the training period, or if self-funded from outside the EEA, to return to their home countries after training. All programmes are committed to equal opportunities legislation, and encourage applications from candidates with disabilities, or who come from ethnic minorities or disadvantaged social backgrounds. Most programmes require at least a high upper second-class degree in psychology, and also look for evidence of sustained motivation for and interest in clinical work, together with a realistic understanding of what the work of a clinical psychologist involves in practice. These aspects can be demonstrated through the candidate having undertaken some relevant employment post graduation (such as working as a health care assistant, care worker, or research assistant), and all programmes do look for this in the application process. It is, however, also important to note that having worked in a formal role such as an assistant psychologist is not a pre-requisite for acceptance onto a training programme, especially since the number of vacancies for such posts is relatively low.

Confidence in, and ability to carry out, research is helpful; however, a research doctorate is certainly not needed in order to apply. An open, friendly, responsible, and empathic personality is a must, as well as a willingness to develop self-awareness and reflective competence.

Training on all programmes comprises an integrated set of learning opportunities for trainees to gain theoretical knowledge and clinical skill by studying and working with patients or clients of all ages and ability in a variety of clinical settings, and applying a range of clinical competencies and theoretical approaches designed to improve the wellbeing of service users and their families or carers. Typically trainees spend around half their time over the 3 years on a series of supervised clinical placements that cover a range of client groups, including adults who have mental health difficulties; people with learning difficulties; older people; and children and families. Placements may also include more specialist populations, such as people with HIV, those in units for spinal injury, paediatrics, and palliative care. The rest of trainees' time is divided between academic teaching (including seminars, lectures, and workshops) and research. All programmes require candidates to complete a number of assignments which normally include essays, case reports, and reports of small-scale research projects, while some programmes also set written exams; in addition there is a doctoral level dissertation which requires the candidate to make a substantial contribution to clinical knowledge involving human participants. All programmes involve a partnership between the university and local clinical services, and trainees typically have both academic and clinical supervisors to support their learning. The quality of clinical supervision provided is particularly pivotal in determining the learning experience of trainees, and all programmes provide additional courses and training for practising supervisors in how to establish supervision contracts, support trainees' unique learning styles, and help trainees to resolve clinical or placement difficulties.

Psychologists who have undertaken professional training in psychology overseas may also apply to the HCPC for registration on the basis of their training. All overseas-trained applicants are assessed on an individual basis against the HCPC's Standards of Proficiency for Clinical

Psychology, although there are specific processes for the mutual recognition of professional qualifications of applicants migrating from within the EEA which are stipulated by European Law (EU Directive 2005/36/EC). If applicants from outside the EEA do not fully meet the HCPC Standards of Proficiency, their application will be rejected, although they may reapply after undertaking further training. Applicants from within the EEA who do not fully meet the Standards of Proficiency have the option to undertake an adaptation period under supervision to develop the required competencies, or undertake an aptitude test.

Detailed information on the application process is available on the HCPC website (<http://www.hpc-uk.org/apply/>).

Further advice is also available from the BPS website (<www.bps.org.uk>), which provides helpful information including answers to frequently asked questions.

Index

A

acceptance and commitment therapy (ACT) 95, 189, 195–6
access to services 257–8
  children/young people 61–2, 63–4
  ethnic differences 241, 242
  intellectual disabilities 123–4
  older people 90
  see also Improving Access to Psychological Services
activity scheduling 92
acute mental health services 74
acute neurology/neurosurgery settings 207–14
acute stress disorder (ASD) 175
addictions 153–68
  associated disorders 155–6
  clinical psychology and 154–5
  role of clinical psychologist 157–67
  treatment systems in UK 156
  vulnerability factors 164–5
adherence, poor 190–1
adolescents see children/young people
Adult Psychiatric Morbidity Survey 262
ageing
  normal 86, 88
  population 85
aggression 146
alcohol-related problems 153, 154, 165
  associated disorders 155–6
  see also addictions
Alzheimer's disease 87, 88
  see also dementia
anorexia nervosa 104–5
  children and young people 62, 108–9
  clinical work settings 109–10
  epidemiology 107
  ethical issues 117
  history and cultural aspects 106–7
  risk factors 108
  therapeutic approaches 112–16
anxiety disorders
  children and young people 61
  older people 87
Approved Clinicians 143

assertive outreach 74
assessment 20–2
  clinical health psychology 192–3
  eating disorders 111–12
  intellectual disability 121, 132–3
  neuropsychological 210–13, 215–16, 218–19
  older people 90–3
  primary health care 41–3
  severe mental health problems 76–7
  see also risk assessment
asylum seekers 178, 240
attachments 54, 93, 128, 175
atypical eating disorders (EDNOS) 106, 107
audit 19
  clinical neuropsychology 214
  primary health care 49–50
auditory hallucinations (voices) 71, 72–3
  therapeutic approach 78
autistic spectrum disorder (ASD) 63
avoidant/restrictive food intake disorder (ARFID) 109

B

Balint, Michael 39
bed wetting 18, 19
behaviour problems
  childhood 59–60
  intellectual disabilities 125
  neurological illness 206
behaviour therapy 29
  addictions 160–1
  clinical neuropsychology 216
  delusions 79
  directed at parents 60
  history of development 8
  older people 93–4
bereavement 89–90, 93
best interests 131
bibliotherapy 92
Big Noise, The 57
Binet, Alfred 4–5
binge eating disorder (BED) 106
biofeedback 188

biological model 28
  severe mental health problems 71, 72
biopsychosocial model 28
  children and young people 58–9
  physical health problems 189, 192
  severe mental health problems 71–3
bipolar disorder 69–70
  causes 71–3
  evidence-based approach 75–6
black and minority ethnic (BME)
    groups 241, 242
borderline personality disorder 106, 176
boundaries, interpersonal 128
brain injury/damage 205, 206–7, 210,
    218–20
brief dynamic interpersonal
    psychotherapy 32, 33
brief interventions
  addictive behaviour 159–60
  primary health care 45
British Psychological Society (BPS)
  Chartered Status 269
  Code of Ethics and Conduct 14–15
  guidance on leadership 235–6
  historical aspects 4, 6–7, 9, 10
bulimia nervosa 105–6, 107
  children and young people 62, 108
  risk factors 108
  therapeutic approaches 112–16
burnout 180
Burt, Cyril 5

C
carers
  dementia 99
  neurological conditions 215
  older people 88, 93
case discussions 96–7
case management 149
cerebral dominance 209
challenging behaviour
  dementia 98–9
  intellectual disabilities 125
child abuse/neglect 54, 60
Child and Adolescent Mental Health
    Services (CAMHS) 56
child guidance clinics 6
Children and Young People's Improving
    Access to Psychological Therapies
    (CYP-IAPT) 64
children/young people 53–65
  access to services 61–2, 63–4

eating disorders 62, 108–9
engagement 64
forensic practice 145
frequency of mental health
    problems 58
historical aspects 5–6
main presenting problems 59–63
need for early intervention 64–5
neuropsychology 214
prevention of trauma 177–8
psychological interventions 57–63
secure services 140–1
wellbeing and resilience 53–6
work settings 56–7
child sexual abuse 181–2, 183–4
chronic pain 188, 195–6, 199–200
chronic physical health problems see
    physical health problems
classical conditioning 29, 93–4
clinical health psychology see health
    psychology, clinical
clinical neuropsychology see
    neuropsychology, clinical
clinical psychologists
  clinical competencies 17, 19–28
  ethics and professional values 14–15,
    264–5
  NHS posts 9, 11, 255
  personal demands on 15–16
  qualifications 2, 9
  reflective scientist practitioner
    model 17–19
  registration 5–6, 269–72
  roles 13–14
  skills mix 259–60
  training by see training/teaching role
clinical psychology 6–16
  cultural issues 243–51
  current context of practice 11–12
  development of profession 6–10,
    253–6
  first use of term 5–6
  future prospects 253–68
  science–practice balance 12–13, 262–4
  training see training, clinical
    psychology
  unique features 14
Clinical Supervisors 143
coaching 231
cognitive-analytic therapy (CAT) 24, 35
  eating disorders 114–15
  older people 95–6

cognitive-behaviour therapy (CBT) 24–5, 29–31
  children and young people 61, 62
  dementia 99
  eating disorders 112–14
  intellectual disabilities 128
  older people 92, 94–5
  physical health problems 189, 193–4
  primary care 45, 46
  severe mental health problems 75–6, 78
  trauma-focused (TF-CBT) 176, 182–3
cognitive biases 78, 173–4
cognitive impairment 87–8, 121, 206
  see also dementia; intellectual disabilities
cognitive models 29–31
  assessment 21
  formulation 24, 30
  PTSD 173, 175, 179
  social anxiety 31
cognitive rehabilitation 216
cognitive stimulation therapy 98
cognitive therapy see cognitive-behaviour therapy
cognitive vaccine concept 12, 179
collectivistic societies 238–9, 246
colour-blind approach 243–4
communication 27–8, 224–5
  older people 91
community approaches, whole 57
community forensic services 141, 148–9
community learning disability team 122
community mental health teams (CMHTs) 74, 88–9
community organizations, local 37–8
community psychology 55, 247
community working
  clinical neuropsychology 214–21
  eating disorders 110
  see also primary health care
co-morbidity 155–6
compassion fatigue 180
competencies, clinical 17, 19–28
compulsory detention/treatment 74, 117, 241
computer game (Tetris) 12, 179
conduct disorders (CD) 60
consultation (consultancy) 27–8, 229–30
  clinical neuropsychology 214
  forensic practice 148–9

consultation model, intellectual disabilities 131–2
context analysis, cultural 246–7, 249
coping effectiveness training (CET) 195
core competencies 20–8
cost-effectiveness, psychological therapies 82–3
counselling, neuropsychological 217
counter-transference 32
Courts
  forensic practice 145, 146, 149
  reporting on trauma/PTSD 178–9
craving, managing 162–4, 166–7
crisis teams 74
cultural competency 244–5
cultural diversity 237–51
  case example 248–51
  clinical psychology 243–8
  eating disorders 106–7
  mainstream psychology 243
  reactions to trauma 174
  social contexts 238–9
culture 237–8, 246–7
culture-blind approach 243–4, 246

D
Dangerous and Severe Personality Disorder (DSPD) programme 147
Davidson, May 7
death and dying 89–90, 194
debriefing 180–1
delusions 70–1, 73
  therapeutic approach 78–9
dementia 86, 87–8, 97–9
  assessment 132
  challenging behaviour 98–9
  psychological interventions 94–5, 98–9
dementia care mapping 98
depression
  children and young people 61
  dementia and 88, 213
  older people 87, 96
developmental problems 60, 63
diagnosis, psychiatric 23
Diagnostic and Statistical Manual (DSM-V) 23, 104, 153, 169
diagnostic overshadowing 125
disaster planning 178
disruptive innovations 260
dissociation 175
dissociative identity disorder 175–6
diversity 238

Down syndrome 132
drug misuse 154, 155–6
  see also addictions

E
early intervention 258–9
  children and young people 64–5
  severe mental health problems 73
eating, selective 108–9
eating disorder not otherwise specified
  (EDNOS) 106, 107
eating disorders 103–17
  across lifespan 108–9
  additional knowledge and skills
    110–11
  atypical (EDNOS) 106, 107
  children and young people 62, 108–9
  clinical work settings 109–10
  definitions and key clinical
    features 104–6
  ethical issues 117
  frequency 107
  history and cultural aspects 106–7
  risk factors 108
  role of clinical psychologist 110–17
  therapeutic approaches 62, 112–16
  see also anorexia nervosa; bulimia
    nervosa
eclectic therapeutic approaches 34–5
education, patient 43–5
Ehlers and Clark model, post-traumatic
  stress disorder 173–4, 175, 179
El Sistema movement 57
emotional problems
  childhood 60–2
  neuropsychological impairment 206
engagement
  addictive disorders 158–9
  children/young people 64
ethical issues 14–15, 264–5
  eating disorders 117
  forensic practice 145, 150
  intellectual disabilities 131
ethnicity 237, 239–40
  mental health services and 243
evaluation 26, 77
  see also outcome measurement
evidence-based practice 58, 75–6
executive dysfunction 206
experimental psychology 3, 4
expert patients 189, 201
expert witnesses 149, 178

eye movement desensitization and
  reprocessing (EMDR) 176, 177
Eysenck, Hans 8

F
false memories 181–2
families
  older people 88, 93
  patients with neurological
    conditions 215
  spectrum of different 54–5
  see also carers
Family Courts 145
family doctors *see* general practitioners
family interventions
  children and young people 56–7, 59,
    61, 64
  neurological conditions 217–18,
    219–20
  severe mental health problems 75–6
  trauma/PTSD 177, 183–4
family therapy 34
  eating disorders 62, 116
  intellectual disabilities 130
food avoidance emotional disorder
  (FAED) 108
forensic psychology 137–50
  demands of 149–50
  mentally disordered offenders 141–3
  range of clients 138–40
  range of work 144–9
  relevant legislation 143–4
forensic services 140–1
formulation 22–4
  addictive behaviour 158
  eating disorders 111–12
  severe mental health problems 77–8
foster care 54
FRAMES model 159–60
functional analysis
  addictive behaviour 157, 158
  intellectual disability field 125, 131
functional disorders 87
fundamental attribution error 228

G
generalized anxiety disorder (GAD) 87
general practitioners (GPs) 37, 40
  problems presenting to 38, 39
  training 49
  working with 46, 47–9
  see also primary health care

Good Lives Model (GLM) 148
Graduate basis for Chartered
 Membership (GBC) 2
group therapy 34
 dementia 98
 primary health care 44–5

H
hallucinations 70–1
 see also auditory hallucinations
harm reduction 153
head injury, severe 206, 218–20
Health and Social Care Professions
 Council (HCPC) 2, 20, 269, 271–2
health anxiety 190, 198–9
health care systems, future trends 256–8
health psychology, clinical 188–202
 assessment 192–3
 case examples 197–201
 key clinical issues 190–2
 shifting themes 189–90
 therapeutic models 189, 193–7
 working in teams and
  organizations 201
 see also physical health problems
health visitors 47–8, 49
Holmes, Emily 12, 179
hospital settings *see* inpatient/hospital
 settings
humanist psychology 9

I
imagery 31
Improving Access to Psychological
 Services (IAPT) 11–12, 129, 259–60
indirect interventions 259
 children and young people 57
 intellectual disabilities 131–2, 133
 older people 96–7
 primary health care 50–1
individualistic societies 238–9, 246
informed choice 42–3
inpatient/hospital settings
 eating disorders 109–10, 116
 forensic practice 146
inpatient mental health wards 74
institutional racism 240–1
integrative therapeutic approaches 34–5
intellectual disabilities 63, 119–34
 case examples 119, 124, 126
 causes 121
 definitions and terminology 120–1

interventions 59, 126–32
 presenting problems and
  difficulties 124–5
 prevalence 121
 role of clinical psychologists 63,
  132–4
 service settings and context 121–4
internalizing disorders, childhood 60–2
International Classification of Disease
 (ICD) 23, 121, 175
interpersonal psychotherapy (IPT)
 adolescents (IPT-A) 61
 eating disorders 115
 older people 96
interpreters 247–8
interventions 24–6
 addictions 157–67
 children and young people 57–63
 clinical neuropsychology 213–14,
  216–21
 dementia 98–9
 early *see* early intervention
 forensic practice 146–8
 indirect *see* indirect interventions
 innovative approaches 260–1
 intellectual disabilities 126–32, 133
 older people 93–7
 primary care 43–9
 severe mental health problems 75–6,
  78–9, 83
 trauma/PTSD 176–8, 180–4
 see also psychological therapies; *specific
  interventions*
IQ (intelligence quotient) 121
IQ tests 5

L
leadership 28, 223, 232–6, 265
 clinical 232–3
 definitions 233
 forensic practice 148–9
 older people 96
 organizational 232, 233, 234–5
 severe mental health problems 82
learning difficulties, specific 120–1
learning disabilities 120–1
 see also intellectual disabilities
legal reports, to Courts 145, 178–9
legislation, mental health 143–4
life review 25
lifespan perspectives 93
life-story books 98, 126

looked after children (LAC) 54
losses, older people 93

M
management, versus leadership 232
marital therapy 34
matched-care approach 92
McNaughten rule 142
medical model 23, 208
medical procedures 191–2
memory, false and recovered 181–2
memory clinics 97
Mental Capacity Act (2005) 144
Mental Health Act (1983) 143
mental health problems
  diagnosis 23
  offenders 141–3
  severe *see* severe mental health
    problems
  substance misuse and 155–6
  see also presenting problems
mental hygiene movement 6
mentoring 231
MIND 7, 82
mindfulness-based interventions
  addictions 165–6
  older people 95
  physical health problems 189, 195
models, therapeutic 28–35
motivational interventions, addictive
  behaviour 158–61
motivational interviewing 159, 160
multi-disciplinary team work *see* team
  working
multi-sensory stimulation 99
music 57

N
narrative work 130
National Association for Mental Health
  (NAMH) 7
National Health Service (NHS)
  clinical psychology posts 9, 11, 255
  improving access to services 11–12
  partnership working 74–5
  see also services
National Institute for Health and Clinical
  Excellence (NICE) 11, 75–6, 82
neuroanatomy, functional 209
neuropsychological counselling 217
neuropsychological impairment 205–7
neuropsychology, clinical 205–21

acute settings 207–14
  assessment 210–13, 215–16, 218–19
  interventions 213–14, 216–21
  rehabilitation/community
    settings 214–21
  services 207
  terminology 209–10
NHS *see* National Health Service
nocturnal enuresis 18, 19

O
offenders 137, 139–40
  mentally disordered 141–3
  providing therapy 146–8
  risk assessment 144–5
  secure services 140–1
older people 85–100
  access to services 90
  assessment 90–3
  cognitive impairment *see* dementia
  context 86
  eating disorders 109
  population changes 85
  psychological difficulties 87–8
  psychological interventions 93–7
  work settings and tasks 88–90
operant conditioning 29, 93–4, 188
oppositional defiant disorders (ODD) 60
oral history projects 98
organic disorders 87–8
organizational leadership 232, 233,
  234–5
organizational skills 234–5, 265
outcome measurement 26, 77, 261–2

P
paranoia 78
parents, behavioural training
  approaches 60
partnership, working in 74–5, 220–1
perpetuating factors 23
personality disorder 69–70
  forensic practice 146, 147
physical health problems 187–202
  children and young people 63
  intellectual disabilities 124–5
  key psychological issues 190–2
  older people 87
  primary health care 40, 41
  therapeutic approaches 189, 193–201
  see also health psychology, clinical
police, working with 149

political astuteness 234
population changes 85, 239–40
post-traumatic stress disorder
    (PTSD) 169, 170–9
  clinical features 172
  cultural influences 174
  Ehlers and Clark cognitive model 173,
      175, 179
  prevention 12, 177–8, 179
  psychological theories 173–4
  risk factors 172–3
  therapeutic interventions 176–8,
      180–4
power therapies 181
practice-based evidence 58
precipitating factors 23
predisposing factors 23
presenting problems 23
  children and young people 59–63
  clinical health psychology 190–2
  clinical neuropsychology 208
  intellectual disabilities 124–5
  older people 87–8
  primary health care 38, 39
prevention 257, 258–9
  relapse, mindfulness-based 165–6
  trauma/PTSD 12, 177–8, 179
primary health care 37–51
  assessment and triage 41–3
  audit and research 49–50
  balancing roles 50–1
  brief psychological treatment 45
  developing systems of care 49
  education and self-help 43–5
  older people 89
  organization and staffing 40–1
  problems presenting 38–40, 41
  standard and intermittent
      treatment 45–7
  working with others 47–9
prisoners 141, 143
prisons 146–7
problem lists 76–7
professional values 14–15, 264–5
profiling, psychological 149
protective factors 23
pseudodementia 213
psychiatrists, working with 57, 79, 89
psychoanalysis 32
psychodynamic approach/therapy 32–3
  assessment 21
  formulation 24

intellectual disabilities 129–30
intervention 25
primary care 46
psychological factors 28
psychological interventions see
    interventions
psychological therapies
  access to see access to services
  cost-effectiveness 82–3
  cultural aspects of acceptability 242–3
  eating disorders 112–16
  eclectic and integrative approaches
      34–5
  forensic practice 146–8
  models 28–35
  neurological conditions 217
  physical health problems 189, 193–201
  primary care 45–7
  see also specific types
psychological wellbeing practitioners 11
psychology
  as academic discipline 3–4, 6, 262
  cultural context 243
  in practice, history of development 4–6
psychometric tests 20, 26
  history of development 5, 6
  neuropsychological 210–12
  severe mental health problems 77
psychosis 70–1
  causes 71–3, 175–6
  continuum with normal
      experience 72–3
  early intervention services 73
  young people 62–3
  see also severe mental health problems
PTSD see post-traumatic stress disorder

Q
qualifications, clinical psychologists 2, 9

R
race 237
racism 240–1
reciprocal intensive communication
    techniques 99
recovered memories 181–2
Recovery movement/model 75, 79–81,
    146
reflective practitioner model 18–19
reflective scientist practitioner
    model 17–19
refugees 240

registration, clinical psychologists 2, 269–72
rehabilitation
  neurological conditions 207, 213, 214–21
  severe mental health problems 74
relapse prevention, mindfulness-based 165–6
relaxation exercises 92
religion 248
reminiscence therapy 98
reports
  legal 145, 178–9
  neuropsychological 212
  psychological 27
research 12–13, 19, 26–7
  clinical neuropsychology 214
  primary care 50
  relevance of competency in 263–4
  severe mental health problems 83
  trauma 179
resilience, psychological 53–6
risk assessment 22, 91
  forensic field 144–5

S
scaffolding techniques 94
schizophrenia 13, 69–70
  causes 71–3
  evidence-based approach 75–6
  prognosis 80
  see also severe mental health problems
schools, working with 59
scientist practitioner model 17–18
secondary health care 37, 39–40
secure units 140–1, 148
selective eating 108–9
self-control training 166
self-efficacy 160
self-harming behaviour 61
self-help, facilitating 43–5
self-management 200, 259
self-report scales 77
services
  acceptability, cultural aspects 242–3
  access to see access to services
  children and young people 56
  developing 82–3, 133–4
  ethnicity and 241–3
  facilitating delivery 27–8, 259
  forensic 140–1
  neuropsychological 207

older people 99–100
  severe mental health problems 73–4
  substance misuse 156
service user movement 75, 79–80, 82, 83
severe mental health problems 69–83
  causes 71–3, 175–6
  conditions encompassed 69–70
  evidence-based approaches 75–6
  positive symptoms 70–1
  Recovery movement/model 79–81
  role of clinical psychologists 75–83
  services 73–5
sex offenders 147–8
sexual abuse, childhood 181–2, 183–4
Shapiro, Monte 8
shattered assumptions 171
shell shock 170
skills mix 259–60
smoking, cigarette 154, 166
SOBER breathing space 166
social anxiety 31
social care model, intellectual disability 123
social care services 37–8, 74–5
social constructionist approach 33–4
social factors 28
social inclusion 80, 123
socialization to the model 30
Socratic questioning 30, 78
solution-focused therapy (SFT) 189, 196–7
Spearman, Charles 3–4
spirituality 248
stepped-care model 11–12, 259–60
  older people 92
  primary care 42, 43
stereotypes, older people 86
stroke 206
substance misuse 153–68
  associated disorders 155–6
  role of clinical psychologist 157–67
  screening for 157
  see also addictions
suicide 61, 88
supervision 19, 81, 116–17, 230–1
surgery, suitability for 191–2
systemic approaches 33–4
  assessment 21
  children and young people 55, 59
  formulation 23
  intellectual disabilities 130, 131–2

intervention 25
  older people 96
systems of care 49, 79

T
teaching role *see* training/teaching role
team working 223–9
  children and young people 56–7
  clinical health psychology 201
  eating disorders 116–17
  older people 88–9, 96–7
  primary health care 40, 47–9
  severe mental health problems 79
therapeutic alliance
  eating disorders 104, 115
  intellectual disabilities 127
therapeutic disdain 126
therapeutic relationship 30, 32
therapies *see* psychological therapies
third-sector organizations 80–1
thought field therapy (TFT) 181
tiers of care 37
training, clinical psychology 2, 269–72
  current debates 259–60, 263–4
  entry requirements 270–1
  history 7–8, 9–10
  personal demands of 15
training/teaching role
  forensic practice 149
  intellectual disability field 133
  primary health care 49
  severe mental health problems 81
transdiagnostic cognitive models, eating
    disorders 112–14
transference 32
trauma 169–84
  biological effects 174
  as cause of psychosis 71–2, 175–6
  complex 175

definitions 169–71
  personal impact 179–80
  psychological effects 170–1, 174–6
  role of clinical psychologists 176–9
  special issues 180–2
  type-I (one-off events) 170
  type-II (repeated) 170, 175
  vulnerability to 172–3
  see also post-traumatic stress disorder
trauma-focused cognitive-behaviour
    therapy (TF-CBT) 176, 182–3
traumatic incident reduction (TIR) 181
traumatization, vicarious/secondary
    180
triage 41–3

U
urges, managing 162–4, 166–7

V
validation therapy 99
values, professional 14–15, 264–5
victims, crime 138–9, 141
vocational rehabilitation 219
voices *see* auditory hallucinations
voluntary sector 38, 74–5

W
wellbeing, psychological
  children 53–6
  forensic settings 146
  measurement 261–2
  whole community approaches 57
willpower, boosting 166–7
Witmer, Lightner 5–6
Wundt, Wilhelm 3, 6

Y
young people *see* children/young people